Eisenhower, Kennedy, and Foreign Aid

Ideas and Action Series, No. 5

W. W. Rostow

Eisenhower, Kennedy, and Foreign Aid

 University of Texas Press, Austin

First Edition, 1985

Requests for permission to reproduce material from this work
should be sent to
Permissions, University of Texas Press
Box 7819
Austin, Texas 78713

Library of Congress Cataloging in Publication Data

Rostow, W. W. (Walt Whitman), 1916–
    Eisenhower, Kennedy, and foreign aid.
    (Ideas and action series; [no. 5])
    Includes index.
    1. Economic assistance, American—Developing countries.
2. United States—Politics and government—1953–1961.
3. United States—Politics and government—1945– .
I. Title.   II. Series: Rostow, W. W. (Walt Whitman), 1916– .
Ideas and action series; no. 5.
HC60.R68   1984   338.91′73′01724   84-20971

ISBN 0-292-74018-2

In memory of
Max Franklin Millikan

Contents

Appendixes

Tables

Charts

Preface

This is the fifth in a series of essays on the relationship between ideas and action. Focusing sharply on particular decisions and policies, they explore, in fact, major facets of recent history: the Second World War and its outcome (*Pre-Invasion Bombing Strategy*); the European dimension of the Cold War (*The Division of Europe after World War II: 1946* and *Europe after Stalin*); inspection and arms control (*Open Skies*); and, here, economic aid to developing countries. In probing these large substantive issues, an effort is made to illuminate, in each case, the relation between ideas and action.

I would define ideas as the abstract concepts in the minds of public officials and their advisers which they bring to bear in making decisions. My experiences as both an academic and a public servant have equally driven home over the years this piece of wisdom from George Santayana's *Character and Opinion in the United States*:

> . . . human discourse is intrinsically addressed not to natural existing things but to ideal essences, poetic or logical terms which thought may define and play with. When fortune or necessity diverts our attention from this congenial ideal sport to crude facts and pressing issues, we turn our frail poetic ideas into symbols for those terrible irruptive things. In that paper money of our own stamping, the legal tender of the mind, we are obliged to reckon all the movements and values of the world.

But there is, of course, a good deal more to decisions in public policy than clash and choice among the "frail poetic ideas" we create to make simplified sense of an inordinately complex and usually disheveled field of action. A decision is, after all, a choice among perceived alternatives. Ideas play a large role in defining those alternatives, but the choice among them involves other factors. The precise setting and timing of the decision evidently matter. So do questions of power, that is, politics and bureaucratic vested interests. So do personalities—unique human beings, controlled by memories and experiences, dreams and hopes which James Gould Cozzens evoked, in *By Love Possessed*, in a definition of temperament:

> A man's temperament might, perhaps, be defined as the mode or modes of a man's feeling, the struck balance of his ruling desires, the worked-out sum of his habitual predispositions. In themselves, these elements were inscrutable. There were usually too many of them; they were often of irreducible complexity; you could observe only results. . . . The to-be-observed result was a total way of life.

And, as we shall see in the story told here, temperaments thus broadly defined sometimes clash at both the working levels and the highest reaches of government, adding a special wild card to the way history unfolds.

This book differs in several significant respects from its four predecessors in the series. First, its initial operational focus is a decision taken by the legislative rather than the executive branch of the U.S. government. In 1958–1959 John Kennedy, joined by John Sherman Cooper, managed to gain the support of his Senate colleagues for a resolution which, in its final form, called on the President to "explore with other free and democratic nations and appropriate international organizations the desirability and feasibility of establishing an international mission to consult with the governments of countries in the area of South Asia on their needs in connection with the fulfillment of currently planned and anticipated development programs. . . ." The resolution played a key role in the creation of a three-man World Bank international mission to South Asia and the emergence of consortia arrangements for India and Pakistan—a pattern subsequently extended to sixteen developing countries. We are examining, therefore, a catalytic initiative of considerable significance.

Second, the book exploits the rich body of documentary evidence now available to trace out, in Chapters 5–9, the inner debates and struggles of the Eisenhower administration with respect to development aid. The somewhat anguished story runs through the whole period 1953–1960, involving not only a direct clash of concepts but also of personalities and of differing views of executive leadership. As often, the emergence of acute crises (in 1957–1958) helps tip the balance of forces at work, setting, in this case, the framework within which enlarged U.S. development lending becomes politically feasible.

Eisenhower emerges as a man torn on this issue. On the one hand, he and his secretary of state share a sense, from at least 1954, that a radical expansion of development lending is required for an effective national security policy. On the other hand, there is strong, articulate opposition from the secretary of the treasury and those associated with him in the executive branch. Eisenhower is also borne down by opposition in the Congress, notably, but not exclusively, within the Republican party. It is put to him strongly on a number of occasions that he has the power to overcome this opposition and move ahead. Year after year he procrastinates. To a degree, Eisenhower probably shared the opposition's concern for the budgetary implications of enlarged development lending; but, in the end, responding to initiatives in the Senate and the pressure of events, his task simplified by a withdrawal from Washington of the major opposition figures in the executive branch, he half acquiesces, half leads in the setting up of institutional arrangements with large budgetary implications beyond his term of office. His final budget submitted to the

Congress includes a large increase in funds for development lending which eases the task of his less inhibited successor.

The portraits of Eisenhower and Dulles which emerge from this tale—and of the complex relationship between them—conform to none of the conventional images of the two men, contemporary or revisionist.

The evolution of executive branch policy toward development lending in the 1950s is, clearly, a significant and essential part of the background to the Kennedy-Cooper initiative, but the account of that transition presented here stands, in a sense, on its own feet.

A third distinctive feature of this book is the effort in Chapter 11 to outline, in first approximation at least, the evolution of development lending from the early 1960s to the early 1980s, including the return of the Reagan administration, in its first phase, to something like the initial ideological posture of the Eisenhower administration.

In Chapter 12 I abandon my stance as advocate and attempt as objective an evaluation as I can muster of the efficacy of development aid over the past quarter-century.

Thus, as befits its ultimate theme, this book is both somewhat longer and more complex in structure than its four predecessors in the Ideas and Action Series.

In this, as in the other volumes, we examine decisions in which I played some role or which I had an opportunity to observe closely at the time. But, as the reader will perceive, this and the other volumes in the series are not exercises in autobiography. It is simply the case that one has a better chance of capturing something of the relationship between ideas and the other elements determining action if one was reasonably close to events than if the whole complex setting has to be reconstructed from the beginning.

On the other hand, my memory of the circumstances, the material in my files, and my knowledge of some of the actors were patently inadequate. In this and the other case studies, my purpose is to bring to bear what public records, communication with participants, and the literature of published memoirs and works of scholarship can now provide. As in the present volume, there is usually a formidable body of relevant material available.

Certain source or other basic materials, hitherto unpublished or not easily accessible, have been assembled in the appendices to this book. They are meant to illuminate facets of the decision examined or to capture something of the moods and temper of the time.

Dr. Ted Carpenter, a scholar of this period, has been of invaluable assistance both in mobilizing relevant primary and secondary sources and as a critic of drafts. Our work on this essay was supported by a grant from the National Endowment for the Humanities, whose indispensable help I wish warmly to acknowledge.

I should also like to thank the participants in these events and the scholars who have generously given their time for guidance and criticism: Robert E. Asher, Charles F. Baldwin, Jagdish Bhagwati, Donald L. M. Blackmer, Robert Bowie, Sidney Chernick, John Sherman Cooper, Eleanor Lansing Dulles, Ralph Dungan, John S. D. Eisenhower, Milton Eisenhower, Oliver Franks, David Harlech, Michael Hoffman, Fred Holborn, Richard H. Immerman, Mrs. C. D. Jackson, F. Tomasson Jannuzi, Burke Knapp, Wilfred Malenbaum, Edward S. Mason, Marie McCrum, Mrs. Max F. Millikan, C. V. Narasimhan, B. K. Nehru, Henry Owen, I. G. Patel, George Rosen, Paul Rosenstein-Rodan, Elspeth D. Rostow, Graydon Upton, and Ann Whitman.

Our task was also eased by the knowledgeable assistance of Mrs. Nancy Bressler, at the Seeley G. Mudd Manuscript Library, Princeton University, by the archivists of the Eisenhower, Kennedy and Johnson presidential libraries and of the World Bank—all of whom reached out to help us. The Massachusetts Institute of Technology [M.I.T.] Center for International Studies made available relevant documents from the files of Max F. Millikan.

Quotations from personal letters and memoranda derive from documents in my files which will, in due time, be transferred to the Lyndon B. Johnson Library. The letter of Harry G. Curran to Eugene Black of March 21, 1960 (quoted pp. 166–168), is to be found in the historical files of the World Bank.

As on many other occasions, I was aided in multiple ways by Lois Nivens. Frances Knape was most helpful in typing the various drafts.

I should add that this series of essays would not have been undertaken without the strong encouragement of my wife, Elspeth Davies Rostow, who believed I might usefully reflect on the large question embedded in those periods in my professional life when I was diverted from strictly academic pursuits.

W. W. Rostow

November 1984
Austin, Texas

I. The Kennedy-Cooper Initiative and Its Background

1. The First Round, 1958

In the autumn of 1957 Senator John Kennedy decided to generate a bipartisan initiative which would lead to enlarged immediate and long-term international support for Indian economic development. We shall consider at a later point the converging concepts and circumstances that brought Kennedy to this decision.

Kennedy sought and easily achieved the collaboration of Senator John Sherman Cooper, a Republican from Kentucky who had been ambassador to India in 1955–1956. From that post and subsequently, he was a steady advocate of larger and more flexible American economic aid to India. Over the winter of 1957–1958 Kennedy consulted a variety of people knowledgeable in Indian affairs, while he and Cooper devised a formula which might permit two senators of only modest power and influence in the legislative branch to set in motion a process which might, in time, achieve their objective. The method chosen was a concurrent resolution of the Senate and the House of Representatives.

On Tuesday afternoon March 25, 1958, Kennedy introduced to the Senate the resolution set out on page 4 in the context of an elaborate speech of some 8000 words.*

*Kennedy's and Cooper's speeches on March 25, 1958, too long for inclusion in the text of this book, are to be found in the *Congressional Record*, 85th Congress, Second Session, Vol. 104, Part 4, pp. 5246–5253 (JFK) and 5253–5255 (JSC).

Kennedy's speech, made in the rather anxious post-Sputnik setting of American politics, with China apparently forging ahead in the Great Leap Forward, contained the following major points:

1. U.S. and Western policy is adrift, focused on Soviet and Chinese Communist achievements and initiatives, not on our own capacities and objectives.

2. As members of the opposition, Democrats are properly searching for and proposing new initiatives related to the military balance and space (Lyndon Johnson), disarmament (Hubert Humphrey), our international role in education (William Fulbright), and other fields.

3. We lack, however, a policy to associate the West con-

85TH CONGRESS
2D SESSION

S. CON. RES. 74

IN THE SENATE OF THE UNITED STATES

MARCH 25 (legislative day, MARCH 17), 1958

Mr. KENNEDY (for himself and Mr. COOPER) submitted the following concurrent resolution; which was referred to the Committee on Foreign Relations

CONCURRENT RESOLUTION

1   *Resolved by the Senate (the House of Representatives*

2   *concurring),* That the Congress recognizes the importance

3   of the economic development of the Republic of India to

4   its people, to democratic values and institutions, and to

5   peace and stability in the world. Consequently, it is the

6   sense of the Congress that it is in the interest of the United

7   States to join with other nations in providing support of

8   the type, magnitude, and duration, adequate to assist India

9   to complete successfully its current program for economic

10   development.

v

structively with the uncommitted world "from Casablanca to the Celebes." A military response is inadequate given the fundamental economic and social problems these nations confront.

4. India is a critically important case: it is an authentic democracy; it is seriously committed to economic and social development; its First Five Year Plan [1951–1956] demonstrated a capacity for progress; its performance relative to that of Communist China will have great political and ideological significance in the developing regions.

5. India's Second Five Year Plan [1956–1961] is in danger of collapse because of a foreign exchange shortage induced, in part, by bad harvests; in part, by the import requirements for industrial expansion. U.S. assistance is far below the minimum necessary to permit the plan to be fulfilled. The question arises, therefore: "Is it not time that India and its foreign friends reach an understanding about the real scope of need?"

6. There are certain immediate, emergency measures the U.S. might undertake to prevent a gross failure of the Plan, but the United States and India's other friends should gear their efforts to the full life of the Plan much as the United States did in relation to the process of reconstruction of Western Europe through the Marshall Plan. The concurrent resolution aims to achieve this result. Required external assistance might be of the order of magnitude of $3 billion for the three remaining years of the Plan.

7. To establish more firmly the order of magnitude of India's external needs over the life of the Second Five Year Plan, a sub-committee of the Organization of European Economic Co-operation (OEEC) should at once be designated to go to India and "to recommend plans by which long-term assistance could be given by all member nations through an international consortium. . . . An OEEC committee, if it could include among its members persons of broad experience such as John McCloy of the United States, Sir Oliver Franks of Great Britain, Professor Tinbergen of Holland, Albert Kervin

[Kervyn] of Belgium, or Erland Waldenström of Sweden, could give a powerful impetus to such an international consortium." It could also provide a model for other, later efforts, perhaps including Pakistan.

8. Kennedy then responded to four criticisms of special action for India:

(a) private investment could and should do the job;

(b) the program should be a joint effort for India and Pakistan;

(c) the recession in the United States precluded such an effort;

(d) Indian acceptance of Soviet economic assistance was problematic.

Kennedy's conclusion, incorporating the large framework in which he set the Indian problem, was as follows:

> Mr. President, let us recall again the profile of the Asian continent. India, with its nearly 400 million souls, and China, a country in the neighborhood of 600 million. India contains nearly 40 percent of all the free peoples of the uncommitted world. Let us not be confused by talk of Indian neutrality. Let us remember that our Nation also during the period of its formative growth adopted a policy of noninvolvement in the great international controversies of the 19th century. Nothing serves the ultimate interests of all of the West better than the opportunity for the emergent uncommitted nations of the world to absorb their primary energies now in programs of real economic improvement.
>
> This is the only basis on which Asian and African nations can find the political balance and social stability which provide the true defense against Communist penetration. Our friendships should not be equated with military alliances or "voting the Western ticket." To do so only drives these countries closer to totalitarianism or polarizes the world in such a way as to increase rather than diminish the chances for local war.
>
> The Russians are trying to repeat in other parts of Asia and

Africa their takeover of China. They are counting on the Indian disenchantment with the inadequacy of Western assistance and democratic methods of planning and economic life.

In considering the economic future of India we shall do well to recall that India has passed the point of economic takeoff and is launched upon an effort which will by the end of the century make her one of the big powers of the world, with the population of just under 1 billion and capable of harnessing all the resources of modern science, technology, and destruction. No greater challenge exists in the future than the peaceful organization of a world society which includes not only the wealthy industrial states of America, Western Europe, and Russia, but also powerful new industrial states in Asia, Latin America, Africa, and the Middle East. How these states emerge from their period of economic transition will not only color but quite likely cast the historic setting of the next generation. This question was recently set in these words by Professor W. W. Rostow before the Senate Foreign Relations Committee:

"Shall these new powerful states emerge to maturity from a totalitarian setting, their outlook dominated by bitter memories of colonialism and by memories of painful transition made without help, while the rich West sat by, concerned only with the problems of defense? Or shall these states emerge from a democratic setting, built on human values shared with the West, and on memories of shared adventure in the decisive periods of transition?"

The answer to this question will not be long in the making if we do not act now and over the next few years, for India, the most important of all the uncommitted states, has entered its formative period. A successful Indian program is important at least as much for the example it can set for the economic future of other underdeveloped countries as for its own sake. The United States, Western Europe, and Japan have it in their power to make a demonstration that the democratic process is a persuasive method of creation, not frustration.

India stands out as one of the few countries in this non-

Communist zone which really believes in the importance of breaking stagnation and acquiring habits of growth. India, like the United States, is engaged in a struggle of coexistence—in its case with China, which is also pursuing a planning effort being put under critical comparison all over the world. India, for better or worse, is a world power with a world audience. Its democratic future is delicately and dangerously poised; it would be catastrophic if its leadership were now humiliated in its quest for Western assistance when its cause is good.

There is no visible political glory for either party in coming to the aid of India, particularly at a time of high taxes and pressing defense needs. The task of "selling" such a program to the American people is far more difficult than that of a decade ago, for we were more familiar with the people and problems of Europe, our ties were closer, their economies were more directly aligned with our own and held more certain promise of success. But the need—and the danger—are as great now as then. India today represents as great a hope, as commanding a challenge as Western Europe did in 1947—and our people are still, I am confident, equal to the effort.

I realize that it is difficult to give resonance to such words and proposals in the mood which has governed the approach to foreign aid and economic policy in both parties during the past sessions of Congress. But this mood has, in part, been induced by the persistent counsels of caution, by the lack of vision the purposefulness [*sic*] with which we have approached the problems of the underdeveloped world. If we are to break the aimless drifts and deadlocks in policy, if we are to regain the initiative in world affairs, if we are to arouse the decent emotions of Americans, it is time again that we seek projects with the power of stirring and rallying our hopes and energies. Once again our national interest and creative magnanimity can merge in the service of freedom.

Cooper then spoke more briefly in support of Kennedy's initiative. He restated in his own way some of Kennedy's basic propositions but concluded on a distinctive note:

I have dealt chiefly with the self-interest of the United States. But I do not want to overlook the deep humanitarian impulses of our people which have led us throughout our history to help peoples throughout the world. We cannot help but know that it is inequitable if democratic countries will not move toward correcting the imbalance of opportunity and living standards which exist in different areas of the world. Humanity and justice dictate the responsibility of the United States, as a favored nation, to do its part to correct this imbalance.

I congratulate the distinguished junior Senator from Massachusetts on the initiative he has taken in bringing these issues before the Senate, and in challenging public opinion. I am glad to be associated with him.

I should like to say, also, that I know, from personal experience, that the President of the United States, and the Secretary of State, Mr. Dulles, have continually shown their deep interest in the problems of India and Asia, and have taken the initiative in supporting their democratic efforts. And it has been evident to all that Mr. Christian Herter and Mr. Douglas Dillon, in their positions of leadership in the Department of State, have given strong and effective support to this aspect of our foreign policy.

In our preoccupation with world communism, we may forget at times the powerful drive for freedom and independence which has swept from the Philippines, across Asia, into Africa. It offers great opportunities. It also offers some dangers. We believe that freedom will prevail, but we know that its spirit is not constantly and uniformly irresistible. The great Justice Holmes said: "The irresistible comes to pass through effort." We have submitted this concurrent resolution to suggest that the United States make its greatest effort for freedom, and in the hope that it may prevail in Asia.

The concurrent resolution was attached to Section 2 of the Mutual Security Act and thus entered formally into the Congressional foreign aid debate of 1958.

As Kennedy's speech of March 25 suggested, he was quite conscious that 1958 appeared to be a difficult year for foreign aid in general and for aid to India in particular. Indeed the *New York Times* account of the Kennedy-Cooper initiative published on March 26 concludes:

> The Kennedy-Cooper resolution's chances of approval by Congress are rated slender for three reasons.
>
> First, Congress has grown increasingly hesitant about making long-term advance commitments on foreign aid.
>
> Second, the Kennedy-Cooper resolution has neither strong Senatorial backing nor a national sense of crisis about India to aid it.
>
> Third, Senatorial opinion is becoming increasingly hostile toward aid to neutralist nations like India and is generally antipathetic to all forms of foreign aid this year.

The embattled senators widely circulated their speeches of March 25, arranged that favorable editorials be inserted in the *Congressional Record*, encouraged outside supporters to set out their views, and mobilized votes in the Senate for the struggle to come. The Foreign Relations Committee on May 21, 1958, supported the concurrent resolution without dissent, but a lively battle took place on June 6 when Senator Styles Bridges, on the Senate floor, moved to strike the proposed concurrent resolution from the bill.

The debate is a vivid and faithful reflection of the conflicting views of the time on foreign aid in general and aid to India in particular. Although the arguments against the Kennedy-Cooper resolution were more deeply rooted (extracted in Appendix B), some opponents echoed the formal position taken by the Department of State in a letter of May 1, 1958, from assistant secretary for Congressional affairs, William B. Macomber, Jr., to Senator Theodore Francis Green, chairman of the Foreign Relations Committee (see Appendix A). Macomber expressed general support for aid to India, but concluded: "We wish to note additionally that these objectives [incorporated in the Kennedy-Cooper resolution] apply equally to many other Free World countries. As a general rule, therefore, the Department believes it desirable to avoid resolutions limited to individual countries."

Bridges' amendment was defeated by a vote of 35 to 47 with 14 paired or not voting. The Kennedy-Cooper resolution was supported by a coalition of Democrats and liberal Republicans, opposed by a coalition of Republicans and conservative Democrats, mainly southern Democrats. Lyndon Johnson, Senate majority leader, supported the resolution. Senator Cooper, in a letter to me of July 1, 1982, recalls that Bridges was astonished at the result.

Things did not go so well in the House of Representatives. The issue had not been systematically debated on the floor; and, for a variety of reasons, the House was less sympathetic to development aid than the Senate (see below, pp. 113–114). In the conference on the somewhat different versions of the 1958 aid bill, which concluded on June 17, the House members rejected the concurrent resolution on three grounds: lack of a House debate; their belief that existing legislation provided an adequate framework for aid to India; and reluctance to single out a particular country. Kennedy and Cooper filed formal statements regretting and rebutting the House position of substance, and chairman Green of the Senate Foreign Relations Committee, in presenting the report, noted: ". . . it was the opinion of most of the conferees on both sides that Indian economic development is of the utmost importance and the act should be administered in a manner which recognized this fact."

Thus, by mid 1958, Kennedy and Cooper had managed to carry the Senate and to heighten somewhat the priority for Indian aid in U.S. policy and public opinion. They had heartened supporters of enlarged aid to India in the executive branch and the international community, including the World Bank; they had provided an element of hope to somewhat gloomy Indian leaders; but they were a long way from their objective of creating an international consortium capable of supplying the foreign exchange required to assure the success of the Second Five Year Plan and to grubstake the Indian development effort in the decade ahead.

So much for the bare bones of the story of how the Kennedy-Cooper resolution of 1958 was launched. We step back now to examine in Chapters 2–5 the forces at work in the 1950s which set the framework for the Kennedy-Cooper resolution of 1958, led Kennedy to seize the initiative on this matter, and in time yielded, as we shall see in Chapter 6, a rather surprising result: a substantial, perhaps even major, change on the world scene set in motion from the Congress rather than the executive branch of the U.S. government.

2. The Communist Challenge, 1953-1958

It is evident that the Kennedy-Cooper initiative launched on March 25, 1958, was, in part, the product of a gathering uneasiness in American political life about both Communist policy toward the developing regions of the non-Communist world and the apparent economic momentum of Communist China. This uneasiness was heightened, as it was in military policy, education policy, and other fields, by the launching of the first Soviet Sputnik in October 1957.

A distinct and explicit Communist policy toward the developing regions had, in fact, begun to take shape as early as 1947, as prospects for a further extension of Soviet power in Europe dimmed and Stalin concluded, rather to his surprise, that Mao was likely to triumph in the Chinese civil war.

Ambitious new objectives were enunciated by Andrei A. Zhdanov at the founding meeting of the Cominform in September 1947. Open guerrilla warfare had begun in Indochina as early as November 1946 out of the region's own dynamics, but in the wake of the Cominform session, Communist insurrections began in Burma in April 1948, in Malaya in June of that year, and in Indonesia and the Philippines in the autumn. The Indian and Japanese Communist parties, with less scope for guerrilla action, nevertheless sharply increased their militancy in 1948. As final victory was won in China in November 1949, Mao's political-military strategy was openly commended by the Cominform to the Communist parties in those areas where guerrilla operations were underway. Stalin and Mao met early in 1950 and confirmed the ambitious Asian strategy, planning in Moscow its climax with Kim Il Sung in the form of the North Korean invasion of South Korea, which took place at the end of June 1950.

The American and United Nations' responses to the invasion of South Korea, the landings at Inchon, the march to the Yalu, the Chinese Communist entrance into the war, and the successful U.N. defense against massive Chinese assault at the 38th parallel in April–May 1951 brought this phase of military and quasi-military Communist effort throughout Asia to a gradual end. Neither Moscow nor Peking was willing to undertake all-out war or even accept the cost of a continued Korean offensive. And elsewhere the bright Communist hopes of 1946–1947 had dimmed. Nowhere in Asia was Mao's success repeated. Indonesia, Burma, and the Philippines largely overcame their guerrillas. At considerable cost to Britain and the Commonwealth, the Malayan guerrillas were contained and driven back. Only in Indochina, where French colonialism offered a seedbed as fruitful as postwar China, was there real Communist momentum. The conventional view is that Ho Chi Minh was finally forced by Moscow and Peking to settle for half a victory at the Geneva conference of 1954 in the interest of the larger policy of the Communist bloc which had begun to shape up in Asia from the summer of 1951. Khrushchev asserts, on the contrary, that the French willingness to grant North Vietnam to the Communists, after Dienbienphu, was "the absolute maximum" the Communist side envisaged, given the gravely weakened position of the guerrilla forces.[1] In any case, there was an interval of four years of relative quiet in Indochina.

It was in this interval, when the initial postwar limits of Communist expansion by force of arms in Asia were reached, that a quite different approach to the developing world was devised in Moscow. It was part of a general strategy broadly enunciated in October 1952 at the Nineteenth Party Congress, but it emerged operationally only in the wake of Stalin's death. It no doubt took account of the U.S. Fourth Point program launched in 1949 as well as the desire of the developing countries, strongly expressed in the United Nations and elsewhere, for external assistance.

The strategy appears to have had three major objectives: to buy time for the Soviet Union to develop fusion weapons and missile delivery capabilities; to weaken the ties between the United States and Western Europe (and to reduce Western allocations for military purposes) by apparently peaceful initiatives; and to expand Soviet influence in the developing regions through expanded trade, loans, and technical assistance as well as more conventional forms of Communist political penetration. The strategy suited well the requirements of Communist China, which, in the wake of the Korean War, felt the need to turn to neglected tasks of economic development.[2] It was also a strategy that held some promise of leapfrogging or diluting the cohesion of the new military pacts formed around the periphery of the Communist world to deter another Korea-like adventure: the Southeast Asia Treaty Organization (SEATO) and the Baghdad Pact. In a larger sense, the new strategy marks the beginning of the Soviet move from status as a Eurasian power to a sustained bid for global power and influence.

The Soviet economic offensive began in 1953 when the new Soviet leaders launched a general program for expanding East-West trade. Between 1952 and 1956 the Communist bloc trade agreement network with the developing areas—which initially touched only Afghanistan, Iran, and Egypt—extended to Argentina, India, Greece, Lebanon, Uruguay, Iceland, Burma, Yugoslavia, Syria, Yemen, Pakistan, and Indonesia. At the same time, the Communist states began to participate with great energy in the trade fairs of the non-Communist world.

While East-West trade expanded, the proportionate share of non-Communist trade with Communist states as a whole remained relatively limited, never rising in this period much above 3 percent. Nevertheless, the post-1953 trade expansion had certain important political consequences. First, although the overall level of East-West trade remained low, trade with certain nations was sufficiently high to constitute a significant source of leverage. In 1956 more than 20 percent of the trade of Afghanistan, Iceland, Egypt, Yugoslavia, and Burma was with Communist countries; 17 percent for Turkey; 12 percent for Iran. Second, the Soviet trade program reinforced the image sedulously cultivated after Stalin's death that the Soviet Union was ending its isolation and emerging as a self-confident world power in the normal, peaceful business of international life. Third, in 1951 the relative prices of basic commodities in the world economy peaked out, after a trend rise begun in the mid-1930s, declined absolutely as well as relatively during the rest of the 1950s. Thus, the Soviet willingness to purchase raw materials and foodstuffs produced in the underdeveloped areas on a stable trade agreement basis, and to provide counterpart goods by barter agreement, often seemed attractive to nations worried by the decline of raw materials and foodstuff prices in world markets, by currency difficulties in the purchase of imports, and by commodity surplus problems. In the latter category, for example, the Communist countries were able to make politically influential deals for Ceylon rubber.

In 1954 the Soviet Union, in addition to expanded trade, began to offer credits and technical assistance to certain selected nations in Asia, the Middle East, and Africa. The scale and spread of Communist bloc credits and technical assistance agreements was fairly impressive, as Tables 1 and 2 indicate, exceeding U.S. aid in a number of cases.

Credit terms granted were easy by international standards. Soviet loans usually ran from ten to thirty years with interest rates at 2 or 2½ percent. Certain loans—as in the case of Yemen—were granted without interest. Moreover, the conditions of repayment permitted in Soviet loan agreements

TABLE 1. Estimated Sino-Soviet Bloc Assistance to Less Developed Countries, as of February 1, 1958 (*millions of U.S. dollars*)

	Economic	Arms	Total
Near East and Africa			
Egypt	235	250	485
Ethiopia	5		5
Syria	194	100	294
Turkey	10		10
Yemen	16	3	19
Total	460	353	813
South and Southeast Asia			
Afghanistan	136	25	161
Burma	42		42
Cambodia	22		22
Ceylon	20		20
India	295		295
Indonesia	109		109
Nepal	13		13
Total	637	25	662
Europe			
Iceland	5		5
Yugoslavia	464		464
Total	469		469
Latin America			
Argentina	6		6
Brazil	2		2
Total	8		8
Grand Total	1,574	378	1,952

Note: The assistance figures shown are all credits except for grants of $56 million by Communist China to Cambodia ($22 million), Nepal ($13 million), Ceylon ($16 million), and Egypt ($5 million).

Substantially all of the arms have been shipped.

Of the economic assistance of over $1.5 billion, probably some $200 million has actually been spent.

Of the total of $1.9 billion in block assistance—arms and economic—over $1 billion comes from the U.S.S.R. and most of the remainder from the Eastern European satellites.

Source: Department of State Bulletin vol. 38, no. 978, March 24, 1958; Table 1, p. 470; Table 2, p. 473.

TABLE 2. U.S. and Sino-Soviet Bloc Economic Assistance to Certain Near Eastern and Asian Countries, July 1, 1955, to February 1, 1958 *(millions of U.S. dollars)*

	ICA Obliga-tions	Other U.S. Govern-ment[a]	U.S. Private Invest-ment[b]	Total U.S.	Total Sino-Soviet Bloc
Afghanistan	33	14	figures not available	47	136
Burma	25	18	"	43	42
Cambodia	94	2	"	96	22
Ceylon	11		"	11	20
Egypt	2	14	"	16	235
India	126	293	"	419	295
Indonesia	27	97	"	124	109
Iran	114	26	"	140	
Iraq	7		"	7	
Israel	51	37	"	88	
Jordan	28		"	28	
Lebanon	16			16	
Nepal	7			7	
Pakistan	204	68	"	272	
Philippines	63	72	"	135	
Saudi Arabia			"		
Syria			"		194
Thailand	73	2	"	75	
Turkey	166	56	"	222	10
Yemen			"		16
Grand Total	1,047	699	213	1,959	1,092

Note: ICA refers to the then current title of the foreign aid agency: the International Co-operation Administration.

Of the private investment figure for the United States— $213 million—it is estimated that not less than 60 percent, or $128 million, is in oil and not more than 40 percent, or $85 million, is in other types of investment. The figures relate to new U.S. private investment during the calendar years 1954, 1955, and 1956. [The degree to which private foreign investment constitutes economic aid is, of course, debatable.]

U.S. Government assistance includes agricultural sales under Public Law 480, ICA obligations, and Export-Import Bank loans.

[a]Includes aid under Public Law 480, Titles I and II, and Export-Import Bank Credits.

[b]U.S. private investment for 3 years 1954–56.

took the form either of commodities normally exported or local currency to be used for Soviet purposes within the country in question.

The distribution of these credits and their scale suggest the variety of Soviet purposes they were designed to sustain. In Afghanistan, the Soviet Union was able to become the major supplier of capital, technical assistance, and military supplies in a region of historic strategic importance. Moscow's aim, obvious in retrospect, was to move gradually toward direct military and political control over the classic gateway to the Indian subcontinent, a project consummated *ad interim* only a quarter-century later.[3] In Egypt a high proportion of Communist aid took the form of arms, a move designed both to exacerbate the tensions within the Middle East and to give Russia a position of general leverage over Egyptian policy. The Soviet arms loan was obviously a prime factor in the events which led to the Suez crisis of November 1956. The Soviet credit arrangements with Belgrade were designed to support the process of weaning Yugoslavia back toward the Soviet orbit and to reverse the consequences of what was judged to have been Stalin's inept handling of the Yugoslavs in 1947–1948—a process subject to many vicissitudes. In India, Soviet aid was purely economic; and it was on a scale sufficient to support the image of the Soviet Union as an authentic friend of India and to achieve several political purposes: to support some increase in popular attachment to the Soviet Union; and to generate increased sympathy for the Indian Communist Party while maintaining, in the short run, friendly relations with Nehru and the Congress Party. Soviet aid in India was not, however, on a scale sufficient to fulfill the foreign exchange requirements of the Second Five Year Plan, the frustration and failure of which Indian Communists evidently counted upon heavily in the latter years of the decade.

In general, then, the Soviet Union placed its credits in the developing areas with an eye to concrete specific advantages both short- and long-run in character. Like Soviet military policy as reformulated after Stalin's death, Soviet economic policy toward the developing countries had the earmarks of a program developed step by step for the long pull, as it proved to be.

The Soviet program of expanded trade, technical assistance, and credits in what were then called "the underdeveloped areas"—now called developing countries—was conducted against a background of policy and propaganda designed to impress the governments and peoples of these areas with the rapid growth in Soviet military and technological strength vis-à-vis the United States. It was altogether typical of this strategy that when Khrushchev and Nikolai A. Bulganin barnstormed through India in 1955 a fusion weapon was test-exploded in Central Asia.

The purposeful offensive in trade, technical assistance, and loans from Moscow, and the assertive peregrinations of Soviet leaders in 1955–1958, served to affirm that Moscow in no way intended to turn Communist leadership over to Peking in these decisive regions. Russia remained a major power in Asia, pressed hard into the Middle East, and began to prepare the way for the exercise of power and influence in Africa. The great relative advantage of the Soviet Union and its Eastern satellites over Communist China in resources, trading potential, and technicians was brought to bear at a time when the economic requirements of Communist China might have absorbed a much higher share of the Communist bloc's exportable surplus than was, in fact, made available to it.

However much Peking may have disliked this effort to assert Soviet primacy—even in Burma, Indonesia, and the other areas close to China's borders—the hard facts of relative military and economic power at this period of history were accepted up to 1958. In the meanwhile, Peking maintained its own ties and apparatus of influence in North Korea, Malaya and Indonesia while contesting Moscow for influence in Hanoi.

This soft strategy in the underdeveloped areas undoubtedly

raised some interesting and difficult questions in Moscow and Peking. Could Communist takeover be envisaged without the massive use of force? After all, it took the combination of civil and external war to lay the basis for the Nationalist disintegration in China; and Communist power had never been achieved elsewhere without major hostilities or physical occupation except in Czechoslovakia, where the threat of occupation operated. And, if force were required to climax the disintegration process envisaged in the new nations, how would the prospective victims then react—and how would the United States? How much risk was it appropriate to assume in carrying forward such ventures? These questions were debated within the inner circles of the Communist world, and they could not immediately or easily be answered. But the prospects for embarrassing the West and for such limited gains as the political disruption of U.S. military base areas were sufficiently attractive in 1953–1958 for Moscow to proceed in good heart.

The whole enterprise could be presented to the developing world in what Douglas Dillon described in 1958 as a "most attractive and colorful wrapping," while the contrast with then current U.S. policy could be drawn by Soviet speakers in passages like these:

> We do not seek to get any advantages. We do not need profits, privileges, controlling interest, concessions or raw material sources. We do not ask you to participate in any blocs, reshuffle your governments or change your domestic or foreign policy. We are ready to help you as brother helps brother, without any interest whatever, for we know from our own experience how difficult it is to get rid of need. Tell us what you need and we will help you and send, according to our economic capabilities, money needed in the form of loans or aid . . . to build for you institutions for industry, education and hospitals. . . . We do not ask you to join any blocs . . . our only condition is that there will be no strings attached.[4]

To the extent that the Kennedy-Cooper resolution of 1958 was a response to Communist policy, it was affected not only by Soviet and Eastern European aid and trade initiatives in the developing world but also—and perhaps even more—by the image in the West of what was transpiring in the People's Republic of China in the period 1953–1958. Statistical estimates of the year-by-year course of the Chinese economy are difficult to construct for this period, and experts differ to a degree. But the simple, universally recognized fact is that the years 1953–1958 witnessed a surge of agricultural and industrial output which, for complex reasons, Chinese society proved incapable of sustaining, as Tables 3 and 4 and Chart 1 indicate. Some Western, Soviet, and Eastern European analysts of the Chinese performance at that time questioned the soundness and long-run viability of the economic policies being pursued on the mainland,[5] but, to a degree, the short-run momentum of the P.R.C. was real and suggested to some that the Chinese Communists had hit upon a formula for the rapid modernization of poor, underdeveloped nations that might exert great attractive power as a model to be emulated throughout Asia, the Middle East, Africa, and Latin America.

This is not the occasion to analyze in detail the basic economic problems of the Chinese mainland in the 1950s and the policies generated under Mao's direction to deal with them.[6] A few observations are required, however, to put in perspective the image of Communist China in relation to India which played a considerable role in the policy debates of the time.

As Table 5 indicates, India and China, as of the early 1950s, were extremely poor countries in terms of real income per capita—at about the level of Meiji Japan before sustained industrialization began in the mid 1880s. Gross birth rates were about 40 per 1000—close to the maximum in the modern world. Very high proportions of the working force were in agriculture. Due to more extensive irrigation, double-cropping, and fertilizer applications, productivity per acre

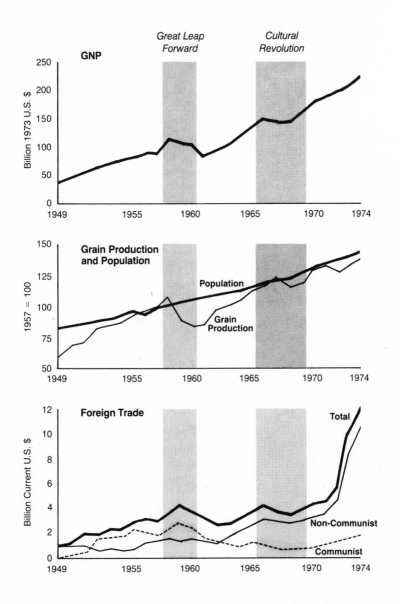

CHART 1. China: Basic Economic Trends, 1949–1974

23

TABLE 3. China: Economic Results, 1949–1974

Period	Overall Results	Industrial Results	Agricultural Results	Foreign Trade Results	Consumer Welfare Results
1949–52 Rehabilitation	Return to pre-Communist level of economic activity.	Reactivation of capacity as flow of raw materials resumes.	Return of fields to operation and distribution of land to peasants.	Imposition of strict government control and switch to Communist partners.	End of civil war, inflation, gross starvation; hope rekindled.
1953–57 1st 5 Year Plan	Successful build-up of industrial base under Soviet auspices.	Increased capacity and output of steel and other basic products.	Gains in output from own resources; collectivization in stages.	Growing volume, with basic products being exchanged for Soviet machinery.	Stabilization of living standards at spartan but improved levels.
1958–60 Great Leap Forward	Disastrous over-straining of the economy's resources.	Ruinous increase in tempo and deterioration of quality.	Precipitous fall in output due to bad weather and ill-fated communes.	Sharp spurt, then downturn caused by domestic problems.	Near starvation and collapse of morale when leap fails.

1961–65 Readjustment and Recovery	Quick and successful recovery of economic balance.	Rationalization of output, with investment in priority.	Quick return to growth pattern with aid of new inputs.	Dramatic shift to Japan and Western Europe, with rising volume.	Restoration of living standards at spartan levels.
1966–69 Cultural Revolution	Short-lived break in economic momentum.	Sharp dip in industrial output with investment continuing.	Continued growth on basis of good weather and larger inputs.	Temporary dip because of domestic dislocations.	Maintenance of living standards in spite of political turmoil.
1970–74 Resumption of Regular Planning	Resumption of economic growth across the board.	Gains in capacity and output, with oil a star performer; coal shortages.	Continued growth on basis of good weather and larger inputs.	Resumption of growth in line with domestic economic gains; use of credit.	Gradual improvement in living standards.

Source: Tables 3 and 4 and Chart 1 were constructed by Arthur G. Ashbrook, Jr. and published in his chapter, "China: Economic Overview, 1975," in *China: A Reassessment of the Economy,* A compendium of papers submitted to the Joint Economic Committee (Washington, D.C.: G.P.O., July 10, 1975), pp. 22–23.

TABLE 4. China: Major Economic Indicators, 1949–1974

Period and year	GNP (Billions of 1973 Dollars)[a]	Population Midyear (millions)	GNP Per Capita (1973 Dollars)	Industrial Production (1957 = 100)
1949–52, Rehabilitation				
1949	40	538	74	20
1950	49	547	89	27
1951	56	558	101	38
1952	67	570	117	48
1953–57, 1st 5 Year Plan				
1953	71	583	122	61
1954	75	596	125	70
1955	82	611	134	73
1956	88	626	141	88
1957	94	641	147	100
1958–60, Great Leap Forward				
1958	113	657	172	145
1959	107	672	160	177
1960	106	685	155	184
1961–65, Readjustment and Recovery				
1961	82	695	118	108
1962	93	704	133	114
1963	103	716	144	137
1964	117	731	160	163
1965	134	747	179	199
1966–69, Cultural Revolution				
1966	145	763	190	231
1967	141	780	180	202
1968	142	798	178	222
1969	157	817	192	265
1970–74, Resumption of Regular Planning				
1970	179	837	214	313
1971	190	857	222	341
1972	197	878	225	371
1973	217	899	241	416
1974 preliminary	223	920	243	432

[a]Note that GNP in this table is presented in 1973 U.S. dollars whereas foreign trade is presented in current U.S. dollars.

[b]Negligible.

Agricultural Production (1957 = 100)	Steel Output (millions of metric tons)	Grain Output (millions of metric tons)	Foreign Trade Exports f.o.b. (billions of current dollars)	Imports c.i.f. (billions of current dollars)	Percent Trade with Communist Countries
54	0.16	108	0.43	0.40	(b)
64	.61	125	.62	.59	29
71	.90	135	.78	1.12	51
83	1.35	154	.88	1.02	70
83	1.77	157	1.04	1.26	68
84	2.22	160	1.06	1.29	74
94	2.85	175	1.38	1.66	74
97	4.46	182	1.64	1.48	66
100	5.35	185	1.62	1.44	64
108	11.08	200	1.94	1.82	63
83	13.35	165	2.23	2.06	69
78	18.67	160	1.96	2.03	66
77	8	160	1.53	1.50	56
92	8	180	1.52	1.15	53
96	9	185	1.57	1.20	45
106	10.8	195	1.75	1.47	34
114	12.5	210	2.04	1.84	30
116	15	215	2.21	2.04	26
123	12	230	1.94	1.95	21
116	14	215	1.94	1.82	22
118	16	220	2.03	1.83	20
129	17.8	240	2.05	2.24	20
134	21	246	2.42	2.30	23
130	23	240	3.08	2.84	22
138	25.5	250	4.90	4.98	17
141	23.8	255	5.90	6.70	15

was higher in China than in India, supporting a larger population from similar amounts of arable land.

Both India under colonialism and China in its more complex interactions with the external world since the Opium War and the Treaty of Nanking (1842) had gradually and erratically developed roughly similar industrial establishments. These establishments were, by 1952, of considerable absolute size; but relative to their populations they were much smaller than those of the Soviet Union in 1928 (on the eve of the First Five Year Plan) or Japan in the 1930s. Nevertheless, the China that Mao effectively unified in 1949 had a foundation of industrial capacity, rail communications, electric power, administrators, and an urban working force on which to build.

The simple facts of peace and unification—including the relinkage, after eighteen years, of the industrial base in Manchuria with the rest of China—permitted rapid increases in output to take place despite the diversion of resources caused by Chinese participation in the Korean War. Substantial idle industrial capacity existed which could quite quickly be re-activated, although the process was somewhat slowed by Soviet removals of equipment from Manchuria as Japanese reparations. By 1952, pre—World War II peak industrial production figures were re-attained, and three successive years of good weather in 1950–1952 probably permitted pre-war agricultural production to be exceeded in the latter year. This was the setting in which the first Chinese Five Year Plan (1953–1957) was launched.

That plan was modeled on the Soviet First Five Year Plan (1928–1933). It centered on rapid expansion of heavy industries as the basis for the modernization of the Chinese armed forces; and, as in the case of the Soviet Union, capital resources were to be extracted from a rapidly collectivized peasantry. The Chinese Communist cadres were, quite literally, instructed to take their guidance from Chapters 9–12 of Stalin's short course *History of the All-Union Communist*

Party, covering both the NEP (New Economic Policy) and the Soviet First Five Year Plan.[7]

As Table 5 suggests, the analogy was inexact: China as of 1952 was a much less industrialized nation than the Soviet Union of 1928; its highly labor-intensive agriculture was of a quite different character; and its people lived closer to the margin of subsistence. Although quite prepared to be ruthless in the collectivization of agriculture, Mao had to proceed with somewhat more care than Stalin who began with the U.S.S.R. enjoying a modest grain export surplus. The Soviet Union could, at great human cost, afford a period of stagnant or even declining agricultural production. China could not. Moreover, the first effect of land redistribution was to increase food consumption in the Chinese countryside and to reduce the flow to the cities. Thus, despite very considerable industrial progress, the Chinese Communist leadership came to face a difficult choice as the result of the passive resistance of the peasants to government claims on their output and the administrative complexity of organizing collective institutions rapidly on a vast scale. By 1955, as Alexander Eckstein concludes: ". . . the Chinese began to realize that the Stalinist model was not applicable to Chinese conditions, *i.e.*, that a development strategy built on industrialization was not viable amidst the resource endowments prevailing on the mainland."[8] The debate, so far as agriculture was concerned, came to rest on whether collectivization should be accelerated or whether it should be slowed down. Those advocating the latter course, foreshadowing policies that were to triumph definitively only in the post-Mao period, also tended to urge increased allocations of fertilizers and machinery to agriculture, increased reliance on material incentives, and priority for technical rather than political expertise in the government and Communist Party apparatus.

Mao decided in 1955 to move firmly in a quite different direction: to mobilize, motivate, and lead China's great abundant resource—manpower—in a maximum collective surge

TABLE 5. Indicators of Comparative Levels of Development in Mainland China, the Soviet Union, Japan, and India

| | | U.S.S.R. | | | |
| | | Approximately 1928 | | Approximately 1950 | |
	Units	Amount	Year	Amount	Year
Gross national product	Billions of 1952 US dollars	35.00	1928	100.00[a]	1952
GNP per head[b]	1952 US dollars	240.00	1928	490.00	1952
Population	Millions	147.00	1926	198.00	1950
Crude birth rate	per 1,000	43.50[d]	1926	25.00 to 34.00	1950–51
Crude death rate	per 1,000	19.90[d]	1926	10.00 to 16.00	1950–51
Proportion in agriculture and fishing	per 1,000	76.50[h]	1926	49.00 to 53.00[i]	1950
Agriculture					
Number of persons dependent on agriculture per acre of cultivated land	Persons per acre	0.20	1926	0.20	1950
Paddy rice yield	Metric quintals per hectare	21.50	1934–38		
Wheat yield	Metric quintals per hectare	7.90	1934–38		
Industry					
Coal	Total in million metric tons	40.10	1929	281.00	1951
	Kilograms per capita	273.00	1929	1,419.00	1951
Pig iron	Total in million metric tons	3.30	1927–28	19.40	1950
	Kilograms per capita	22.00	1927–28	98.00	1950
Crude steel	Total in million metric tons	4.30	1927–28	24.80	1950
	Kilograms per capita	29.00	1927–28	125.00	1950
Finished steel	Total in million metric tons				
	Kilograms per capita				
Generating capacity of electric power	Total in thousand kilowatts	1,900.00	1928	16,000.00	1949
	Kilowatts per capita	0.01	1928	0.08	1949
Cotton spindleage in industry	Total in thousands	7,465.00	1929	10,000.00	1949
	Units per capita	0.05	1929	0.05	1949
Cement	Total in million metric tons	1.90	1928	19.40	1950
	Kilograms per capita	13.00	1928	98.00	1950

Source: Alexander Eckstein, *China's Economic Development* (Ann Arbor: University of Michigan Press, 1975), p. 214.

[a] 1950 GNP was $87 billions, or $440 per head.

[b] To nearest $5.

[c] 1938 GNP was $24.6 billions, or $355 per head.

[d] European Russia.

[e] Not official statistics, but based on the interpretation of Irene B. Taeuber and Frank W. Notestein, "The Changing Fertility of the Japanese," *Population Studies*, I, No. 1, pp. 1–28.

[f] Official statistics (implying some understatement of both).

[g] Estimated from the official returns by applying the Kingsley Davis figures; estimates by Davis for 1931–41 are 45 per 1,000 birth rate and 31.2 per 1,000 death rate. See his book, *The Population of India and Pakistan* (Princeton, 1951).

Japan				India		China	
Meiji		1930's					
Amount	Year	Amount	Year	Amount	Year	Amount	Year
2.20	1878–82	22.60[c]	1936	22.00	1950	30.00	1952
65.00	1878–82	325.00	1936	60.00	1950	50.00	1952
35.56	1875	69.25[f]	1935	358.00	1950	582.00	1953
39.00[e]	1885	31.20	1931–37	38.00[g]	1949	40.00	1930–35
32.00[e]	1885	17.90	1931–37	24.00[g]	1949	34.00	1930–35
84.80[j]	1872	42.10[k]	1940	68.00[l]	1931	80.00	1952
2.00	1872	1.60	1936–40	0.60	1931	1.90	1953
21.60	1880–84	36.30	1934–38	13.30	1934–38	25.30	1931–37
		18.80	1934–38	6.80	1937–39	10.80	1931–37
0.60	1875	41.80	1936	34.90	1951	53.00	1952
17.00	1875	604.00	1936	97.00	1951	96.00	1952
0.01	1877	2.00	1936	1.90	1951	1.60	1952
0.20	1877	29.00	1936	5.00	1951	2.75	1952
none				1.50	1951	1.20	1952
none				4.00	1951	2.00	1952
none		4.50	1936			0.70	1952
none		66.00	1936			1.00	1952
none		6,777.00	1936	2,409.00	1951	2,850.00	1952
none		0.10	1936	0.01	1951	0.005	1952
8.00	1877	11,823.00	1936	10,144.00	1952	5,000.00	1952
negligible		0.17	1936	0.03	1952	0.01	1952
negligible		4.30	1929	3.20	1951	2.30	1952
negligible		63.00	1929	9.00	1951	4.00	1952

[h] Distribution of the male labor force. The figure is 77.6% for the distribution of population and 81.8% for the distribution of the total labor force.

[i] Distribution of the male labor force. The figure is 53–57% for the 1950 distribution of the total labor force. It was 53.8% for 1939.

[j] Distribution of the total occupied population, including females. Some estimates place the 1872 percentage at 77.1%.

[k] Distribution of the total occupied population, including females. The 1936 figure for the occupied population, excluding women in agriculture, is 30.1%.

[l] Distribution of the total population.

of human effort in both industry and agriculture to compensate by political means for the nation's lack of capital. A poor harvest in 1956–1957 slowed things down but, against the background of an abundant harvest in 1957–1958, the Great Leap Forward was in full cry. Agriculture as well as industrial production did, indeed, surge ahead as the world watched in authentic fascination. But the application of Mao's political theories to economic development proved wasteful and, in the end, counterproductive. A good deal of the industrial output generated proved unusable, and labor was diverted from agriculture. The whole somewhat manic enterprise proved extraordinarily sensitive to the vicissitudes of weather and the harvests. In 1959 agricultural output collapsed; in 1960, industrial output. China, its people exhausted by the extraordinary effort, underwent a severe economic decline which bottomed out in 1963 when agricultural production was 17 percent below its 1958 peak, industrial production 26 percent below its 1959 peak, real GNP per capita down by perhaps 21 percent (see Table 4). The human impact was sufficient to raise death rates and slow down the increase in Chinese population. This surge and collapse interwove the emergence, early in 1958, of acute tension between Moscow and Peking centered on the nuclear issue, leading to a progressive deterioration of relations including, in mid-1960, the withdrawal from China of Soviet technicians and the cessation of deliveries of Soviet industrial aid.

For our limited purposes, however, the point is that as of early 1958, when the Kennedy-Cooper resolution was launched, the Chinese economic development effort appeared to most observers a formidable, original, and apparently successful enterprise; indeed, the whole Chinese Communist economic performance since 1949 seemed impressive.

At a later point in this essay we shall look back from the 1980s at the relative economic performance of China and India over the past three decades (see below, pp. 208–212). At the moment, it is sufficient to note that, as of 1958, Indian economic development since independence (1947) was much less glamorous. For one thing, India did not experience the expansion that came, as it were, automatically to China from the ending of civil war, the re-linking with Manchuria, and the reactivation of idle industrial capacity. On the contrary, there were some significant economic costs to the separation of India and Pakistan on the previously unified sub-continent. Moreover, all the imperfections of the Indian development effort were open to view and, indeed, debated vigorously in the Indian press and parliament. Table 6 provides a roughly accurate shorthand view of how economic growth proceeded in the two countries from 1952 to the mid 1960s. It dramatizes clearly the simple fact that China did better in the first round (1952–56 to 1957–59), India did better in the second (1957–59 to 1961–65). But it was during the first round that the intellectual and policy debate on foreign aid was intense and that formative institutional decisions were made in Washington.

The adequacy of U.S. policy towards the developing regions was increasingly challenged during the 1950s under a wide variety of impulses, of which the rise of Soviet foreign aid programs and the apparent high momentum of the Chinese economy were only two. As noted earlier, the launching of the first Soviet satellite belongs among the array of such impulses. The connection was not, of course, direct, although the peoples in the developing regions and their political leaders were much impressed with the Soviet feat. The major impact, so far as the subject of this essay is concerned, was the effect of Sputnik in shifting the balance of forces in American political life. Within the two parties as well as in inter-party debate there had been since 1953 tension between what might be called the conservatives and the activists. Books 3 and 4 of this series (*Europe after Stalin* and *Open Skies*) are, in part, concerned with this tension. The conservatives (including some in the Democratic party) were, by and large,

TABLE 6. Rate of Growth of Production Sectors, China and India, 1952–1965 *(% per year)*

| Sector | China | | | India | | |
	1952–56 to 1957–59	1957–59 to 1961–65	1952–56 to 1961–65	1952–56 to 1957–59	1957–59 to 1961–65	1952–56 to 1961–65
Agriculture	4.2	1.6	2.8	2.3	2.6	2.5
All nonagricultural sectors	6.2	0.5	3.1	3.9	5.2	4.6
Net domestic product	4.8	1.4	3.0	3.1	4.0	3.6

Note: Swamy's calculations of Chinese growth rates are towards the lower end of the range of experts' calculations. They are, however, useful because he alone has done the laborious work of trying to render Chinese and Indian data roughly comparable by making calculations in terms of the price structure of both countries.

Source: Subramanian Swamy, "Economic Growth in China and India, 1952–1970," *Economic Development and Cultural Change*, Vol. 21, No. 4, Part II, July 1973, p. 63.

content with the military and foreign policy posture that had emerged from the Eisenhower administration's dispositions of 1953: overwhelming reliance for deterrence on the nation's nuclear delivery establishment; emphasis on military pacts, and military aid and support as reinforcement for those pacts, to enlarge and strengthen local ground forces in sensitive strategic areas; a commending of private foreign lending as the principal source of capital from abroad; and a reserved or negative diplomatic stance towards those governments adopting a neutralist position in the Cold War. The conservative policy was framed by a general view coloring domestic as well as military and foreign policy: that budgetary restraint was a fundamental, overriding imperative.

The sufficiency of these dispositions was questioned from within, as well as outside, the Eisenhower administration from its early days. And, by the autumn of 1957, the activists, including the proponents of development aid, had, piecemeal, gained some ground, as Table 2, above, and Chapter 9 suggest. Their hand was strengthened on all fronts by the Soviet launching of the first satellite—a fact of which Kennedy was quite conscious as he began the India initiative on March 25, 1958.

3. The Conceptual Debate of the 1950s about Development Aid Policy

U.S. policy toward development aid in the 1950s evolved not only in response to policies and events in the Communist world but also, to a degree, in response to a debate in the advanced industrial countries on three quite complex matters: the nature of the process of modernization in developing countries; the relation of external assistance to it; and the U.S. (and Western) interest, if any, in the success or failure of the developing nations in achieving sustained economic and social progress.

Many of those who addressed themselves with reasonable intellectual rigor to these questions were also involved in political crusading and, in some cases, in formulating and carrying out policy at one time or another. Conceptual analysis is a related but distinctively different kind of business from lobbying for a change in policy, policy formulation in a government, or day-to-day operations. Nevertheless, the main lines of conceptual argument are clear enough and can be abstracted from their sometimes polemical or operational context.

It may be well to begin with the arguments against U.S. development aid; that is, aid outside the framework of U.S. military security arrangements. They represented, on balance, the majority view within the Congress and the executive branch for most of the 1950s.

One version of the opposition to development aid was, in

its own way, positive. It suffused, for example, the 1954 Randall Commission report on foreign economic policy (see below, pp. 92–93). It took the view that the task of U.S. policy was to lead the world economy, as rapidly as possible, back to an approximation of the world before 1914: liberal if not free trade; unrestricted movement of private long-term capital; convertible currencies. The pre-1914 world economy did not, in fact, operate in such an engagingly uninhibited way, but the somewhat romanticized memory of that era exercised a powerful hold over many minds. And the influence of that memory had some positive consequences; for example, it encouraged those who accepted the concept to struggle against protectionist impulses in the United States and helped set in motion the succession of global negotiations to reduce trade barriers. But, implicitly at least, this vision of the task did not recognize that distinctive and difficult problems existed in the developing regions for which free trade, free private capital flows, and convertible currencies were not sufficient answers. By and large, holders of this view, while opposing development aid, were willing to support technical assistance, narrowly defined.

Among those who recognized the distinctive problems of the developing regions, P. T. Bauer was, without doubt, the most sophisticated intellectual analyst who took a reserved stance toward development aid and set explicit, highly restrictive economic and political criteria for expanding such aid. A Hungarian-born British academic at the London School of Economics, Bauer wrote, among other things, a short book analyzing the development process in India and urging, explicitly, the rejection of the Kennedy-Cooper resolution.[9]

Bauer argued that the West should not support the Indian Second Five Year Plan on the dual grounds that the Indian development strategy was technically ill-conceived and that the ultimate domestic political objectives of the Indian government were contrary to Western interests.

His technical argument began with a vivid and essentially

accurate portrait of India's poverty and the extent to which technical backwardness in the countryside, and social customs and attitudes, including the caste system, constituted serious but not insurmountable blocks to sustained progress.

Against this background, Bauer attacked the bias of the Indian Second Five Year Plan toward development of heavy industries, on the one hand, and inefficient cottage industries, on the other. In his view, India, as of the mid 1950s, should have concentrated its efforts on agriculture, education, transport and other infrastructure while creating a setting in which the private sector (mainly, but not exclusively, light industry) was encouraged to expand as higher incomes in agriculture, improved transport, etc. enlarged the domestic market.

Bauer's most explicit target was Professor P. C. Mahalanobis, a physicist who became for a time India's chief economic planner. Here Bauer quotes Mahalanobis and comments:[10]

> "In the long run [wrote Mahalanobis], the rate of industrialisation and the growth of national economy would depend on the increasing production of coal, electricity, iron and steel, heavy machinery, heavy chemicals, and the heavy industries generally which would increase the capacity for capital formation. One important aim is to make India independent, as quickly as possible, of foreign imports of producer goods so that the accumulation of capital would not be hampered by difficulties in securing supplies of essential consumer goods from other countries. The heavy industries must therefore be expanded with all possible speed [*Second Plan Papers*]."
>
> Yet in no meaningful sense [Bauer responded] is the prior development locally of a capital goods industry necessary either for material prosperity, or for the subsequent development of manufacturing industry itself. This is clear both on general grounds, and also from ample empirical evidence from the experience and position of many developed and underdeveloped countries, including that of Japan, in the rapid industrialization of which consumer goods industries

and the production of small-scale equipment were in the forefront.

Bauer summed up his technical indictment of the Second Five Year Plan with precision:

The Second Five-Year Plan is a glaring paradox, or rather series of paradoxes of which the following is an incomplete list. . . . There is the massive expenditure of heavy industry, regardless of cost and of prospective demand for its output, at a rate at least eight times the expenditure on the development of elementary education, when about four-fifths of the population are illiterate; the expenditure on a single steel plant is more than double the development expenditure on elementary education. There is the comparatively small expenditure on agriculture, and the restrictions on the movement of agricultural products, in the face of manifest, urgent and indeed desperate need to increase agricultural productivity and to extend production for the market. There are the severe restrictions, or complete bans on the supply of both imported and even locally produced consumer goods, in the face of the urgent need both to raise living standards, and to provide incentives to agricultural production for the market. There are the restrictions on the extension of efficient industrial capacity and the subsidization of inefficient cottage industry and of cooperative production and distribution, in the face of manifest need to economize on resources and satisfy wants at low costs, and in the face also of official statements on the importance of industrial progress and the raising of living standards. There is the exclusion of private Indian and foreign enterprise and investment from a wide range of industrial and commercial activity, in the face of urgent need to encourage viable economic activity. There is the neglect of roads, the official restrictions on the establishment of road transport enterprises, and on the movement of agricultural products, in the face of the urgent need to widen markets and to facilitate the movement of men, ideas and commodities. There are the severe restrictions on the establishment of all enterprises, in the face of the need to widen opportunities. And these measures and policies not only affect adversely the standard of living, but also restrict further any economic demand there might be for the output of the capacity created under the heavy industry program.[11]

Having disposed of Mahalanobis to his satisfaction, Bauer then turned to his political charge, the heart of which was that India, under its existing political leadership, was on the road to socialism and that western democratic governments had no business supporting that transition. His policy conclusions are captured in passages like these:

> The suggestion that foreign aid should be granted specifically to underwrite Indian economic planning should be rejected—not so much because of the cash cost to the United States, but because of the cost to India. For this would make it inevitable that the country is pushed further in the direction of the establishment of a completely socialized economy, in the direction of an economy in which the range of choice of individuals is severely circumscribed both as consumers or producers, and in which the state is all powerful. . . .
>
> One approach would be a policy under which American aid would be varied in accordance with the overall economic policy pursued by the Indian Government over the previous period. The amount of aid could then be made to depend on the performance of the Government in pursuing a policy designed to raise living standards and to promote an anti-totalitarian society, insofar as these aims can be promoted by government policy.[12]

To Bauer's political criteria for the granting of U.S. and Western assistance to India, others added the issue of the diplomatic orientation of India's foreign policy. They found it difficult to allocate U.S. taxpayers' money to a neutralist government, often critical of American foreign policy, which compounded the felony by cultivating friendly relations with the Soviet Union.

As the 1958 Senate floor debate on the Kennedy-Cooper resolution indicates (see Appendix B), arguments like Bauer's were widely diffused. Behind them was a concept of what the objectives of U.S. assistance should be, articulated, for example, by John Davenport, an able journalist, in a memorandum he sent to Kennedy on May 29, 1958, opposing the joint resolution:

> The purpose of foreign aid should be to help other peoples to help themselves. This will be accomplished as the U.S. lends its influence to favoring sound currencies, balanced budgets, and the limitation of government functions to their proper sphere. It will also be accomplished as we make plain our belief in the institutions of private property and the market system of economy as the bulwarks of higher political freedoms. In many cases aid has and will be given even where these principles are not today honored. But it would be a tragedy indeed if they were lost sight of in our foreign aid program, and if that program became an engine and an instrument for actively *encouraging* unsound and politically dangerous economic experiments.[13]

The lines of argument thus far described do not exhaust the opposition case. There were some who took the view that the U.S. had no interest worth the allocation of public resources in the economic, social, and political fate of the developing regions and/or that U.S. loans and grants would not affect the outcome and/or that normal private lending would suffice.

The opposition argument—notably Bauer's—was not trivial; and, indeed, certain aspects of it were shared by some who, on balance, disagreed with his conclusions; some of his strictures on Indian development policy hold up quite well in retrospect, as we shall later see. But there was an alternative perspective on India and the developing regions as a whole in the 1950s, and alternative criteria for U.S. and Western assistance. In presenting that perspective, I shall confine this exposition mainly to work of the Center for International Studies at MIT (CENIS).* It should be said immediately that the interest of CENIS in economic development analysis and policy was by no means unique. On the contrary, as the 1950s wore on, development analysis became something of an intellectual fad in American academic life; the policy debate on these matters was conducted on an increasingly crowded stage, including persons of experience, judgment, and sophistication that certainly matched the MIT team.

Nevertheless, CENIS attracted and, in a loose, academic way, organized a diverse range of talents in the analysis of development problems; its agenda required it to give sustained thought to the nature of U.S. interests abroad; it was active in policy formulation; it lobbied for its view with a patient stubbornness; and its contacts with politicians, the federal bureaucracy and the media were good. CENIS represented a kind of critical mass of somewhat over-active students and crusaders on the subject. Although I am not a wholly objective judge of the matter, in retrospect I would guess Russell Edgerton's observations on the Millikan–Rostow (i.e., CENIS) proposal are more or less correct: "Nothing else on the scene in Washington rivaled the grand scale of the Millikan–Rostow proposal nor the sophistication of its presentation. . . . As the different parts of the Executive and Congress launched reappraisals of aid in different directions with different motives, Millikan and Rostow supplied them all with a common theme."[14] Edgerton's evaluation proves nothing, of course, about the correctness of CENIS' views.

The CENIS role in the evolution of policy will be addressed in Part II. Here I shall try to evoke briefly the intellectual

* For a more detailed account of the role of CENIS, notably its work in India, see George Rosen, *Western Intellectuals and South Asia* (forthcoming). Rosen was a member of CENIS who spent considerable time in India. His study is an account and evaluation of Ford Foundation programs on economic development.

strands that were generated within CENIS and the synthesis which emerged bearing on its outcome.

CENIS' work on development began formally in 1952, including intensive studies of India, Indonesia, and Italy. Aside from Millikan and me, the members of the senior staff engaged in economic development problems were: P. N. Rosenstein–Rodan, Everett Hagen, Benjamin Higgins, and Wilfred Malenbaum. We were also closely in touch with our colleague Charles Kindleberger, whose wide portfolio of interests included the field of economic growth in both a historical and contemporary context. Harold Issacs, Dan Lerner, Ithiel Pool, Lucian Pye, and James E. Cross contributed insights from political science and sociology. Younger economists, including George Baldwin, Francis Bator, Richard Eckaus, and George Rosen, also got into the act, as did a then junior political scientist, Donald Blackmer, and a remarkable former schoolmaster and novelist, Richard Hatch, who served as critic, editor, and conscience of CENIS. Brooding sympathetically over our efforts, while he conducted studies of the Soviet Union, was a dedicated scholar, Alexander Korol, with a colorful career that included at one time piracy in the South China Sea. As Note 15 suggests, the senior economists of CENIS working on development problems came at them from quite different perspectives.[15] We were a strong-minded as well as variegated lot held together by a common commitment to the problems of development, by ties of mutual respect and affection that often grow out of such common commitments to large purposes, and, above all, by the graceful and sensitive leadership of Max Millikan.

The views generated by the members of CENIS on the process of development, development policy, and external assistance were articulated during the 1950s on many occasions in forms ranging from academic essays and books to congressional testimony and articles in the press. Moreover, our ways of presenting what became a reasonably common view varied in emphasis and even in technical vocabulary.

The most complete synthesis of our argument was incorporated in a short book entitled *A Proposal: Key to an Effective Foreign Policy*, completed in August 1956, published in 1957. It represented the fruition of a draft written in the wake of a meeting in Princeton in May 1954 (see below, pp. 95–98). It passed through a series of stages over the subsequent two years, responding to specific occasions traced out in Chapters 6–9. Its collective character is suggested by its authorship: Max Millikan and W. W. Rostow with collaboration of P. N. Rosenstein–Rodan and others. The names of eleven others at CENIS are mentioned in the Preface as contributors.

The central, distinctive feature of our approach was that we placed economic growth and foreign aid systematically within the framework of the process of the modernization of societies as a whole. With some oversimplification of a reasonably complex exposition, the argument of *The Proposal* can be paraphrased as follows:

1. The bulk of the world's population, for the first time in history, is caught up in a revolutionary transition which is "rapidly exposing previously apathetic peoples to the possibility of change." The transition presents the United States "with both a great danger and a great opportunity:"

> The danger is that increasing numbers of people will become convinced that their new aspirations can be realized only through violent change and the renunciation of democratic institutions.
>
> . . . The dangers of instability inherent in the awakening of formerly static peoples would be present even in the absence of the Communist apparatus, as is demonstrated by the existence of trouble spots like Kenya and Morocco—apparently relatively unconnected with Communist subversion. But the danger is, of course, greatly intensified by the focus which both Communist thought and Communist organization give.
>
> The United States has not presented a consistent and persuasive alternative in terms of the democratic process.

2. U.S. assistance should not aim "to insure friendship and gratitude," or "to enable the recipient countries to carry a much larger burden of military buildup against Communist armed forces," or "to stop Communism by eliminating hunger." U.S. assistance should contribute to "the evolution of societies that are stable in the sense that they are capable of rapid change without violence."

3. This judgment flows directly from a definition of the U.S. national interest which is taken to be "to preserve a world environment within which our form of democratic society can persist and develop. . . ." Two priority tasks follow from that definition:

> The first of these is to meet effectively the threat to our security posed by the danger of overt military aggression, a threat . . . to be met primarily by maintaining or increasing U.S. military strength and by solidifying alliances with other countries in a position to contribute significantly to that strength. . . .
>
> The second priority task of U.S. foreign policy is to promote the evolution of a world in which threats to our security and, more broadly, to our way of life are less likely to arise. Success in this task would mean the freeing of a large volume of resources from military to more constructive uses. More important, it would mean protecting our society from the pressures inevitably associated with a garrison state, pressures which threaten our most cherished values. It is this task with which this book is mainly concerned.

4. External economic assistance can be effective only if it is meshed with and designed in ways which contribute to the society's own efforts to move towards "political maturity." This implies that six conditions be met in the process of economic and social modernization:

> A. There must be posed for the leadership and the people of each country challenging and constructive internal tasks which will look to the future of their societies. . . .
>
> B. The constructive tasks to which united national efforts

are to be devoted must relate to the emerging aspirations of all classes and regions in the society. . . .

C. The new countries must find ways of developing young and vigorous leadership. . . .

D. Related to the recruitment of new leadership is the need for greatly increased social, economic, and political opportunity. . . .

E. Related to this fact is the requirement, if these countries are to achieve mature political development, of finding ways to bridge the existing gulf between the urban classes, often Western educated, and the countryside. . . .

F. Perhaps the most critical requirement for the growth of political maturity is that the people of the new nations develop confidence, both as a nation and as individuals in small communities, that they can make progress with their problems through their own efforts."

In its widest sense, economic development is seen as a potentially constructive outlet for nationalism, a social solvent, a matrix for the development of new leadership, a means for generating at the grass roots confidence in the democratic process and for imparting a strand of reality to the concept of international solidarity.

5. Technically, aid programs must be geared to the particular circumstances of each developing country. In general, developing countries were viewed as constituting a wide spectrum at different stages of economic growth. Where they stood in the spectrum determined the amount of capital and technical assistance they could efficiently absorb. Broadly speaking, three stages were distinguished: the preconditions for take-off; take-off; and self-sustained growth: "the long period of regular if fluctuating progress . . . [when] the structure of the economy changes continuously—sometimes painfully—as technique improves. The character as well as the scale of appropriate external assistance will vary with these stages, rising and becoming more diversified in take-off, fall-

ing gradually away with the attainment of self-sustained growth when, in time, developing countries could come to rely on normal commercial sources of international finance."

6. Against this background the proposal consisted in an international plan to generate sufficient resources to meet all requirements for external assistance which could be justified by absorptive capacity plus enlarged technical assistance to accelerate the increase in absorptive capacity.* Tables 7 and 8 indicate the roughly estimated annual price tag.[16]

7. Four reasonably objective criteria were defined to test whether the overriding standards of absorptive capacity and credit worthiness were being met:

A. It must be within the technical and administrative capabilities of the receiving country to carry out its proposed project with reasonable efficiency, over the time period of the loan or grant.

B. Steps must have been taken to insure that the rest of the economy of the receiving country is being developed sufficiently to make the proposed project fully productive in the time period envisaged by the loan.

C. The receiving country must have an overall national development program designed to make the most effective possible use of its resources; this should include not only a series of interrelated capital projects but also necessary educational and training programs.

D. The receiving country's national development program must be consistent with the requirements of expanding world commerce and the international division of labor.

---

*The phrase "absorptive capacity" emerged in the 1950s as a rough measure of a society's ability to employ efficiently additional capital resources. It embraced such diverse factors as the availability of necessary transport and electric power facilities, a working force of adequate skill to deal with the relevant technologies, indigenous foremen, engineers, etc.

TABLE 7. CENIS Estimate of Absorptive Capacity for External Capital [a]

	billions of dollars per year
India, Pakistan, Ceylon	0.8–1.0
Balance of non-Communist Asia (excluding Japan)	0.4–0.6
Middle East (excluding Pakistan but including Egypt)	0.3–0.5
Latin America	0.8–1.0
Africa (excluding Egypt and Union of South Africa)	0.2–0.4
Total	2.5–3.5

[a]To put these figures in perspective it should be noted that $3.5 billion was .8 percent of U.S. gross national product in 1956 and about $10 billion in 1980 U.S. prices.

TABLE 8. CENIS Estimate of Possible Sources of External Capital

Grants:	
U.S. contribution	$ 360 million
Other country contribution	240
Direct private investment	500
Additional international bank loans	400
Public loans:	
U.S. contribution	1,700
Other country contribution	300
Total	$3,500 million

8. Administratively it was proposed that the program be conducted mainly by existing institutions, but that the World Bank create a special instrument "to co-ordinate information, set the ground rules, and secure acceptance of the criteria for the investment program." The exposition of the plan closed with this admonition:

> We cannot emphasize too strongly that this program will not achieve its basically political and psychological purposes

unless its fundamental features are preserved. Dilution could prove extremely dangerous. The sharp edges of policy which must be preserved appear to be these:

A. The additional sums envisaged must be large enough to remove lack of capital as a bottleneck to growth, while maintaining the tough criteria of productivity envisaged.

B. There must be no tie between economic aid and military pacts, and no explicit political conditions within the Free World beyond the requirement that national development goals be democratically established. An aid program with strings yields satellites, not partners.

C. The plan must look to a long future and envisage a sustained U.S. effort.

D. There must be a real measure of international contribution and international administration.[17]

This paraphrase of our grand scheme is necessary to understand CENIS' advocacy of sustained international assistance to Indian development. Evidently our approach was, fundamentally, political and psychological rather than narrowly economic. We believed that a concentration of talents and energies in the developing countries on the tasks of modernization was likely to maximize the chance that they would transit the inherently revolutionary experience through which they were destined to pass without excessive domestic or external violence and cope with the blandishments and pressures that might arise from Communist activities of various kinds. India seemed particularly important in this context because its government, under Nehru, had decided in the wake of independence and the division of the subcontinent to accord economic and social progress an extremely high priority. And, by a kind of miracle, this vast, complex, impoverished society began its national life with an extraordinarily strong commitment to the democratic political process. Rightly or wrongly, we believed the success or failure of India with respect to both its development and its politics would be widely influential. In varying degree, perhaps, the members of CENIS working on

India were inclined to share the judgment in the opening paragraph of Barbara Ward's special supplement on India published in *The Economist* of January 22, 1955:

> The Indian economy today is the subject of what is, without doubt, the world's most fateful experiment. Its problems may be expressed in economic terms—in so many millions of investment, in such and such a percentage of national income—but the outcome is nothing less than the demonstration that underdeveloped economies can—or cannot—achieve progress by Western and liberal means.

As for the linkage between economic development and the emergence of stable political democracies, we may, in retrospect, have been a bit too hopeful, but we were by no means naive. One CENIS publication of 1955 posed and answered bluntly the question of linkage: "Is there any guarantee that the free Asian nations will emerge from rapid economic growth politically democratic? No such guarantee can be made. The relation between economic growth and political democracy is not simple and automatic. More than that, the decisive take-off process involves complex and often unsettling effects on societies, which must transform their institutions and ways of doing things." [18] Our consciousness of the lack of automatic linkage was heightened by knowledge of the troubled political evolution of Latin America where, on the whole, the major countries were more economically advanced than in the other developing regions. [19] Lucian Pye's work on Malaya and Burma, Dan Lerner's on the complexities of modernization in the Middle East, Ithiel Pool's on communications, James E. Cross' on guerrilla warfare in the Phillippines and elsewhere, and similar academic work going forward in CENIS and other institutions in the 1950s impressed on us the truly revolutionary character of the modernization process, the length of time it was likely to take, and the unlikelihood that Western-style democracies would inevitably and universally emerge. For an economic historian like myself who had vicariously lived through the usually painful process of modernization of many countries in the longer past, including the early modern history of Western Europe, the conclusions of my colleagues in political science were not difficult to accept.

On the other hand, we were firmly convinced that a concentration of scarce resources, talents, and political energies on the tasks of development was likely to maximize the chance that societies would move through the modernization process with minimum violence and human cost. The obverse of this proposition was borne in on CENIS rather directly through its short-lived Indonesia project. Sukarno was a leader who dissipated his own and his nation's resources in many directions, among which he accorded development a low priority indeed. We soon concluded that no useful purpose was served by continuing the CENIS program in Indonesia.

In any case, our direct, as well as vicarious, knowledge was sufficient to take the view that, while the Indian example might well be influential, its early attachment to democracy was unlikely to be typical. On the other hand, we judged that societies concentrating seriously on their development tasks had a better chance than others to emerge with political systems increasingly responsive to the will of the governed.

Evidently, CENIS' perspective was somewhat different than that which analysts like Bauer brought to the problem. The CENIS perspective differed both technically and in its notion of the U.S. and Western interest.

Technically, CENIS agreed with Bauer that the Mahalanobis influence on the Indian Second Five Year Plan had not been benign. There was, I recall, a polite but rather sharply drawn debate in Millikan's office at MIT with Mahalanobis. At its core, Mahalanobis' extreme emphasis on heavy industry was based on an inexact analogy with the Soviet First Five Year Plan. Another factor also had some influence: simplistic interpretation of the policy implications of the fact that productivity per man was generally higher in industry than agriculture. On that view, a higher rate of growth in real GNP would result from a concentration of investment in industry. As the quotation on p. 38, above, suggests, there was also a strong strand of economic nationalism in Mahalanobis' view and, perhaps, an element of military policy in Nehru's acceptance of it.

Although we thought the Second Five Year Plan was somewhat distorted—notably in its relative neglect of agriculture—we were not about to make a technical judgment of that kind an overriding criterion for support or refusal of support.[20] Nor did we believe Bauer's citation of the Japanese case (see above, pp. 38–39) disposed of the argument that India should include the expansion of heavy industry in its early plans. Mid nineteenth-century France, Belgium, and Germany and pre-1914 Russia, for example, had built their take-offs on heavy industries as did the United States in the period 1840–1860.

Similarly, we did not believe that the degree of public versus private enterprise in the Indian industrial sector was a decisive criterion. In responding to the kind of argument evoked here by the quotations from Bauer and Chamberlain, CENIS had a good deal to say in *A Proposal*.[21] The quotation below is included because the issue loomed large in the debate on development aid in the 1950s and remains a contentious matter in the 1980s.

> The expectation that American aid programs can and should be used to halt or reverse the trend toward "socialism" present in many underdeveloped areas may find expression in either of two kinds of policy attitudes.
>
> Some argue that we should use offers of assistance to force countries to abandon proposed government enterprises and to establish conditions favorable to the maximum degree of domestic and foreign private investment. . . . The second group believe that, although a country may adopt any philosophy it likes, no U.S. resources should be devoted to assisting governments which have socialist objectives.

The authors believe that both of these attitudes are likely to frustrate what we conceive to be the basic purposes of economic assistance. We agree with those who hold a private market system with opportunity and incentive for individual enterprise will in the long run promote self-sustaining growth better than a highly bureaucratized system dominated by central government. But we believe that we shall ultimately promote reliance on private incentives more effectively by not insisting on any particular economic philosophy as a condition of aid than by attaching private enterprise strings. In many situations a favorable environment for private investment can be established only after a period of rather heavy capital formation under government auspices. This is what happened in Japan in the decade after 1868. More recently, the whole set of measures instituted by the Indian government in the period starting in 1951 have, by 1956, created an environment in which Indian private enterprise is undergoing rapid growth.

Thus we believe on the one hand that crude attempts to force a free private enterprise philosophy on recipient countries as an explicit or implicit condition for aid are almost certain to be self-defeating; on the other hand we believe there are good reasons for expecting countries now avowedly socialist but determinedly democratic to move toward greater reliance on private enterprise as their development proceeds. . . .

Therefore, although one must not fall into the error of employing our aid program to dictate another nation's economic philosophy, we can appropriately insist that we will aid only countries dedicated to advancing standards of living and encouraging widespread local initiative. With this condition, we need not be too concerned in the long run if some large-scale ventures are started under government auspices or if there is a preference for describing economic goals in socialist language.

Thus, the conceptual differences between the Bauer and CENIS views can be summarized in these propositions:

(a) Bauer believed the objective of foreign aid should be to promote democracy by promoting private enterprise; CENIS held that the objective of foreign aid was to encourage the development of societies capable of undergoing rapid change with minimum violence, and that such societies were most likely to evolve in democratic directions, although the early achievement of Western-style democracy was not guaranteed.

(b) Bauer believed foreign aid should be used as a lever actively to promote development programs which maximized promptly the role of the private sector and the market mechanism, whereas CENIS believed that this was a second order criterion, that its strict application would be politically counterproductive, and that the ultimate role of the private sector would be determined by the dynamic evolution of the economy and its political system.

(c) Bauer and CENIS agreed that a modern, high productivity agriculture was essential for sound development and that the Second Indian Five Year Plan was somewhat out of balance, although CENIS held that the vitality of the Indian private sector, and its consequently increasing foreign exchange requirements, was one of the causes of the strain on India's foreign exchange resources and that enlarged foreign aid would permit the private sector to go forward with increased élan. In fact, throughout the developing regions one major technical factor which led in the 1950s and beyond to excessive state intervention was foreign exchange shortage and consequent government allocation of foreign exchange.

The differing views summarized here were part of an insiders' debate among those who felt that the destiny of the developing world mattered to the West. A great many political figures (and, indeed, economists), implicitly or explicitly, simply ignored the issues involved; and when politicians of negative bent were forced by events to take a position, they reached out, as Appendix B indicates, for the kind of rationale Bauer formulated.

Nevertheless, the underlying question was serious and fundamental, and it has proved to be an abiding question: What interest did the United States and the West, as a whole, have in the fate of the developing regions worth the allocation of scarce resources painfully extracted from the taxpayer? After all, if one felt human, moral, or religious concern for the poor, aspiring people of the South, institutions of charity existed to which one could contribute. And if one commanded economic or other training and talents, one could go as an individual and, if accepted, work side by side with the men and women in a developing country. In the old missionary tradition, some citizens in the North during the 1950s did these things; that is, gave money through their churches or other institutions or went to work in developing regions. And others turned their professional talents to the analysis of and prescription for problems in the developing regions.

These impulses, rooted in the values and culture of the West, were strong enough to constitute one strand in the effective political support for foreign aid, but, by themselves, they were clearly insufficient. Political support for military aid was, of course, not difficult to rally for countries where the U.S. strategic commitment commanded a substantial consensus. Similarly, so-called "defense support" proved politically viable in the 1950s; that is, economic aid to developing countries in compensation for disproportionately high military outlays in areas judged to be strategically important. After all, economic aid could be presented in such cases as an alternative to the direct commitment of U.S. military forces. And, as we shall see in Chapter 4, political support for economic aid rose sharply for countries experiencing political and social unrest which Communists were seeking to exploit in areas judged to be strategically sensitive. The problem was to make a case for steady, long-term development aid, in general, in terms of the abiding vital interests of the United States and the West.

It was appropriate for CENIS to attempt to do this, engaged

as it simultaneously was in studies of Communist societies, the development process, and the interplay of American life and foreign policy. In elaborating a reasonably coherent and defensible definition of the national interest which embraced development aid, it made a distinctive, if evidently debatable, contribution to thought and policy in the 1950s and beyond.

4. JFK and the Developing World, 1951-1958

We turn now to a much narrower element in the background to the Kennedy-Cooper Resolution of March 1958: how it came about that John Kennedy decided to launch this somewhat unlikely enterprise in support of Indian economic development.

Kennedy was to be the first of the American presidents to take the developing regions of the world seriously, day after day, not merely when the dynamics of the Cold War or purely indigenous conflicts generated crises in those regions with which Washington inescapably had to deal. In fact, I believe it is fair to say that, to date, he and Lyndon Johnson have been the only two post-1945 presidents who not only believed that the security of America and the whole advanced industrial world was bound up in a fundamental way with the path those regions would follow but also acted systematically on that judgment.

It is, moreover, clear that Kennedy came to the presidency with a rather fully elaborated perspective on the developing regions. When, for example, he defined in ten chapters of *The Strategy of Peace* (1960) the "Areas of Trial" ahead in foreign policy, eight came to rest on specific problems in Asia, the Middle East, Africa, and Latin America.

What accounts for this emphasis on the importance of the developing regions? On a matter of this kind one cannot be dogmatic. The files of a senator are much less complete and less suffused with a self-conscious duty to history and historians than those of a president; and, unfortunately, the major contemporary biographies of Kennedy did not focus on the evolution of his thought on foreign policy.[22]

I would guess that the following four factors are a significant part of the background to his decision to launch the 1958 resolution in support of Indian development:

First, the trip he took with his sister Patricia and his brother Robert to the Middle East and Asia in the fall of 1951, including stops in Israel, Pakistan, India, Indochina, Malaya, and Korea. This experience was clearly a bench mark shifting perceptibly Kennedy's view of the world. In his first five years as a congressman (1947–1951), Kennedy was a somewhat erratic supporter of Truman's foreign policy. He voted for most of the administration's measures (except, initially, Point Four), but he was also a rather sharp critic. The Communist takeover of China led him to attack head-on Roosevelt's decisions on Asia at Yalta as well as Truman's policy toward China. He concluded a one-minute address on January 25, 1949, with this sentence: "This House must now assume the responsibility of preventing the onrushing tide of Communism from engulfing all of Asia." He attacked Truman's pre-Korean War military budgets as inadequate. After the Korean War began, however, he expressed fear that the U.S. might be so diverting forces to Asia as to be unprepared to deal with a military crisis in Western Europe, which he predicted was on its way. After a trip to Western Europe early in 1951, he gave testimony in the Senate in support of the Vandenberg Resolution assigning U.S. forces to NATO.

On economic foreign policy he opposed for a time the Trade Agreements Extension Act, supported cuts in aid to both Europe and the developing regions, and, as noted, opposed Point Four. Although American political labels often conceal as much as they illuminate, it is roughly fair to categorize Kennedy's initial positions in foreign policy as nonisolationist conservative but colored, especially in the period

1949–1951, by a fear that the 1930s were about to be re-played with Stalin in Hitler's role and the United States as inadequately prepared as pre-1939 Britain. In all this there were echoes of his experience of living in Britain during part of the 1930s and his reflections as set down in the book derived from his undergraduate thesis, *While England Slept.*

In 1952, after his trip to the Middle East and Asia, Kennedy's position sharply reversed. He supported assistance under the Point Four program and expressed the view that the United States had concentrated its attention excessively on Western Europe at the expense of the two-thirds of the world beyond. His statement in the House on June 28, 1952, reversing his previous position on technical assistance, is worth quoting among other reasons because it already reflects a concern for India.

> Mr. Chairman, last year when this bill was before the House, I offered a motion to cut technical assistance in the Middle East. But, this fall, I had an opportunity to visit that area and southeast Asia and I think we would be making a tremendous mistake to cut this money out of the bill. Many of us feel that the United States has concentrated its attention too much on Western Europe. We will spend several billions for Western Europe in this bill. Yet, here is an area, Asia, where the Communists are attempting to seize control, where the money is to be spent among several hundred million people, and where the tide of events has been moving against us. The Communists are now the second largest party in India. The Communists made tremendous strides there in the last election. The gentleman from Montana [Mr. Mansfield] pointed out that the life expectancy of people in India is 26 or 27 years, and they are increasing at the rate of five million a year—at a rate much faster than the available food supply.
>
> The Communists have a chance of seizing all of Asia in the next 5 or 6 years. What weapons do we have that will stop them? The most effective is technical assistance. The gentleman from Michigan [Mr. Crawford] is right, that the amount

of money involved here is not sufficient to prevent their being attracted to the Communists, but it gives them some hope, at least, that their problems can be solved without turning to the Communists. We are planning to spend a very large amount of money in this area for military assistance, which is of secondary importance compared to this program. To cut technical assistance when the Communists are concentrating their efforts in this vital area seems to me a costly and great mistake.[23]

Robert Kennedy observed that the trip, including the visit to Indochina, had made "a very major impression on his brother";[24] but something else had happened in 1951. The widespread fear in the Atlantic world that the Korean War was a prelude to a Soviet attack in Europe had dissipated. SHAPE was in place, giving substance and credibility to NATO; the Chinese Communist forces had been stopped at the 38th parallel in Korea in April–May 1951; the American political system had survived Truman's firing of MacArthur (which Kennedy supported); the Korean truce negotiations had begun in June; Western Europe had clearly passed beyond reconstruction into a new phase of rapid economic growth. In short, the nightmare which haunted a good many Americans in the wake of the Communist takeover of China followed by the Communist initiation of war in Korea had substantially passed. Other, less dramatic but deeply rooted problems could more clearly be perceived.

The second relevant factor is that the seriousness with which Kennedy began to take the developing regions after his trip in the autumn of 1951 was increasingly vindicated as the 1950s wore on. As noted elsewhere (see above pp. 14–21), the period after Stalin's death (which coincided roughly with Kennedy's accession to the Senate) was relatively quiet from, say, London east to Tokyo, but it saw the emergence of a new Communist strategy addressed to the developing regions. From the Suez crisis in the autumn of 1956, that strategy, interacting with the inherent volatility of the developing regions and the inadequacies in U.S. and Western European policy, yielded a succession of substantial crises. In short, events in the 1950s successively underlined the legitimacy of the insights Kennedy drew from his 1951 trip.

Third, quite particularly, the visit to Indochina impressed indelibly on Kennedy the corrosiveness of the French effort to maintain an imperial position against the will of the people and the opportunities French policy afforded the Communists. In November 1951 he said:

> In Indochina we have allied ourselves to the desperate effort of a French regime to hang on to the remnants of empire. There is no broad, general support of the native Vietnam Government among the people of that area. To check the southern drive of Communism makes sense but not only through reliance on the force of arms. The task is rather to build strong native non-Communist sentiment within these areas and rely on that as a spearhead of defense rather than upon the legions of General deTassigny. To do this apart from and in defiance of innately nationalistic aims spells foredoomed failure.[25]

In a major intervention, at the height of the Indochina crisis in 1954, he recalled and reinforced this judgment.

> The hard truth of the matter is, first, that without the wholehearted support of the peoples of the associated states, without a reliable and crusading native army with a dependable officer corps, a military victory, even with American support, in that area is difficult, if not impossible, of achievement; and, second, that the support of the people of that area cannot be obtained without a change in the contractual relationships which presently exist between the associated states and the French Union.[26]

This was, of course, the matrix for, perhaps, Kennedy's most famous speech as a senator: his intervention on July 2, 1957, urging independence for Algeria.

For our purposes in this essay, the linkage between Kennedy's views on Indochina, Algeria, and foreign aid are particularly relevant. With respect to Vietnam, Kennedy spoke on June 1, 1956, in a context where Diem's surprising success in consolidating South Vietnam after the Geneva conference of 1954 led, in Kennedy's view, to a period of neglect in American policy. He deplored the tendency of American policy to focus sharply on acute crises but fail to generate longer run programs:

> Like those peoples of Latin America and Africa whom we have very nearly overlooked in the past decade, the Vietnamese may find that their devotion to the cause of democracy, and their success in reducing the strength of local Communist groups, have had the ironic effect of reducing American support. Yet the need for that support has in no way been reduced. . . .
>
> Much more needs to be done. Informational and propaganda activities, warning of the evils of Communism and the blessings of the American way of life, are not enough in a country where concepts of free enterprise and capitalism are meaningless, where poverty and hunger are not enemies across the 17th Parallel but enemies within their midst.
>
> I shall not attempt to set forth details of the type of aid program this nation should offer the Vietnamese—for it is not the details of that program that are as important as the spirit with which it is offered and the objectives it seeks to accomplish. We should not attempt to buy the friendship of the Vietnamese. Nor can we win their hearts by making them dependent upon our handouts. What we must offer them is a revolution—a political, economic, and social revolution far superior to anything the Communists can offer— far more peaceful, far more democratic, and far more locally controlled. Such a revolution will require much from the United States and much from Vietnam. We must supply capital to replace that drained by centuries of colonial exploitation; technicians to train those handicapped by deliberate policies of illiteracy; guidance to assist a nation taking those first feeble steps toward the complexities of a republican form of government. We must assist the inspiring growth of Vietnamese democracy and economy, including the com-

plete integration of those refugees who gave up their homes and their belongings to seek freedom. We must provide military assistance to rebuild the new Vietnamese Army, which every day faces the growing peril of Vietminh Armies across the border.

This is the revolution we can, we should, we must offer to the people of Vietnam—not as charity, not as a business proposition, not as a political maneuver, nor simply to enlist them as soldiers against Communism or as chattels of American foreign policy—but a revolution of their own making, for their own welfare, and for the security of freedom everywhere.[27]

With respect to Algeria and North Africa, he called on July 2, 1958, for a U.S. willingness to undertake sustained economic support for development:

United States policies in these areas—to provide an effective alternative to these forces, who aided Tunisian and Moroccan independence while we remained silent—cannot be tied any longer to the French, who seek to make their economic aid and political negotiations dependent upon the recipient's attitude toward Algeria. We cannot temporize as long as we did in 1956 over emergency wheat to Tunisia. We cannot offer these struggling nations economic aid so far below their needs, so small a fraction of what we offered some of their less needy, less democratic, and less friendly neighbors that even so staunch a friend as Premier Bourguiba was forced to reject Ambassador Richards' original offer—just as he had rejected an offer of Soviet aid more than thirty times as great. In Morocco, too, our aid has fallen short of the new nation's basic needs.

We must, on the other hand, avoid the temptation to imitate the Communists by promising these new nations automatic remedies and quick cures for economic distress—which lead only too readily to gathering disillusionment. But we can realistically contribute to those programs which will generate genuine economic strength as well as give relief from famine, drought, and catastrophe. The further use of agricultural surpluses, and the new revolving loan fund making possible long-term planning and commitment, should be especially well suited to the requirements of Morocco and Tunisia, which have moved beyond the point of most under-developed states but not yet attained the strength of most Western economies. . . .

The United States must be prepared to lend all effort to such a settlement [involving both Algerian independence and association with Tunisia and Morocco], and to assist in the economic problems which will flow from it. This is not a burden which we lightly or gladly assume. But our efforts in no other endeavor are more important in terms of once again seizing the initiative in foreign affairs, demonstrating our adherence to the principles of national independence and winning the respect of those long suspicious of our negative and vacillating record on colonial issues.[28]

Fourth, the need for Kennedy to formulate and articulate a coherent foreign policy position was heightened by his assignment in January 1957 to the Senate Foreign Relations Committee. With Lyndon Johnson's support he won out in the Senate Democratic steering committee over the more senior Estes Kefauver for the seat vacated when Walter George retired.

He soon took the occasion to publish a piece in the October 1957 issue of *Foreign Affairs*, "A Democrat Looks at Foreign Policy." The article dealt with a good many matters: Germany, East-West relations, military policy, the organization of national security affairs, the role of the Congress, and the potentialities and limits of bipartisanship in foreign affairs. But something like three-fourths of the text concerns the inadequacy of policy towards the developing regions. And a good deal of the argument comes to rest on the linkage between the power of nationalism in the developing regions and a wise foreign aid policy:

To an observer in the opposition party there appear two central weaknesses in our current foreign policy: first, a failure to appreciate how the forces of nationalism are rewriting the geopolitical map of the world—especially in North Africa, Eastern Europe and the Middle East; and second, a lack of decision and conviction in our leadership, which has recoiled from clearly informing both the people and Congress, which seeks too often to substitute slogans for solutions, which at times has even taken pride in the timidity of its ideas. . . .

. . . In the years immediately ahead we face a challenge in how to help the new and underdeveloped nations bear their economic burdens. Again we must strike a balance between what Denis Brogan has labelled "the illusion of American omnipotence" and a somber contemplation of the impossibility of absolute solutions.

It is sobering to realize that population curves turn steeply upwards in underdeveloped lands, that as a result the economic backwardness of much of the world is increasing, and that the process of social disintegration intensifies with the rising curve of expectations among many peoples. Old liberal bromides have no appeal to nations which seek a quick transition to industrialization and who admire the disciplined attack which Communism seems to make upon the problems of economic modernization and redistribution. The more immediately persuasive experiences of China and Russia probably approximate what lies ahead for states such as Indonesia or Egypt, suffering from deteriorating economic standards and steeply rising populations.

The United States is economically capable of increasing aid for development purposes, but it cannot scatter its assistance on each parched patch of misery and need. The first step would seem to be to make a small number of investments through aid and loans, selected with an eye to their likelihood for success. There is no need for us to be neutral as to the objectives which it should serve. Successful foreign aid must be selective; otherwise a large amount of aid goes into projects designed to enhance the prestige of the receiving government and into military panoply which may only perpetuate feudalism. The general approach furnished in the Millikan-Rostow proposals (though too much patterned on the Indian economy and perhaps too sanguine about the possibility of freeing economic assistance from political objectives) furnishes some useful guideposts, particularly in stressing the need for more durable aid commitments and for finding methods which minimize political blackmail and indiscriminate handouts. In this regard the Senate has made beginnings this year in providing a long-term basis for assistance, which has the advantages not only of permitting better planning and a more rational evaluation of the political and psychological effects of aid, but also will tend to avoid the disadvantages of making annual aid appropriations which cannot be spent effectively.

In future years, other nations can probably make larger contributions in skills and money to world-wide economic development. Germany already is a sizable foreign investor and lender, and other nations will grow in such capacity. The development of atomic power has given Great Britain the prospect of becoming a prime exporter of atomic reactors. Chances for developing oil await the French in the Sahara if they can establish a political settlement in North Africa. With opportunities like these opening up, a wider system of multinational aid, pioneered in Asia by the Colombo Plan, can become a reality.[29]

By this time, also, Kennedy had begun to focus sharply on the critical role of India:

> India, which itself represents a pole within the Commonwealth, is the leading claimant for the role of a "broker" middle state in the larger bipolar struggle; she is also a centerpiece in a "middle zone" of uncommitted nations extending from Casablanca to Djakarta.[30]

So much by way of broad background. That background suggests why Kennedy, as of 1957–1958, would be in support of development aid to the southern continents—like many of his Democratic contemporaries in the Senate—and it suggests some of the reasons why his interest came to rest on India and the possibility of a consortium in which a revived Europe might play a role. The *Foreign Affairs* article foreshadows to a degree the Kennedy-Cooper resolution, but it does not explain its somewhat curious and limited form.

Kennedy, like all serious politicians, was interested in ideas. Politicians understand better than most that ideas are an essential raw material for effective action. But he was not an intellectual in the usual sense. He did not enjoy the elegant elaboration of ideas for its own sake. Ideas were tools. He picked them up easily, like statistics or the names of local politicians. He was a resourceful political innovator, not an inventor or scientist. He wanted to know how ideas could be put to work. His most typical response to an idea was "What do you want me to do about it today?" His disciplined courtesy and good manners were strained by the extensive exposition of ideas with which he was already familiar, as was usually the case. He would tap his teeth and fuss with his tie. His personal intellectual interest was in history and, especially, in the history of politics and politicians in the Anglo-American world. He saw the politician as hero; often frustrated, sometimes confronted with choices that tested and strained the fabric of his character and spirit, but striving to do great things.

He sought out experts, but he was also systematically suspicious of them. He was conscious that his course of action, even as a senator, required him to orchestrate a great many different ideas and considerations that no single adviser or expert could take fully into account.

Thus, as he found his feet as a senator and member of the Foreign Affairs Committee in 1957, Kennedy was looking for some concrete things to do which advanced broad policies in which he believed. As Chapters 8 and 9 make clear, enlarged development aid was in the wind. In 1957 the Eisenhower administration resolved its inner conflict and achieved the creation, at a modest level, of the Development Loan Fund (DLF). Monroney was pushing inconclusively for what was to become International Development Association (IDA). Clearly, however, the greatest unresolved development challenge was India where, putting China aside, about 40 percent of the population of the developing regions lived. Bowles, Humphrey, and others were talking about a Marshall Plan for India, but the political facts of life in the executive branch and the Congress made an immediate radical enlargement of long-term aid to India unrealistic. On the other hand, Kennedy perceived that the situation might be quite different if it were clear from the beginning that the United States was entering a commitment to support India shoulder-to-shoulder with the major countries of Western Europe and Japan. Multilateralism appealed to him—and to other senators—for a reason George Humphrey's attack on the concept in his letter to Eisenhower (see below, p. 116) did not take into account: it eased the problem of justification to the voters. A communal venture looked less like a unilateral giveaway. And, besides, it eased some of the inevitable frictions between borrower and lender. Thus, as a concrete initial move, the notion of a high-level international team to survey India's needs appealed to him as a double step in a direction he wished U.S. policy to go.

What part did politics play in Kennedy's decision to use up some of his political capital in support of Indian development? I have no doubt that every substantial decision Kennedy made from, say, January 1957 forward took into account, among other things, his probable bid for the presidential nomination in 1960. In 1958 he took on two major foreign policy initiatives: the Kennedy-Cooper resolution and a revision of the Battle Act which would have permitted wider and more flexible trade between the United States and Eastern Europe. Both, I believe, were chosen because he believed they were significant and correct moves in foreign policy and because they were "liberal" in terms of the political spectrum. It is wholly typical that Kennedy had Holborn assemble for him, in a memorandum of July 9, 1959, the votes on some fourteen foreign aid issues of the four major Senate candidates for the Democratic nomination: Humphrey, Johnson, Kennedy, and Symington. Commenting on the political dimension of Kennedy's India initiatives, Ralph Dungan wrote, in a letter to me of February 13, 1981:

> Support for India was a cause with which "liberals" identified and that was an uncertain and inconstant constituency for him at that time. Conversely those who were opposed would have been opposed to him in any event for a host of reasons.[31]

Right down to his election as president, Kennedy was generally viewed as a rather conservative Democrat although he drew to him increasing liberal support after the failure of Stevenson's bid for the nomination and his stance on national issues was more fully defined.

Early in 1959 I visited Oliver Franks in Oxford. I had been a fellow of The Queen's College in 1946–1947 when he was provost. I had corresponded with him from MIT about CENIS' views on foreign aid in general and on India in particular in 1956 and 1958. A year later, I explained to him in Oxford the circumstances which had led to his name emerging on the floor of the Senate in the context of a speech about India. He asked why an evidently ambitious young politician was spending so much time on the Indian aid program. It did not seem to Franks a vote-getting issue. I replied that, while marginally it might help Kennedy alter his image favorably among the Democratic liberals who were giving him considerable trouble, it was basically because the question of aid to India was something important and creative that he could influence from where he was. Politics was his chosen medium; he was a senator, and this was something a senator could do that might not otherwise get done. As nearly as I can make out, in retrospect that assessment, which wholly converges with Dungan's, is about right.

Once Kennedy came into focus on India, towards the close of 1957, he looked for technical help. At that time Kennedy's staff was not large, and his ties to the academic community were rather limited. Sorensen evokes lucidly how he sought supplementary assistance on substantive issues.

> The Kennedy Senate staff, even when supplemented in later years by the part-time or full-time efforts of Fred Holborn, Harris Wofford and Richard Goodwin, could not keep pace with his demand for new speech ideas and material. Professor Archibald Cox of the Harvard Law School (later Solicitor General) headed a team of outside experts on labor reform. Professors Max Millikan and Walt Rostow of the Massachusetts Institute of Technology (the latter was later Assistant Secretary of State) were among many advisers on foreign policy. For material on a speech on nuclear tests, he directed me to call his friend Sir David Ormsby-Gore (later U.K. Ambassador to the U.S.) in the British UN delegation. His 1954 speech on Indochina was checked with Ed Gullion of the Foreign Service (later his Ambassador to the Congo) and with an old family friend, Arthur Krock of the *New York Times* (later the chief critic of his policy in the Congo). Columnist Joe Alsop helped on a defense speech. Jacqueline translated French documents for his Vietnam speech. Law professors Freund and Howe were consulted on civil rights. Occasionally he would turn to his father's associate, New Dealer James Landis. In short, while the Senator was a brainy man, his intelligence included the ability to know his own limitations of time and knowledge and to draw on the brains of others.[32]

CENIS became Kennedy's major, but not unique, source of staff work and advice on the India resolution in November 1957. Frederick Holborn, who had joined Kennedy's staff a few months earlier, came to visit us at MIT. I remember meeting him in an office where he was already talking with Paul Rosenstein-Rodan and Wilfred Malenbaum. I joined in the discussion which went on for some time. We offered our assistance. Holborn later called to say Kennedy wished to meet me on my next trip to Washington. We had lunch on February 26, 1958, with Holborn, the day before I gave testimony before the Senate Foreign Relations Committee. I had gone to

Washington earlier in that week for Eric Johnston's two-day conference in support of foreign aid (see below, p. 159). Among a good many other things, we discussed the kind of questions he might raise at the Senate hearing to elicit material on India relevant to his planned initiatives with Cooper. From that time, my tie to Kennedy gradually expanded to issues beyond India and development aid.

To complete the historical record, it would be useful to know when and under what circumstances the idea of a high level international mission to India arose. I simply do not remember, nor does Holborn. I do recall contributing to the drafting of Kennedy's March 25th speech and suggesting to him the names used to illustrate the appropriate level for the mission.

From the autumn of 1957 CENIS was in regular contact with Kennedy, mainly through Holborn, and generating a quite steady flow of analytic material, responses to specific questions, and information on attitudes in India and Western Europe. Millikan, Rosenstein-Rodan and I were the principal contacts, as well as Wilfred Malenbaum, who contributed some detailed analyses of the comparative economic performance of India and China. An oral history interview with Barbara Ward of June 28, 1964, captures both the intensity with which Kennedy pursued a subject, once committed, and the character of the tie he developed with CENIS in this period:

> . . . he'd read the [*Economist*] supplement [on India; see above, p. 50] he wanted to follow up, what had happened since, what was going on, what were the chances of the Indian plans, what was the influence of the various politicians. Again, I suppose he was really a sort of "show me" politician in the feeling that this intellectual curiosity was overwhelmingly strong and utterly disinterested. That's the thing that always struck you about him was that whatever of himself was engaged, it was never engaged at the intellectual level, that he simply wanted what was accurate, what reflected the truth, and what could be given to him in a com-

pletely unbiased way. And I saw that even more vividly a few
weeks later when I attended a meeting of Max Millikan's
small group at lunch—I think at the Harvard Faculty Club
Max conducted. . . .

I think Wilfred Malenbaum was there, anyway, a group of
MIT people. He did not appear a young aspiring politician
carefully asking for help, advice, and information of a group
of sage academicians; it was a fellow academician putting
them through the hoops. I've never seen anything like it. It
was a brilliant performance from the point of view of his
grasp on the subject and the kind of things he wanted to
know. The nuances introduced were fully as subtle and fully
as well-informed at that time as anything the true academics
were discussing and it was an enormously impressive performance on the India resolution.[33]

Having decided to commit a limited but not trivial part of
his political capital to the cause of Indian economic development towards the close of 1957, Kennedy carried through,
without loss of momentum after his rather limited success in
1958, to renew the struggle in 1959 (see Chapter 10).

II. U.S. Foreign Aid Policy, 1945–1958

5. Foreign Aid, 1945-1952

Kennedy's India initiative of 1958 reflected not only an American reaction to Communist policies of the 1950s and the image they projected out on the world, not only the conceptual debate about development, not only the evolution of his own thought and political circumstances, but also the realities of foreign aid policy as it evolved in the executive branch and the Congress.

Foreign aid—the voluntary transfer of resources or technology from one country to another at less than market rates—has a long history, indeed. For example, in the early phase of the Delian League, in the fifth century B.C., members provided money rather than ships and men to maintain an Athenian navy capable of continuing to contain the power of Persia—a defense support arrangement, in later U.S. parlance, that corroded in time with tragic results for Athens and Greece. The use of money to gain or hold the support of allies runs through the history of the next twenty-four centuries in many parts of the world, including its crucial role in the Napoleonic, First, and Second World Wars.

From the sixteenth century forward, the acquisition from abroad of technologies which might strengthen the economy and military potential was endemic in mercantilist Europe. And when financial inducements did not suffice, espionage was occasionally invoked to effect the transfer—a method not unknown even in the late twentieth century.

The nineteenth century saw the rise of missionaries and a more diffuse missionary spirit carrying with it private support in the economically more advanced Christian nations for education and medical services as well as for the promulgation of faiths in what were to become the developing regions. And this impulse remains a living force in the politics of the Atlantic world. But there was at least one case of an intergovernmental offer of aid in the reverse direction. In 1861, the great modernizing leader of Thailand, King Mongkut, conscious that the government of the United States was caught up in a civil war, offered President Lincoln elephants to strengthen the American economy and military potential.[34]

After the First World War, the United States government engaged in substantial relief operations—notably, in supplying food—to both Western Europe and the Soviet Union. But it was only after the Second World War that intergovernmental loans and grants, from the more advanced (or more affluent) to less developed nations, became an institutionalized feature of the world community. By World Bank calculations such transfers ("official development assistance") approximated $27 billion in 1983, from the members of the Organization for Economic Cooperation and Development (OECD); perhaps $7 billion in 1982 from the Organization of the Petroleum Exporting Countries (OPEC).[35] Aid from Communist governments to non-Communist developing countries approximated $2.6 billion in 1979.[36]

In a world still dominated by fierce attachment to national sovereignty, these figures represent a limited, but real, recognition of the facts of interdependence and, even, to a degree, of human community. The period we examine in this essay—essentially, 1953–1961—was the interval when the phenomenon took shape and was institutionalized in a more or less stable way; and the Kennedy-Cooper initiative was a part of that larger process. The purpose of Chapters 5–9 is to evoke something of how the process occurred in the arena of American politics.

The proximate beginning of modern development aid was the agreement at Bretton Woods in July 1944 to create an International Bank for Reconstruction and Development.[37] Behind its creation were memories of the inter-war uncertainties in the flow of U.S. long-term capital exports, the patent future capital requirements of nations damaged or disrupted by the war, and a third, new strand: the notion of an international institution to assist in the development of the less developed countries. Of the seventeen countries engaged in the negotiation, only seven fell in the latter category: Brazil, Chile, China, Cuba, Greece, India, and Mexico. Their minority status, the palpable urgency of the tasks of reconstruction, and the caution of an ultimately dominant U.S. delegation, acutely conscious of the need to obtain Congressional approval, yielded an institution quite different from the World Bank which subsequently emerged:

> . . . Its initial, if not primary, function was the financing of reconstruction and only afterward of development; its capital subscriptions were relatively small, but its guarantee fund was intended to be large. Its dependence for funds therefore was mainly on private investors, which underlined the importance of establishing its position on capital markets; and the consent of the concerned government was required to raise funds in particular markets. The Bank was intended to operate mainly by guaranteeing private investors against loss, but it could also lend directly and participate in private loans. It was to lend primarily for specific projects and ordinarily only for the financing of foreign exchange costs; its loans were not to be tied to procurement in any particular countries, and the proceeds of the loans were to be used with due attention to considerations of economy and efficiency. Finally, its loans were to be made solely on the basis of economic considerations.

> On the whole it was a conservative institution—considerably more conservative than its framers had intended, since it was not the size of the guarantee fund that mattered but what private investors thought of the nature of the guaran-

tee. It was also, at least in its initial stages, far from being a bona fide international institution, since the United States supplied most of its loanable funds and was by far the predominant market for Bank securities. Its location in the territory of its largest stockholder further undermined its international status.[38]

The early days of the Bank were a study in slow motion. Its first loans were made to four European countries in 1947: France, Netherlands, Denmark, and Luxembourg. Its first loans to less developed countries were to Chile in 1948; Mexico and Brazil in 1949. But an institution had come to life capable of evolution in directions not initially envisaged; by 1980 it was lending some $12 billion annually for development purposes.

So far as American policy was concerned, Truman's enunciation of his Fourth Point in his inaugural address of January 20, 1949, was the next benchmark:

> Fourth. We must embark on a bold new program for making the benefits of our scientific advances and industrial progress available for the improvement and growth of underdeveloped areas.
>
> More than half the people of the world are living in conditions approaching misery. Their food is inadequate. They are victims of disease. Their economic life is primitive and stagnant. Their poverty is a handicap and a threat both to them and to more prosperous areas.
>
> For the first time in history, humanity possesses the knowledge and the skill to relieve the suffering of these people.
>
> The United States is pre-eminent among nations in the development of industrial and scientific techniques. The material resources which we can afford to use for the assistance of other peoples are limited. But our imponderable resources in technical knowledge are constantly growing and are inexhaustible. . . .
>
> We invite other countries to pool their technological resources in this undertaking. Their contributions will be warmly welcomed. This should be a cooperative enterprise

in which all nations work together through the United Nations and its specialized agencies whenever practicable. It must be a worldwide effort for the achievement of peace, plenty, and freedom. . . .

Such new economic developments must be devised and controlled to the benefit of the peoples of the areas in which they are established. Guarantees to the investor must be balanced by guarantees in the interest of the people whose resources and whose labor go into these developments.

The old imperialism—exploitation for foreign profit—has no place in our plans. What we envisage is a program of development based on the concepts of democratic fair dealing. . . .

Democracy alone can supply the vitalizing force to stir the peoples of the world into triumphant action, not only against their human oppressors, but also against their ancient enemies—hunger, misery, and despair.

Point Four reflected two facts aside from a typically presidential impulse to make a mark in history in an inaugural address: the evident progress in European reconstruction as the Marshall Plan took hold; and the gathering pressure of the less developed nations for assistance which they came to feel was being allocated rather inequitably to the more advanced nations. This pressure had resulted, for example, in the creation of a small United Nations technical assistance program at the meeting of the U.N. General Assembly in Paris late in 1948 which, after the announcement of Point Four, evolved into the (still exceedingly modest) Expanded Programme of Technical Assistance approved in the summer of 1949. The emergence from colonialism of a number of nations, including India and Pakistan, played an important role in the process, yielding also the Colombo Plan. It was generated at a meeting in Ceylon in 1950 as an important component in the emerging concept of the British Commonwealth, and went into effect the following year.[39]

The character of the American national interest in the economic progress of the underdeveloped areas was less clear-cut than the British concern with the future of the Common-wealth; and it was not made clear in Truman's exposition. He leaned mainly on a combination of humanitarianism and American economic self-interest; he also linked successful economic development to the conditions for peace and the spread of the democratic process. He did not, however, in scale or in urgency elevate the Point Four program to the level of, say, the Marshall Plan or national defense policy.

The importance of the underdeveloped areas of the world to the American interest and the need to meet their power-ful aspirations for the modernization of their societies was, however, increasingly appreciated in 1949–1950, as Euro-pean recovery gathered momentum and the military position there appeared to be stabilized, while Communism moved to victory in China, shaking the fragile foundations of non-Communist Asia. Acheson's speeches on Asia of January and March 1950, Gordon Gray's report in November 1950, and Nelson Rockefeller's "Partners in Progress" report of March 1951 all reflected a gathering awareness of the strategic importance to the United States of long-run development in the underdeveloped areas.[40] And in October 1951 Chester Bowles went as ambassador to India and plunged wholeheart-edly into the adventure of the First Indian Five Year Plan.

The Point Four concept was well rooted in parts of Amer-ica's values and tradition. It appealed to the missionary spirit still powerful in the land, and it represented the kind of con-crete, constructive response to problems which instinctively caught the nation's imagination. On the other hand, there was no clear general understanding that the Point Four enterprise represented a major aspect of the task of protecting the na-tional interest. It was treated by the Congress as a low pri-ority matter in the first half of 1950, and then it was all but overwhelmed by the Korean War.

The fact of Communist military aggression immediately focused attention on actions designed to hold the line in the short run at the sacrifice of action designed to yield wholesome political and economic change for the longer run. Moreover, the neutralism of many poltical leaders in the new nations (and their recognition of Communist China)—which could be regarded as reasonably harmless when, for example, Nehru visited the United States in 1949—took on a different and, for many Americans, a more sinister cast by 1951 when the Korean War was at its height. When the issue was put to the test in Congress by the India grain bill (designed to relieve the famine of 1951), a loan was granted, but it was clear that the nation found it difficult to pursue simultaneously its immediate interest in frustrating Communist military aggression and its long-run interest in the evolution of successful, relatively stable societies, less vulnerable to external intrusion, less prone to violence, when the two interests did not yield neatly convergent lines of action.

In terms of resources and attention, then, the short-run military aspects of the struggle against Communism in the underdeveloped areas rose sharply in priority in 1950–1952 (see Chart 2). Military aid, which had been well under 10 percent of economic aid in (fiscal) 1950 and less than a quarter of the total in 1951, was more than two-thirds of the total authorization for 1953. And in the underdeveloped areas this aid flowed overwhelmingly to areas of military crisis—to Korea, Taiwan, and to assist the French in the struggle against the Viet Minh forces in Indochina. In effect, what Chart 2 reflects is a rapid decline in economic aid to Western Europe, made possible by European recovery and rapid growth, substituted for by enlarged military and economic aid (in the form of defense support) to selected, less developed countries judged to be under military threat.

The changing pattern of outlays in foreign aid in the late phase of the Truman administration reflected the main directions of diplomacy; that is, the build-up of NATO (including German rearmament) and the beginning of the effort to

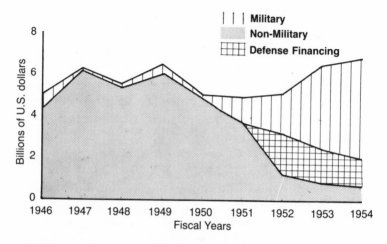

CHART 2. U.S. Gross Foreign Aid, 1946–1954

spread the NATO pattern of alliances and bases around the whole periphery of the Communist bloc. In 1951 NATO itself came to embrace Greece and Turkey; and Yugoslavia was brought bilaterally within the Western security system. Arrangements were made for air bases in Morocco and in Saudi Arabia. Bilateral arrangements were made or expanded with Japan (in the context of the treaty negotiation) as well as with the Nationalist forces on Taiwan and with the Philippines, Australia, and New Zealand.

In general, then, American diplomatic and economic foreign policy shifted its course in June 1950 away from the path marked out by Truman's Fourth Point and took as its central task in the following two and one-half years the problem of building a structure of alliances calculated to prevent another Korean War. Included in that effort was the creation of SHAPE which gave operating military substance to NATO. But, as Chapter 2 indicates, it was at just this time that Communist strategy and tactics began to move towards alternative, and less overtly military, means for advancing the power and influence of Moscow and Peking. Thus, the creative and anticipatory dimension in foreign policy, symbolized by the Fourth Point, was throttled back while the nation continued in its familiar style to institutionalize its emergency response to the last crisis.

6. The Failure of the World Economic Plan, 1953-1954

This, then, was the state of affairs when the Eisenhower administration came to responsibility in 1953. In the course of its eight years of stewardship, American dispositions toward the developing regions were destined to change quite substantially; and the change was rendered explicit, heightened, and dramatized with the arrival of the Kennedy administration. The turning point occurs, as we shall see, in 1957–1958, the interval when the Development Loan Fund was created and the Kennedy-Cooper resolution was launched along with several other initiatives. The purpose of Chapter 9 is to suggest how that turning point came about. Chapter 10 deals with its aftermath up to 1961.

A useful place to begin is with the statistical data on foreign aid set out in Tables 9 and 10 which exhibit in detail the transition in U.S. development assistance up to 1960 (Table 9) and, more broadly, from 1960 up to 1980 (Table 10).

Table 9 (1953–1960) exhibits the following major features:

(a) Military aid subsides as the war in Korea ends but remains substantial in support of the SEATO Treaty and other military pacts of the period.

(b) The bulk of economic aid remains defense support up to 1957 when it is two-thirds of the total.

(c) Development loans rise modestly after the creation of the DLF in 1957, reaching about 13 percent of total economic assistance in 1960.

(d) Overall, however, economic aid declines during the Eisenhower administration: 19 percent in terms of current dollars; 23 percent in real terms.

Table 10, which covers most of the period dealt with in Chapter 11 (1961–1982), exhibits in compressed style the principal developments of the two decades:

(a) The surge of development aid, by about one-third in the Kennedy years to a U.S. (and OECD) peak in fiscal year 1965.

(b) The fall of the U.S. proportion of ODA (and rise in the proportion provided by others) after 1965, accompanied by the erratic but clearly evident shift of aid towards multilateral institutions.

(c) The approximate leveling off of OECD ODA after 1965 in real terms (1978 prices) until the increases of 1975–1980 to help meet the balance of payments consequences for oil-importing developing nations of the rise in the international price of oil.

The pattern of foreign aid in the period 1953–1960 (Table 9) faithfully reflected the dominant thrust of the Eisenhower administration's policy towards the developing world in this period, although, as we shall see in Chapter 9, Table 9's modest shift of 1958–1960 in no way captures the drama of the policy breakthrough that lies behind the statistics.

The primary objective of American policy in Asia and the Middle East in the period 1953–1956 was to reduce the American burden in cost and manpower of holding the line around the periphery of the Communist bloc. Although there was increasing evidence of the new Communist strategy and tactics in the underdeveloped areas, the administration continued to base American policy on the assumption that the primary danger was a recurrence of the type of invasion launched against South Korea in June 1950; and the avoidance of another direct engagement of American ground forces was central to the administration's domestic political

TABLE 9. The Changing Scale and Composition of U.S. Foreign Aid, 1953–1960
(millions of current U.S. dollars)

	1953	1954	1955	1956	1957	1958	1959	1960
Military Aid	3954	3629	2292	2611	2352	2187	2340	1609
Defense support					1110	874	881	741
Development loans & grants								202
Technical assistance & cooperation	1960	1241	1928	1587		2	66	202
Agriculture (P.L. 480)		74	91	94	187	146	113	107
Contingency and other special assistance		3	3	22	341	408	407	369
Total economic assistance (including P.L. 480 and defense support)	1960	1318	2022	1703	1752	1570	1636	1591
In $ 1978	5026	3295	4932	4055	4074	3568	3636	3454
Total official flows (DAC definition)[3]				1996[1]	2091	2410	2310	2322
In $ 1978				4752	4863	5477	5133	5048

(DAC definition,
including private
investment)[4]

In $ 1978

| 3236[2] | 4100 | 3685 | 3276 | 3818 |
| 7705 | 9535 | 8375 | 7280 | 8300 |

Note: DAC figures for official flows of development assistance include Export-Import Bank loans and certain other forms of lending not included in the regular U.S. foreign aid budgets. The price correction in this table is from U.S. implicit GNP deflator, 1978 = 100.

Sources: Except as specified below, all data are from *The Budget of the United States Government,* for specific fiscal years ending on June 30, as follows: 1953 data, FY 1955, pp. M55 and M56; 1954, FY 1956, pp. M38 and M41; 1955, FY 1957, pp. M31 and M33; 1956, FY 1958, pp. M33 and M34; 1957, FY 1959, pp. M21 and M23; 1958, FY 1960, pp. M39 and M41; 1959, FY 1961, pp. M29 and M30; 1960, FY 1962, pp. M34 and M35.

1. *1963 Review—Development Assistance: Efforts and Policies of the Members of the Development Assistance Committee* (OECD), p. 79.

2. *1967 Review—Development Assistance: Efforts and Policies of the Members of the Development Assistance Committee* (OECD), p. 183.

3. *1969 Review—Development Assistance: Efforts and Policies of the Members of the Development Assistance Committee* (OECD), p. 297.

4. Ibid., p. 296.

TABLE 10. Official Development Assistance (ODA), 1960–1981: Net Disbursements, U.S. and OECD (note deposit basis, billions of U.S. dollars)

Year	Total U.S. ODA	U.S. as % of Total OECD	U.S. Multilateral ODA	Multilateral ODA as % of Total	Total U.S. ODA (in 1978 prices)	Total OECD-ODA (current dollars)	Total OECD-ODA (in 1978 prices)	U.S. dollar GDP Deflator (1978 = 100)[a]
1960	2.7	58	.26	9	7.7	4.6	13.2	.35
1961	2.9	57	.28	10	8.3	5.2	14.7	.35
1962	3.3	60	.27	8	9.2	5.5	15.4	.36
1963	3.6	62	.15	4	9.7	5.7	15.5	.37
1964	3.6	61	.22	6	9.5	5.9	15.6	.38
1965	4.0	62	.67	17	10.3	6.5	16.6	.39
1966	3.8	59	.44	12	9.3	6.4	15.7	.41
1967	3.3	52	.13	4	7.9	6.3	15.1	.42
1968	3.8	56	.84	22	8.8	6.9	16.1	.43
1969	3.4	49	.62	18	7.7	6.9	15.8	.44
1970	3.1	45	.50	16	6.6	7.0	14.8	.47
1971	3.1	41	.22	7	6.2	7.5	15.0	.50
1972	4.0	43	1.23	31	7.3	9.2	16.7	.55
1973	2.7	29	.30	11	4.3	9.1	14.4	.63
1974	3.7	32	1.11	30	5.4	11.6	16.7	.69
1975	4.2	30	1.22	29	5.4	13.8	18.0	.77
1976	4.4	31	1.52	35	5.5	13.9	17.4	.80

1977	4.7	30	1.78	38	5.4	15.7	20.0	.87
1978	5.7	28	2.19	39	5.7	20.0	20.0	1.00
1979	4.7	21	.61	13	4.3	22.4	20.4	1.10
1980	7.1	26	2.77	39	5.9	27.3	22.7	1.20
1981	5.8	23	1.50	26	4.2	25.5	21.2	1.38

Note: Since the U.S. and OECD ODA figures have been rounded to U.S. $ billion, and the percentages calculated with unrounded data, the percentages may differ from those calculated from rounded data.

ªThe dollar GDP deflator is based on price increases in OECD countries (excluding Greece, Portugal, Spain and Turkey) measured in dollars. It takes into account the parity changes between the dollar and national currencies. This differs from the standard U.S. implicit GNP deflator used in Table 9.

Sources: Data for 1960–1975 supplied to the author by the World Bank; for 1976–1980, World Bank, *World Development Report, 1981*, p. 164 (Table 16), supplemented and with 1982 revisions supplied by the World Bank. The World Bank figures vary, in some years, from those produced by the Development Assistance Committee (DAC) of the OECD. This is the case for the year 1960 which appears in both Table 8 and Table 9. The U.S. data for 1981 were provided by AID.

strategy as well as to its foreign policy. The American government after 1953 became deeply committed, in effect, to defend the national interest within the limit, if possible, that no American rifleman again fight in Asia or elsewhere along the non-European periphery of the Communist world.

The principal method for deterrence was to extend the pattern of bilateral and regional military alliances created in Europe by the Truman Doctrine and NATO to those other areas where Communist military aggression might occur and which had not been brought within the orbit of direct American alliance in the latter days of the Truman administration. In the Middle East a pact of mutual defense between Turkey and Pakistan was signed in May 1954; and the United States became directly linked to Pakistan when SEATO was set up in September 1954 in the wake of the Geneva conference on Indochina. The Baghdad Pact was negotiated with American support but under British leadership early in 1955, linking Iran and Iraq to Turkey and Pakistan. Bilateral security relations between the United States and Japan, provided for in the Japanese Peace Treaty, were consolidated in a Mutual Defense Pact in March 1954; and Formosa was linked to the United States by a mutual security pact in 1955. The mantle of explicit American military commitment was thus spread over a vast new area, and these nations were offered American military and economic aid to enlarge, sustain, and modernize their armed forces.

The Korean War had, then, a curious, paradoxical effect. The success of the American Eighth Army and its associated forces in the spring of 1951 in decimating the massed attacking armies of Communist China convinced Moscow and Peking that the military phase of the exploitation of postwar instability was about at an end, and that a sharp shift in tactics toward diplomacy and ideological competition was called for. On the other hand, the heavy casualties, indecisiveness, and controversies of the Korean War launched the United

States into a protracted phase during which, with almost obsessive single-mindedness, American diplomacy and resources were devoted to creating the kind of military arrangements around the periphery of the Communist bloc which were judged by Eisenhower most likely to discourage a second Communist venture along the lines of the Korean War.[41]

The adequacy of this policy was challenged within the Eisenhower administration as well as without from 1953 forward. The protracted debate on foreign aid for development purposes was, in a quiet way, one of the most dramatic strands in the Eisenhower administration. The unfolding of this inner struggle—in part a struggle within the minds of some of the key participants—is, perhaps, best illuminated by summarizing its chronology.

Eisenhower's first articulation of a policy embracing the developing regions as a whole came in his speech of April 16, 1953, in the wake of Stalin's death, the central subject of Book 3 in this series:

> This Government is ready to ask its people to join with all
> nations in devoting a substantial percentage of any savings
> achieved by real disarmament to a fund for world aid and
> reconstruction. The purposes of this great work would be:
> To help other peoples to develop the undeveloped areas
> of the world, to stimulate profitable and fair world trade,
> to assist all peoples to know the blessings of productive
> freedom.[42]

Safely protected by the caveat of prior "real disarmament," this statement had no operational consequences whatsoever. The administration proceeded to reorganize the foreign aid program in a new Foreign Operations Administration (FOA) headed by Harold Stassen. The foreign aid program, as it emerged from the Congress, consisted of appropriations of about $4.5 billion, of which 70 percent was direct military assistance, 20 percent defense support. There was a marked shift in allocations from Europe to Asia. The sums available for development assistance outside the structure of military pacts was exceedingly modest and thinly spread as Dulles acknowledged in an address on June 1, 1953.[43]

Outside the administration, the inadequacy of these dispositions was articulated by a good many figures, including Adlai Stevenson and Chester Bowles, within the administration, by Milton Eisenhower (for Latin America) and a good many of the professionals in the State Department, notably those working on Asia. A sense that a fresh look at economic foreign policy was required was shared within the administration, although there was no clear substantive consensus. As often happens in such circumstances, a presidential commission was appointed, headed by Clarence B. Randall, an articulate steel executive. It contained members of Congress as well as a representative group of citizens. Its report was filed with the president and the Congress early in 1954.

On the face of it, 1954 was a quiet, somewhat regressive year in foreign aid. Reflecting the balance of opinion in the Randall report, Eisenhower tersely summarized his views in a March 30 message to the Congress on foreign economic policy:

> Aid—which we wish to curtail;
> Investment—which we wish to encourage;
> Convertibility—which we wish to facilitate;
> Trade—which we wish to expand.

The focus was on the rapid movement of the world economy towards liberal goals in which U.S. private investment and expanded imports would permit the still present element of dollar shortage to be ameliorated and currency convertibility attained.

In his lectures on foreign economic policy, delivered in the wake of the publication of his report, Clarence Randall delineated clearly the tightly circumscribed role he envisaged for development aid.

> If one holds that economic aid other than that devoted to the immediate considerations of security shall terminate, there should be, it would seem, one clear exception. That is what is known as technical assistance. . . .
>
> . . . If the programs are sharply limited to education and training in the knowledge and techniques required for economic development abroad, including the administrative skills needed to create and manage modern industrial institutions, the moderate sums of money involved would seem to be altogether proper as a part of our total national effort.[44]

The foreign aid request of the administration was for only $3.5 billion. Given a substantial backlog of unobligated prior appropriations ($2.5 billion), Congress appropriated only $2.4 billion in 1954, of which 86 percent was for military assistance and defense support. So far as the formal record showed, the only aberration was Stassen's initiative for a regional development program in Asia, the rise and fall of which was well chronicled by Richard Stebbins in his annual review of American foreign policy for 1954:

> . . . Mr. Stassen became the principal exponent of a new concept of the "Arc of Free Asia" which was said to extend from Pakistan around to Japan and to afford a possible basis for a cooperative organization like the OEEC in Europe—one in which Japan's industrial and technological preeminence would play a particularly vital role. Such an arrangement, it was said, would form a logical counterpart to the new Southeast Asia Collective Defense Treaty, but might include not only countries allied with the United States but also neutral countries whose economic growth and democratic future needed to be further assured.
>
> But the bold scope of these proposals aroused considerable misgivings both in Congress and within the administration, and the scale of the proposed assistance began to be

whittled down even before work on the new Mutual Security appropriation got seriously under way. Mr. Dulles said on December 7 that the administration would probably submit a program for Asian economic development to the next Congress, since the emphasis of the East-West struggle had "shifted to some extent, for the time being perhaps, more to economic competition." But the President indicated next day that the question of reconciling such a program with the objective of a balanced budget had not yet been thought through. Mr. Stassen explained (December 9) that it was hoped to carry out the program with a minimum of American funds and maximum participation by Western European nations. By the end of the month it was apparent that the over-all Mutual Security request for fiscal year 1956 would be further reduced as compared with the year preceding, and that the sums to be sought for Asian development would certainly not exceed $500 million.[45]

Stassen was not acting irresponsibly. The administration did, indeed, formally staff out and approve, with Dulles' support, the concept of a special Asian development fund. Stassen's concept of the scale of such a fund exceeded that of some of his colleagues, notably the undersecretary of state, Herbert Hoover, Jr.; and his advocacy was judged excessively ardent. (Appendix D, supplied by former Ambassador Charles F. Baldwin, details the inner struggle of the administration over this issue at the working level in the second half of 1954.) Stassen's bit of enterprise helps explain the creation, at the end of 1954, of a new Council on Foreign Economic Policy, headed by a rather tight-fisted former director of the budget, Joseph Dodge, and Stassen's subsequent transfer to the less budgetary field of disarmament negotiations.

Two substantial but not decisive events, widening the scope of development lending, occurred in 1954. First, Public Law 480 was passed by the Congress and signed by the president. Title I of the act authorized the U.S. government to accept inconvertible local currencies in repayment for surplus agricultural commodities and to make loans or grants with the proceeds for economic development purposes. The Agricultural Trade Development and Assistance Act had its roots, of course, in the emergence of large U.S. agricultural surpluses and the desire of farmers to move their products out into world markets. U.S. agricultural prices fell from 125 in 1951 to 105 in 1954 (1967 = 100). P.L. 480 appeared a way both to mitigate the downward pressure on prices and to supply useful resources to developing countries; although, as noted below (p. 218), it had its costs.

Second, a Congressional reaction against executive branch constraints on the Export-Import Bank imposed in 1953, led by Senator Homer Capehart, yielded both greater independence in its operations and enlarged borrowing authority. Like P.L. 480 these moves were related to domestic economic problems and pressures: the sharp recession of 1954 and the desire of certain U.S. exporters to have the benefit of enlarged public support in financing sales abroad.

Beneath the surface, however, 1954 was the year in which a little-known, major, head-on confrontation occurred on the issue of development aid at the highest level of the Eisenhower administration.[46]

The battle of 1954 begins on March 25. John Foster Dulles invited to lunch C. D. Jackson, with whom Millikan and I had been in touch on a number of matters, including foreign aid policy. Jackson, after service on the White House staff since January 20, 1953, was about to return to a post in the Luce magazine empire. Robert Bowie, head of the State Department planning staff and one of Dulles' closest advisers, was also present. Jackson's terse diary entry was the following:

> JFD asked me to lunch with him and Bowie. Discussed sad state of affairs. He repeated the statement that only real things done in foreign policy had been April and Dec. speeches [Eisenhower's April 16, 1953, speech in the wake of Stalin's death and his Atoms for Peace speech of Decem-

ber 8, in both of which Jackson was a central figure]. Asked for a new idea. Uncorked world economic plan and new Princeton Conference.[47] Very enthusiastically received. Later went over possible names with Bowie.[48]

As I recall Jackson's contemporary account of the lunch, Dulles was deeply depressed by the impending setback in Indochina and the gathering momentum of the Soviet economic and political offensive in the developing regions. He said that, as secretary of state, he was being forced to defend the interests of the United States with one arm tied behind his back; namely, the nation's economic strength. U.S. military power—the other arm—was not enough and was, indeed, largely unusable. Dulles asked for Jackson's help.

On March 30 Jackson had lunch with Millikan and solicited his assistance in organizing the proposed Princeton meeting. The notion was to assemble a representative group from within and outside the government to see if a consensus could be established that development aid should be substantially increased, and to outline a plan to accelerate growth in the developing regions which could be used as the basis for a presidential initiative. Jackson's telegram of invitation and the list of those attending the Princeton meeting of May 1–16 are in Appendix D.

At the Princeton Inn a rough-and-ready consensus did emerge that an enlarged global initiative by the United States in support of development was required. Millikan and I, on the basis of some preliminary drafting on the night of May 15, were commissioned to produce a coherent proposal to go in to the government. An interim draft of twenty-five pages, reflecting the May 16 responses of the group to our initial draft, was finished by May 25; and a fifty-two-page paper, entitled "A Proposal for a New United States Foreign Economic Policy," by July 23. This essay contained essentially the same calculations on the order of magnitude of required development aid as those published three years later in *A Proposal* (see above,

p. 48). It was the July 23 draft that circulated widely through the executive branch in the summer of 1954 and became the focus of intense debate.

Jackson, with the assistance of John Jessup of *Life* magazine, Millikan, and me, drafted, early in August, a speech for Eisenhower which might have launched the enterprise, the essential points of which he summarized in a letter to Dulles of August 3 as follows:

> I propose that the President early in September make a speech along the following lines:
>
> 1. It should recall his statement of April 1953 on his intent to increase the resources allocated to economic growth.
>
> 2. It should recall his statement of December 1953, appealing for Soviet cooperation in the peaceful use of atomic energy.
>
> 3. It should review the events of the last six months covering both progress and set-backs, ending with a powerful reassertion of the continuity of American intentions, which I would describe simply as follows:
>
> a. Peace.
>
> b. An expansion, not a contraction, of the area of freedom.
>
> c. Stimulus to the economic well being and the economic *independence* of all free peoples. In particular our willingness to foster an enlarged, long-term development of underdeveloped areas without military or political strings, designed to raise the personal welfare status of the individuals in those underdeveloped areas in order to have them appreciate on their own, and not by edict or mimeograph machine, that the Free West offers more than the Communist East.
>
> d. A sharing of scientific development for peaceful purposes.
>
> e. A reduction of the armaments burden.
>
> 4. A specific announcement of the U.S. willingness to enter into a World Partnership for Economic Growth along the lines of the attached draft.
>
> 5. A specific announcement, as part of the scientific as-

pect of the plan, of U.S. willingness to install forthwith four atomic power plants outside the U.S.

As part of the latter two announcements the President would indicate his intent to seek Congressional support and appropriations promptly.

The speech draft and the text of the proposal on which it was based were sent to Robert Cutler, director of the NSC staff, Brigadier General Paul ("Pete") Carroll, a presidential aide, as well as to Allen Dulles. Cutler, who attended the Princeton meeting, appeared to be in strong support and passed the documents to John Eisenhower "to interest his father." [49] On August 7 Jackson had a long session with John Foster Dulles in which the difficulties began to emerge:

> Two and a half hours with Foster, starting with Beaver [World Economic Plan], which he is all for although had not given it full reading yet, but promised to do it over the weekend. . . .
>
> Raised difficulties regarding presenting such a package while Congress was away, and without pre-conditioning. Also difficulty of economy-minded Congress against further grants. Countered by telling him that if President wanted to he could call in carefully selected group of Congressmen and Senators before adjournment and tell them what he proposed to do.
>
> On money, the proposal is partly a substitute for FOA type of thing; also it is loans rather than grants; also the capacity to absorb capital not up to amt [amount] made available, therefore cash drain probably 50% of authorization.
>
> Argued back and forth with Foster repeatedly saying, "Don't misunderstand me, I am for this, not against it."
>
> Then got into real hairdown session on Administration, Prexy, and foreign policy. Agrees with me that foreign policy by Presidential speech without follow through impossible. Further agrees direct tie-in between domestic actions and foreign actions. Confirmed textually Ann's [Ann Whitman, Eisenhower's personal secretary] statement Prexy has sold out to [Congressional] liaison boys until November. . . .

[Reference is to November 1954 Congressional elections.]

JFD is sincerely devoted to Prexy, but makes two important points:

1. When JFD is away, Prexy falls apart from other pressures;

2. His exaggerated desire to have everybody happy, everybody like him, prevents him from making clean cut decisions and forces him to play ball with the last person he has listened to.

Conclusion: Is wonderful man, every right instinct, the man to fulfill Arthur Vandenberg's "bipartisan leadership America-out-of-crisis" dream. May well go down to ignominy and defeat."[50]

On August 11 Jackson spent three quarters of an hour with Eisenhower focused, in part, around the administration's desire to induce Jackson to return to Washington.

. . . I have lived through fifteen months of what I would call foreign policy by Presidential speech, with no follow-through afterwards, and I know it doesn't work. . . .

. . . I have been doing quite a lot of work the last months on a Plan and a Speech. . . . But I happen to know that you have not seen it yet. Now, that is the kind of thing that is going to be torn to pieces by the Indians; it won't ever be made; it won't even be put to you in the form in which you can make your own decision—unless *you* want to do it, unless you say "I want to say this. . . . I like it"—and then argue out the difficulties.

For instance, you will be told that it will be difficult to put this plan across with Congress. All right. Difficulty with Congress is an occupational hazard for the President of the United States. It is built in. For me or anybody else to propose something to you that was NOT going to make difficulty with Congress would be to suggest something ridiculous or innocuous that no one will pay any attention. . . .

What you need is something that will capture the imagination. The prestige of the United States is at a low point today, and will not be captured or enhanced by dribbling out little bits and pieces.

. . . I suggest that you read it, and you decide whether you want to get excited about it. If you do, then something is likely to happen. If you don't, nothing is likely to happen. . . .

If there is action and follow-through, then the psychological warfare boys can do things. But if they are expected to do things in a vacuum and then nothing happens, you might as well not have them around.

The President seemed to take it all right. . . .

We fenced around for a bit, and then the President said, "Look, I don't want to force you to come down here. You have been here for more than a year, more than you agreed to originally, and I am grateful for that, and I certainly don't want to drag you away from anything. But what happens in this Government is that unless there is one person in the setup who is really concerned about these things and pulls the others together, things just simply don't get done—and that is the lack and that is what I would like to have you do. You don't have to come down regularly, but every now and then when you know something ought to be done, if you could come down it would be wonderful, and then I would relieve Pete Carroll of his present duties and he would be sort of in residence and be able to follow through, and you and he could check with each other, and I think we could get somewhere. . . ."[51]

In terms of administrative style the clash of conceptions is clear: Jackson requested an unambiguous command decision from the President which would force unified action; Eisenhower envisaged a subordinate to "pull the others together" into consensus.

By August 16, Eisenhower, having read the speech draft and the supporting papers, sent Jackson the following serious but troubled reply:

Over the week end, I read the entire sheaf of papers that you left here during your recent visit. This morning I have your personal letter.

First of all, let me say that I am more than impressed with

the careful analysis you made of the subject. Likewise, I admire the skill with which you presented your conclusions. I am frank to say that the documents gave me an insight into some phases of the general subject that had never before occurred to me.

In considering the impact upon the American people of the kind of talk of which you speak, I have a feeling that it will take some doing to make the whole plan appear as a new bold and broad approach! The cynic will describe it as "bigger and better give-aways." The presentations made in prior years in Congressional committees and on the floors of both Houses in behalf of Point IV, Mutual Security, the Marshall Plan and NATO frequently made use of some of the facts and conclusions that appear in your paper.

The new concept in your paper is the breadth and depth of your attack; but that these factors make the entire project something new and different will be difficult to sell.

All of this, of course, does not argue for shutting our eyes to the opportunity and the project, or of dodging the burden of making a speech—to the contrary, these things tend to emphasize the importance of "educating" ourselves and then our anticipated associates.

This thought introduces some specific questions that should be directed toward the composition and the details of the first speech to be made. (This is not a criticism of the draft you submitted—just thinking in type!) Since no speech can comprise an entire education in itself, it is important that in a case like this it should be inspiring as to purpose and should avoid alarming as to cost. With this in mind, the question of detail becomes highly important.

I realize that you do not want to miss the impact of a concrete proposal. By definition, a concrete proposal requires specifics.

The question in my mind is whether these two considerations—(a) to educate our own people, and (b) to have a dramatic effect upon the world—do not create considerable difficulties in the exact terminology of the initial speech.

At the moment there is no use pursuing this line of

thought. I have not yet talked the whole subject over with anyone except my son—who is vastly impressed. I will get at it when I can and you will hear further from me. . . ."[52]

Jackson responded, in effect, to Eisenhower's concerns in a letter to Dulles with a copy sent to Carroll at the White House. I was brought in to help on this letter. Evidently, Jackson's judgment was that Eisenhower was worried by two things: the money involved in the proposal, and the Congress.

> Dear Foster:
>
> . . . I had a very long and very frank talk with the President last week on this and related subjects, and managed to cover several of the target points you and I had discussed the previous Saturday afternoon.
>
> Although election rabies seem to have seized practically everyone in his entourage, I feel that he himself is developing considerable immunity, and is unquestionably conscious of the crisis, of the dangers, and of the opportunities. But this consciousness will require fairly constant reminding in order not to get snowed under by the almost overwhelming political lapel-tugging to which he is being subjected. . . .
>
> In connection with the economic and political analysis of the speech, I have a few points which may be of help in some of the arguments you will undoubtedly have.
>
> We have always known that there would be a price tag on any such constructive effort, and that the price tag would raise important political hurdles. Following are four points on the cost and the politics:
>
> First, the cost to the U.S. economy. It may not help with some of the more difficult gentlemen on the Hill, but it is a comfort to look at the price tag in terms of the country's income, growth, and outlays for other purposes. We propose additional U.S. loans and grants (mainly loans) of about $10-billion, over five years; that is, about $2-billion per year. This is about 1/7th of the normal increase in national income, as the economy grows. This is less than 5% of the present annual outlay on national security. Even taking the whole amount in one lump, $10-billion is about 1/3 of the present

unused capacity in the economy. We can take it that the country can afford the program without significant sacrifice of welfare or other measures of national security.

Second, this is primarily an investment program, not a giveaway. It is extremely important that this fact be appreciated and dramatized in presentation. This is not a repetition of the Marshall Plan, where we covered balance of payments deficits by gifts. The Plan figures that additional grants should only be made to the tune of $360-million per annum, out of the total U.S. annual contribution of $2-billion. There may even be some form of Bureau of the Budget presentation for making clear the serious investment character of the effort.

Third, the political problem on the Hill would be measurably eased if we get the other industrialized nations to contribute to the pool. The Plan suggests that they commit themselves to putting in more than a half billion a year in loans and grants. This is a substantial chunk. They can now afford it (largely due to earlier U.S. aid in reconstruction).

Fourth, a possible gimmick. It seems to me that a part of the capital for the loans should be raised by small Liberty Bond type loans all over the United States and the Free World.

I don't for a moment under-estimate the problem of the price tag and the Hill. But I would add this. We Americans can be tight with a dollar but we also enjoy shooting for large objectives and taking on big jobs. I sense in the country now an end to the post-Marshall Plan let down, an end to the mood of stock-taking and letting the dust settle. I believe the country is prepared to move forward constructively again in a big way, if the challenge is explained, if the goals are firmly set by the President, and if it is not, simply, more of the same. There will be in-fighting on the Hill, of course. And, like yourself, I have a wholesome respect for $2-billion a year. But I'm pretty well convinced the hurdles can be taken. . . .[53]

At this point Jackson's assessment, as reflected in a letter to John K. Jessup on August 20, was not exuberant but something short of total discouragement:

The matter is in one of those twilight situations that I have seen so often that they don't worry me any more. The essential has been accomplished in that the idea has gotten under Prexy's skin, and I am confident that it will emerge in some form or other, possibly not the way we have pitched it for September. Conceivably it might be the core of January's State of the Union.[54]

A letter from Dulles to Jackson of August 24 clearly revealed his fundamental dilemma: his strong support for the plan on anti-Communist grounds and his determination not to lead the battle against its opponents in the administration and the Congress.

As far as I personally am concerned, it is just not practical for me to be a crusader for some particular program however good it may be. I can plan, and I can support, and I am 100% behind your type of investment program. I spent most of last Saturday discussing it with Bob Bowie and we are going to try to get some studies under way. However, the task of fighting these things out with Treasury, Budget, World Bank, Ex-Im Bank, not to speak of Congress, is itself a full-time job, and not only a full-time job for *somebody* but a full-time job for someone who can speak on a basis of equality with Cabinet Ministers, Senators and the like.

I have become personally convinced that it is going to be very difficult to stop Communism in much of the world if we cannot in some way duplicate the intensive Communist effort to raise productive standards. They themselves are increasing their own productivity at the rate of about 6% per annum, which is about twice our rate. In many of the areas of the world such as Southeast Asia, India, Pakistan and South America, there is little, if any, increase. That is one reason why Communism has such great appeal in areas where the slogans of "liberty," "freedom" and "personal dignity" have little appeal.[55]

By the autumn, the defeat of the proposal became increasingly clear. A Millikan note to Jackson on October 1 reported his impression, while in Washington, that "something would definitely be done for Asia; but that there was an almost equally definite decision not to launch anything on a broader geographic scale." Then, again, Millikan wrote on October 28:

> . . . My conversations [in Washington] depressed me profoundly as it was quite apparent to me that the Treasury has skillfully and effectively sabotaged all efforts to produce a program which will cost anything. In addition to this effective sniping from the economy boys the lack of any high-level energetic leadership has led to just what we were afraid it might lead to, namely a set of bureaucratic squabbles at a relatively low bureaucratic level as to who should handle any program that might be launched and how it should be organized. . . .[56]

To which Jackson replied on November 2:

> . . . Your advice on the corridor status of the World Economic Plan is terribly discouraging, particularly as it pretty well confirms what my grapevine was carrying. However, as you certainly know, it is not a unique Washington phenomenon, nor does it reveal any exceptional bureaucratic animosity in this particular case. Every single thing of any real importance requires one guy, feeling very strongly, and in a position to speak with authority at all levels—and that fellow just doesn't exist today, or at least doesn't exist with the freedom from administrative responsibilities essential to give him the time to "walk" such a project through the Washington labyrinth.
>
> Dulles is a perfect illustration of this situation. He has repeatedly told me that he is 100% for this idea, but that he simply cannot assume the responsibility of pushing it through, nor does he dare turn it over to any one of his people who might have time to devote to it. . . .
>
> I am afraid that if it is left at that, what will eventually emerge will be as inconsequential and undramatic as the special economic message based on the Randall Report, which was itself the least common denominator of what

Clarence Randall thought Senator X and Congressman Y would buy. . . .

Before the year was out, Jackson made several further efforts. He wrote to Herbert Hoover, Jr., a determined, even ruthless opponent of the proposal. This venture yielded an impeccably correct reply of December 10, with Hoover saying, in effect, that there might be a U.S. program for Asia "appropriate to our responsibilities and capabilities" but not a global effort.[57] Jackson had a livelier and, initially, more hopeful exchange with Dodge, as the latter assumed his new coordinating role in foreign economic policy. In the end, however, it emerged that Dodge's priorities were quite different from Jackson's: to dismantle FOA and distribute its functions; and to avoid U.S. rhetoric which would lead "foreign countries to expect a great deal more from us than we could or would provide":

> I was very much interested in the points you make in your letter. However, one thing we have to bear in mind is the damage that has been done by public statements that have led foreign countries to expect a great deal more from us than we could or would provide.
>
> Several important members of the Congress, who have been traveling abroad this fall, telephoned me about this. One put it this way—we have got to stop inviting those nations to come with suitcases and send them home with a cigar box. This man had just completed an extensive trip through the Far and Middle East, is extremely well informed on foreign affairs, and is a very important member of the right Committee. . . .
>
> It is not clear yet, but I believe the President will expect me to submit to him some kind of a recommendation on future policy which, in whatever form is accepted, may be used in a later message to the Congress. I have not seen a draft of the proposed State of the Union message so have no knowledge so far of the kind of presentation intended in that about foreign aid. I believe it will be rather restrained from what I have heard about it.[58]

My end of year reaction to Dodge's view, incorporated in a letter to Jackson of December 27, is in Appendix F. In the course of it I tried to evoke the Humphrey-Dodge view in sympathetic terms before responding:

Economic development is a complicated matter. Other people's money is only one of the things involved, and perhaps the least important. You need orderly government, vigorous entrepreneurs, plant managers, foremen, engineers. You need tax systems that collect taxes, a forward-looking middle class, a hard-working working class. Any fool knows that, unless you are going to give the money away to finance imported Cadillacs and trips to Paris for some official's nephew, there are only limited openings for new capital investment in many areas, if you really mean investment. Any fool knows that the men in these underdeveloped countries are only too ready to talk and act as though U.S. dough will solve their problems when, in fact, they have to solve them at home. So let's keep cool and keep them cool. Let them work along at home. Let us help them with technical assistance. Let them learn that capital is other people's money which must be respected and put to use only under conditions which will yield a solid return.

I then went on to argue against this perspective.

On December 13, the editors of TIME, with Jackson's encouragement and Luce's support, had laid out in some detail the case for "Partnership-for-Growth"; but 1954 was a year when we, who believed in such a program, tried hard but clearly failed. We had formulated the case for development aid as well as we were capable of doing it. Jackson, prodded by Dulles in March, had led the charge within the executive branch with courage and resourcefulness. The proposal had supporters within the administration, including both Dulleses, Cutler, John Eisenhower, and a good many in the State Department, except Hoover. But Eisenhower was not prepared to overrule its opponents within the administration—notably Humphrey, Hoover, and Dodge; and he was not prepared to take on the opposition in the Congress, much of it within his own party. Moreover, he was honestly concerned about the cost of the effort. And so 1954 ended with foreign economic policy firmly in the grasp of the opponents of a large scale U.S. effort in support of development. Its advocates, bloody but unbowed, could only live to fight another day.

7. Foreign Aid Doldrums, 1955-1956

Dodge's assessment that Eisenhower's State of the Union message of 1955 would be "rather restrained" on the subject of foreign aid proved prescient. Eisenhower's address of January 6 and a special message on foreign economic policy of January 10 focused, in the spirit of the Randall Report, almost exclusively on lowering barriers to trade and investment and moving towards convertible currencies.

The previous pattern of military assistance and defense support continued, increasingly focused on a few parts of Asia: Korea, Taiwan, and Indochina. Stassen's large vision of a program for "the Arc of Free Asia" emerged as an exceedingly modest Fund for Asian Economic Development of $200 million to be used over a three-year period.

Again, as Dodge had forecast in his exchange with Jackson, FOA was terminated and an International Cooperation Administration (ICA) set up within the State Department. Its first director was John B. Hollister, a Republican ex-Congressman and former law partner of Senator Robert Taft, who proved, in time, more moderate than had been anticipated but distinctly not a crusader for development aid.

Although the Democrats had regained control of the Senate and House in the congressional elections of 1954, this fact did not significantly affect the congressional dispositions of foreign aid in 1955 which remained cautious, skeptical, and pretty much in harmony with the proposals laid before Congress in that year. Once again, however, there was an unpublicized battle within the administration on foreign aid. This one was brief and decisive.

As Book 4 in this series details, the Quantico Panel, organized by Nelson Rockefeller, which generated the Open Skies proposal in mid 1955, dealt also, in its background analyses, with larger issues of military and foreign policy. These included the possibility of mounting "with NATO countries a joint policy for accelerating economic growth in the underdeveloped countries of the free world" and a special development program for Asia. These passages had, I suspect, little impact.

The report of a second Rockefeller-led meeting at Quantico in September 1955 focused more sharply on foreign aid. Millikan, who played a major role in Quantico II (as well as Quantico I), provided a substantial supplementary paper for the report entitled "Economic Policy as an Instrument of Political and Psychological Policy." [59] It reflected explicitly the paper we had developed in the wake of the May 1954 Princeton meeting, focusing, in particular, on what a global development plan could be expected to accomplish and not accomplish. It incorporated an estimate that a concerted program, looking ahead ten years, and matching the absorptive capacity of the developing world, might involve additional annual investments of $2–3 billion, of which the U.S. budgetary share might be $1.5–2 billion. These figures were included in the final report, backed by Rockefeller, and were met with the same frigidity they generated when presented by Jackson. At a climactic meeting at Eisenhower's office in the Post Office at Gettysburg on December 5, 1955, it became clear to Rockefeller that Eisenhower would not advocate substantial increases in either military expenditures or foreign aid. Rockefeller decided to take his case to the public through the panels organized by the Rockefeller Brothers Fund.

While the 1955 debate within the administration was kept quite firmly within the family, the basic issues were widely discussed outside. There was, for example, a proposal of Christian Herter, then Governor of Massachusetts, that the U.S. offer to join with the Soviet Union in a common program of assistance to developing nations, thus removing the issue from its Cold War environment.

In 1955 CENIS published its recommendations for an American policy in Asia in the wake of its study of the prospects for Communist China.[60] One of the basic conclusions of the latter book was the following:

> The effectiveness of this [the Chinese Communist] program obviously hinges on the military and political performance of Free Asia. . . . if Free Asia does not substantially improve its performance, an indifferent outcome on mainland China could still represent an important relative achievement both to the Chinese and to Asians generally.
>
> On the other hand, the evolution of solid military, political, and economic policies in Free Asia could deny Peking its claim to military and ideological primacy in Asia, and help force, over a period of time, a fundamental re-evaluation of the Chinese Communist regime's domestic and foreign policies. . . .[61]

In the policy volume, we applied to Asia the criteria of the proposal developed in 1954 out of the dynamics set in motion by the Princeton meeting (see Appendix E). The operational conclusion was the following:

> . . . the United States should consider enlarging its program of technical assistance and loans to Asia, looking ahead at least five years, at a rate of about $1.3 billion per year; and the other industrialized areas of the Free World should put up about $0.7 billion.[62]

But undoubtedly, the most important events of 1955, so far as aid policy was concerned, were the Soviet (nominally

Czech) arms deal with Egypt and the barnstorming, month-long visit of Bulganin and Khrushchev to Afghanistan, India, and Burma in November–December. Referring to Western claims that Soviet aid offers were without substance, Khrushchev said in India:

> To those who write this, we say: Perhaps you would like to compete with us in establishing friendship with the Indians? Let us compete. (Applause.) Why have we come here? We come with an open heart (applause) and with honest intentions. We are glad of it. Perhaps you have not sufficient experience? Then apply to us, and we shall help you. (Applause.) You want to build electric power stations? If you have not the necessary know-how, if you need technical assistance, apply to us and we shall help. (Applause.) You want to send your students, your engineers to our country for training? Please do so. (Applause.)[63]

And a considerable array of Soviet-financed projects, including a steel mill, were set in motion in India early in 1956.

These and other similar events, rather than the arguments of Quantico II and CENIS, led Eisenhower in a letter to Dulles sent from Gettysburg on December 6, 1955, to observe: "I am delighted that you are calling attention to the economic phase of the Cold War"; and to note in his May 3, 1956, report to the Congress on the Mutual Security Program: "The last six months of 1955 saw Soviet tactics shift increasingly from threats and violence to more subtle methods for extending Communist influence across new borders. The underlying purpose of this shift requires careful study."[64]

The fact is, however, that, despite Eisenhower's and Dulles' increasing awareness that U.S. policy was deficient, 1956 was another year in which nothing much of substance happened in the field of U.S. foreign aid policy; although "the implications of Soviet tactics as they bear on the conduct of the Mutual Security Program" were carefully studied both within the executive branch and in the Congress.

The foreign aid appropriation requested of the Congress was, indeed, $2 billion higher than the previous year's authorization; but this increase merely reflected the fact that Congress, appropriating a good deal less than the level of expenditures, had permitted the military aid pipeline to be run down for several years. In the end, Congress imposed a considerable reduction in the level of military aid requested, forcing a slight (about $150 million) reduction in expenditures in fiscal year 1957. Economic assistance stayed at just about its existing level. Two modest innovations requested by the administration were turned down: authority to commit up to $100 million per year (for not more than ten years) to economic development projects where the continuity of American support was judged essential; and the second $100 million installment for the president's fund for Asian development. A third requested innovation—a special $100 million fund for the Middle East and Africa—was converted into a sum appropriated conventionally for the year.

Congress was quite aware that within as well as outside the administration there was a good deal of uneasiness about the direction and adequacy of the administration's foreign aid program. The reactions of the two houses of Congress to this fact differed. The Senate set up a special committee to study the foreign aid program embracing members from the committees on appropriations and armed services as well as foreign relations. The House of Representatives was less constructive, tending to cut the executive branch foreign aid requests but acquiescing in more or less livable compromises in Senate-House conference committees. In a letter to Jerry Persons, an Eisenhower aide with responsibility for liaison with the Congress, Jackson evoked the reasons for this stance as articulated by a senator's assistant.

> Politically it is very simple. The House is simply trying to wash its hands of the whole business, and go to its constituents on strictly domestic affairs. There was a time when

they would have found it difficult to go through this hand—washing act, but as they look around today, what do they see?

The first thing they see on foreign aid is that the Administration has selected a man, Hollister, to head up the non—military aspects, who by his own admission does not believe in the thing itself. (I hope you read the transcript of Hollister's television appearance that I sent to Shepley in Florida.) In the second place, neither the President nor the Secretary of State have evidenced, in public, anything but the most routine pressure on this subject—no new ideas, no new words, no drive. So the House says to itself, "Why the hell should we be front man for carrying this torch, particularly as we are not at all sure that our own people back home give much of a damn."[65]

There may well have been another factor at work in the House as opposed to the Senate. The Democratic leaders and their staffs in the Senate were, by and large, authentically sympathetic to development aid and responsive to the arguments for its expansion. Influenced by Otto Passman and others, the mood was, by and large, quite different in the House. As Russell Edgerton observed:

> The hearing rooms of the Senate Foreign Relations Committee and the House Foreign Affairs Committee are not physically very far apart. But the mental distance between the two committees is considerable. . . . The staff of the Foreign Affairs Committee privately referred to Millikan and Rostow as the "cloud nine boys."[66]

In the spring of 1956 CENIS produced a further draft of its proposal which received widespread public attention in May and June with articles in the *New York Times*, *Washington Post*, *Washington Star*, *St. Louis Post Dispatch*, *Christian Science Monitor*, and other journals. It circulated widely in both the executive branch and the Congress, finding a supporter, among others, in Robert Jackson, who had succeeded Nelson Rockefeller on the White House staff. The special Senate committee on foreign aid asked CENIS to submit, under contract, a paper on "The Objectives of United States Economic Assistance Programs." Millikan, in fact, was the lead witness when public hearings opened under Fulbright's chairmanship on March 20, 1957.

In counterpoint to the CENIS effort, C. D. Jackson kept up a flow of letters to Dulles urging, among other things, that the U.S. approach to foreign aid be positive, in terms of its own plan, rather than responsive to Soviet initiatives; and he offered to mobilize citizen support if the administration should be serious. And there was a good deal stirring elsewhere in the administration which George Humphrey sensed. He tried to warn Dodge on the telephone; but the latter's departure on a trip outside Washington led Humphrey to drop him a note on April 27, 1956, which records for history something of the flavor of the opposition:

> I had a talk with Foster this morning about multilateral aid. He says he has no idea of getting into anything of the kind at the present time; yet in his conversation it is perfectly plain that it keeps recurring to his mind. He is sending me a note about his views and when it is received, I will send a copy to you.
>
> With Hoffman, Lodge, a whole small coterie in the State, and most of the foreign countries all promoting the project, we are going to have to be pretty agile or we will wind up with both feet in the trap.[67]

The reference to Paul Hoffman and Henry Cabot Lodge stems from activity in New York, where Hoffman had taken on the administration of the technical assistance work of the United Nations and Lodge was the U.S. ambassador. A proposal for a Special United Nations Fund for Economic Development (SUNFED) had been formulated to supply additional capital for developing countries on attractive terms.

On May 7 Humphrey addressed himself directly to Eisenhower in opposition to SUNFED and all other multilateral soft

lending schemes in perhaps the most full exposition of his
views available—views which were substantially to be echoed
by the Reagan administration a quarter-century later (see below, pp. 191–192).

These are a few thoughts to have in mind in considering
the relative advantages and disadvantages of new proposals
for multilateral aid.

There are two main fields for aid. One is to advance our
military objectives with direct or indirect support required
to finance or maintain military strength of the recipients.
The other is designed to promote the economic strength
and freedom of friendly countries by helping them to help
themselves and so increase their independence of action and
avoid reliance upon Russia. . . .

In discussing multilateral aid we are, therefore, concerned
principally with economic aid. This, however, is so closely
related to military aid that in most cases they are insepar-
able. In the remaining cases which clearly permit separate
consideration, we already have instruments to handle them
satisfactorily, either multilaterally or bilaterally as our own
best interests may dictate. [Humphrey then cites the World
Bank, the IMF, and existing U.S. programs.]

. . . Despite these very substantial provisions for multilateral lending, there are several current suggestions for new
organizations:

Cabot Lodge is urging that we support SUNFED primarily
as a direct maneuver to put Russia in the hole. He suggests
that we start in a very small way, but experience has shown
us that such a scheme once started never ends and continually grows—with the great bulk of the money always
coming from us.

There are proposals for an Asian Corporation in which a
number of countries interested in that area would start a
new lending organization there.

Then, there is always the recurring request for a bank or a
finance company for South America.

These all follow the same pattern. We put up the great

bulk of the convertible dollars. They put in their own inconvertible currencies or promises to pay at some future time. We supply the money. They supply the majority of the board of directors to dispense it.

If we engage in any one, we will be set upon immediately for the others, and unless we join with them, we will make more enemies than friends.

If new organizations are established to make loans on a looser basis than the International Bank or Fund, it will clearly undermine their work.

Much of the success of the banks' operations lies in the aid they have given member countries in working out sound economic programs. Without such programs, funds lent by looser methods might be largely wasted.

There is nothing any of these proposed schemes can do which cannot be done better by a combination of the World Bank, the Monetary Fund, and the International Finance Corporation, as multilateral agencies, supplemented by our own Export-Import Bank, the ICA, and P.L. 480 agricultural sales and loans.

. . . The only thing missing is authority to make commitments of funds to be appropriated in future years.

It is to cover this lack of authority to make long-term commitments out of future appropriations that you have asked for the extra legislation that is now pending in this Congress.

I think it is a very wholesome thing that such funds must be obtained from the Congress as a part of the budget so that they are under constant review and subject to the limitations of continuing legislation and criticism by the public. Otherwise, the pressures on the Executive are so great that it would be extremely difficult to resist unjustified expenditures.

I have a growing conviction that we will better promote our own global purpose; that we will more nearly comply with the growing public demand for tightening up aid activities; and that we will better serve the interests of those peoples whom we are trying to assist by gradually, but firmly, shifting our financial relations with them to sound, constructive, commercial relations, including sound but imaginative loans.

In this way, I think we will gain in their respect and we will help them develop sound enterprise. This program will not be popular with the politicians temporarily in control of such countries as are currently receiving our support; they want our money to spend for their own purposes and in their own way. But such a program will certainly increase the respect for us of all sound thinking citizens everywhere. And in the long run it will accomplish more.[68]

Meanwhile, out of his contacts with Dulles and others, C. D. Jackson had generated (with John Jessup of *Life* magazine drafting) yet another possible speech for Eisenhower on a world economic plan. Jackson described the mixed and indecisive reaction on May 22, 1956 to the draft in a memorandum to Henry Luce, concluding that any new initiatives would have to wait until "next year" (see Appendix F). The fact was (see Appendix G) that Eisenhower had decided early in 1956 that he would undertake no major divisive initiative until after the presidential election.

In the midst of his fruitless activism within the administration in the spring of 1956, C. D. Jackson spent an hour and a half with Dulles on a Saturday afternoon (April 14). He reported in a letter to Henry Luce, fully reproduced in Appendix G. It is a rare portrait of Dulles' view of the Russians as of the mid 1950s, of Eisenhower, the state of the bureaucracy, and his frustration by the Humphrey-Dodge-Hoover axis.

Nevertheless, by September the indefatigable Jackson was already focusing on Eisenhower's January 1957 State of the Union message. He wrote to Emmet Hughes, who had been brought back to the White House for speech-writing during the campaign, providing him material to buttress his recommendation that a world economic plan be a major focus of the State of the Union address; and on December 27 he addressed Dulles, who was recovering from a cancer operation, recapitulating the long road since 1954 and urging that the State of the Union message of 1957 at last launch the global development plan.

> . . . For a lot of reasons, well known to you and the President, World Economic Policy never got off the ground. Hopeful and sometimes strong paragraphs were included in State of the Union messages, but the project was not what I would call "orchestrated." Various commissions and committees studied WEP and reported on it, but their recommendations either wound up in a Capitol Hill tangle or for budgetary or other reasons were compromised into more or less ad hoc emergency aid. (None of the above, of course, refers to the military or semi-military aspect.)
>
> So much for the past.
>
> Now, once again, we are confronted with another State of the Union message and another Legislative year. But—something has been added of paramount importance.
>
> (1) President Eisenhower has been reelected by such an overwhelming mandate that the Eisenhower vote can only be construed as the clearly expressed wish of the majority of the American people that he proceed forthwith to propose and to drive through the Eisenhower program. . . . While it would be politically unsophisticated for me to pretend that WEP would have completely smooth legislative sailing, at the same time if the Administration's tactics are carefully planned and vigorously pursued, they will be met with an infinitely greater grass roots response than would have been possible before. . . .
>
> (2) The Soviet Union has at long last told us itself that it is no more immune to certain economic laws than anyone else. This morning's headlines on the economic personnel shakeup and the changes in the current Five Year Plan heavily underscore the economic predictions of so many thoughtful experts both in and out of Government. . . .
>
> Therefore, a World Economic Policy by the U.S. which was in the past desirable as a defensive measure against further

Communist encroachment, has now become the one *essential* offensive measure to roll back imperial Communism.

Furthermore, if coupled with a strong and visibly alert military position, it is just about the only way in which we can go on the offensive with the minimum risk of precipitating a final military convulsive reaction by the Kremlin. . . .

On the practical side, I can assure you that our publications would give whole-hearted support to an Administration World Economic Policy that was a world program rather than a regional project. And if you felt the need of private, articulate support throughout the nation, both on the level of individual citizens and the great private national organizations, I would be delighted to help organize this.[69]

8. The Log-Jam Breaks: The DLF, 1957

For the development crusaders, 1957 began with a bang. Eisenhower's second Inaugural Address of January 20 included the following rousing passage:

> We must use our skills and knowledge and, at times, our substance, to help others rise from misery, however far the scene of suffering may be from our shores. For wherever in the world a people knows desperate want, there must appear at least the spark of hope, the hope of progress—or there will surely rise at last the flames of conflict. . . .
>
> . . . We do not fear this world of change. America is no stranger to much of its spirit. Everywhere we see the seeds of the same growth that America itself has known. The American experiment has, for generations, fired the passion and the courage of millions elsewhere seeking freedom, equality, opportunity. And the American story of material progress has helped excite the longing of all needy peoples for some satisfaction of their human wants. These hopes that we have helped to inspire, we can help to fulfill.

In the wake of this pronouncement C. D. Jackson was invited on February 6 to present the World Economic Plan to a meeting organized by Clarence Randall. (Randall had succeeded Dodge as coordinator of foreign economic policy and had moved beyond the position taken in the report of the commission he chaired toward support for development aid.) Here are the key passages from Jackson's vivid, somewhat disabused account of the session as reported to Luce the next day.

Report on Meeting Organized by Clarence Randall
for me to present World Economic Plan
Washington, Feb. 6, 1957

Around the table, chaired by Clarence Randall, sat John Foster Dulles, George Humphrey, Sinclair Weeks, John Hollister, Gabe Hauge, Robert Cutler, True Morse (Agriculture), Steve Saulnier (successor to Arthur Burns as Chairman of the Council), C. D. Jackson.

Although it was never asked in terse Gallup fashion, the question "Do you or do you not propose to do anything to follow through (implement) the promise in the President's Inaugural address?" would have received the following vote:

YES – 1 (Randall)

NO – 9 (all the others).

These negative votes ranged all the way from really closed minds like Humphrey and Hollister, through the Hauge, "Well, we really are doing quite a lot of this sort of thing, you know; in South America we discovered that twenty beggars don't make a bank, but I for one am very hopeful about the Colombo Plan," to a kind of groping hopelessness voiced by John Foster Dulles.

From the start, it was a session in which I could not possibly win. If I talked about opportunity and theory, someone would demand nuts and bolts. If I started on a nut or a bolt, before any plan could emerge it was under quick attack and the thread was lost.

Typical of this see-saw: After a fairly emphatic statement by me relating to the President's Inaugural Address and the necessity for follow-through, or this would go down as just another amiable speech, George Humphrey said, "All right, I am all excited, I am ready to buy—but what is it you want me to buy?" To which I replied, "I have been trying to get down to the nuts and bolts of this thing, and am delighted to proceed. However, before doing that, I would like to ask you if after the President's Inaugural, you went to him and told him that you were excited and prepared to buy, but what

122

was it exactly he was proposing." George replied, "I did exactly that, and I got just as much of an answer out of him as I expect to get out of you."

The other end of the see-saw appeared during a discussion of the advisability of moving from grants to loans. Before I could get more than a few sentences out, Saulnier interrupted to say, "Every time I listen to one of these plans, it always seems to wind up with a proposal that besides everything else we are doing, the U.S. Government should go in for soft loans. We don't like soft loans."

Another moment of deliberate confusion came when several of them piled in on me saying that I was apparently proposing that we should give up the Korean type aid and the brush fire emergencies in order to concentrate on under-developed countries. When I tried to explain that we were faced with three types of aid—(1) the albatross type, like Korea, (2) the emergency, like Saudi Arabia, (3) the loans for productive development, which was the best way eventually to cut down on (2) and also (1)—Humphrey jumped in to say, "You don't seem to realize the jam that we are in. Our major allies are bust, repeat bust; we are pouring money into the pockets of cheap politicians who are taking their countries further and further away from the American way of doing things. Practically everybody is 'gone' against our way of life, and we just can't go on this way."

Lost in this particular shuffle was the fact that out of the $4-billion of the aid program, something between $200-million and $600-million was all that was left after defense, defense support, and types (1) and (2) above. . . .

The Millikan-Rostow book, which I did not mention, also came in for a panning. At one point, Saulnier said, "I have just finished reading that book by Millikan and Rostow. I didn't find anything new or interesting in it. It is just some more of the same kind of thing we have heard so often before."

I had been told by Randall that the session had to wind up in an hour. When everybody had had his say, it was five minutes past the hour, but Randall turned to me and asked if I cared to give a summary answer to the points made. I told him that while I was not running away from the invitation, it would inevitably take more than five minutes, and I did not feel that I had the right to take more of the time of this high powered group. Therefore, I proposed to have a brief and strictly nuts-and-bolts paper in their hands before the end of the month. Randall assumed responsibility for distribution.

At that, the meeting broke up, I crawled onto my shield and was carried out.

*　　*　　*

One way of analyzing the above is to say that, given a golden opportunity, I did a lousy job. Maybe so.

But I don't think it is just vanity which makes me add that I do not think anyone short of the President, in a command-decision mood, could have made a real dent on that group. Although there were three different types of minds present, they all formed an instinctive alliance.

One type, led by George Humphrey, does not believe that we should do anything beyond strictly military defense unless the proposed recipient country promises to behave like a God-fearing Middle Western businessman.

A second type, led by Foster Dulles, will take no initiative, won't even approve in principle, unless his client, the President of the United States, tells him to damn well pick up that ball and run with it.

The third type, part Hollister, part Hauge, thinks that actually we have not done too badly, and is mildly irritated that someone should suggest something more, given the difficulties on Capitol Hill, the problems of the budget, and the difficulty of coordinating so many divergent and Departmentally protectionist points of view.

As I said, although their attitudes were quite different, they easily formed an instinctive alliance against W.E.P.

*　　*　　*

I should be discouraged to the point of "To hell with it." But I am not—quite.

In the next three weeks I have to come up with a paper, and assuming that I can get some help here and in Cambridge, I am quite confident that a good one can be prepared. But, we have got to drop that word "World." It is too big for the boys who have to handle it, and it frightens them.

As a matter of fact, I have great sympathy for all of those guys who gave me my lumps yesterday afternoon. They are so overwhelmingly beset with the daily crisis requiring an ad hoc decision that they can't help an "Oh my God, as though I didn't have enough already!" when some cheerful world saver comes down from New York and starts talking about a *World* Economic Policy.

This has got to be brought down to pilot project size, and then let it spread.[70]

Jackson's conclusion that, in the environment of the Eisenhower administration, the only practical way to proceed was by small steps—by pilot projects that spread—proved to be correct. That is what began to happen in 1957. But it may not have happened if two men had not left the administration: Herbert Hoover, Jr., on February 21, succeeded by Christian Herter; George Humphrey, on July 28, succeeded by Robert B. Anderson. Herter was genuinely pro-development aid and quite knowledgeable about the situation in Washington, as Millikan and I discovered when briefing him on our proposals in Boston before he took up his new post in the State Department. Anderson was, by and large, a conservative political figure, in conventional parlance; but he proved to be considerably less rigid than his predecessor and, indeed, on several occasions, constructive and resourceful, as we shall see. In addition, the balance on foreign aid policy was shifted significantly by the return to Washington from his ambassadorial post in Paris of Douglas Dillon as deputy undersecretary of state for economic affairs.

The pilot project of 1957 proved to be the Development Loan Fund. The rather complex story of its creation is well told in a monograph by Russell Edgerton, *Sub-cabinet Politics and Policy Commitment: The Birth of the Development Loan Fund.*[71]

So far as U.S. foreign aid policy was concerned, the intellectual, ideological, and political debate over the period 1954–1957 came to rest operationally on the question of whether tax resources should be explicitly set aside in support of economic development in countries not allied with the United States in military pacts. The scale of such a program and whether it should take the form of a multi-year fund or annual appropriations were also involved; but the issue of principle had become quite clear.

The foreign aid Special Committee of the Senate, led by Fulbright, had emerged in 1957 in support of such a program. Two citizens' committees, both linked to the Eisenhower administration, split cleanly on the issue. The International Development Advisory Board (IDAB), chaired by Eric Johnston, was strongly in support. Millikan and I, as well as various other like-minded characters, worked closely with the IDAB. The President's Citizen Advisers on the Mutual Security Program, chaired by Benjamin Fairless, was against such an innovation. The latter was, at the time, the more prestigious effort—in effect, a well-publicized counterweight to the Senate Special Committee. The IDAB had been in existence since 1950. Its report on foreign aid had been initially envisaged (in September 1956) as a private communication to the administration. On the other hand, Eric Johnston had good ties to the White House and was a strong, articulate personality when fully committed to a cause.

The Fairless report was delivered to the White House on March 1, and released to the press on March 5. The Johnston report, although dated March 4, was delivered earlier and had, in fact, been made available to the Fairless committee. When Sherman Adams learned of the substance of the Johnston report, he ordered all copies locked up to avoid undermining the Fairless report. The device did not work. Johnston saw Eisenhower on March 4 and, perhaps with Dulles' backing, persuaded him that the IDAB report should be released by the administration. On March 7, Johnston held an effective press conference as his report was released. It proposed a fund which would operate for a minimum of three years without requiring additional financing; appropriations would be substantial and would include the developmental portions of defense support; the major emphasis would be on loans, many of which would be soft; and the administrator of the fund would be given broad discretionary powers in setting interest rates. The fund would not meet requirements that could be filled by private investors, the IBRD, or other institutions lending in hard terms, but would participate with these institutions in joint financing arrangements. The IDAB recommendations were well reported in the press which contrasted its findings with those of the Fairless committee. Johnston appeared before the Senate Special Committee on April 13, Fairless on April 5.

This was the schizophrenic background against which an administration, long schizophrenic on the subject, made its 1957 dispositions on the question of development aid and a U.S. fund to support it. Debate on that issue was cross-cut by a more narrowly bureaucratic question: whether military aid should be separated from military support and other forms of economic aid and assigned to the military budget. But the heart of the inner battle centered on a quite specific proposal arising from the policy planning staff, headed by Robert Bowie, who took development aid very seriously indeed. Two members of his staff, Henry Owen and Philip Trezise, had generated by May 1956 a proposal for an Economic Development Corporation with about $5 billion in initial capital, which would operate on strict development criteria but would be empowered to make grants and soft loans. It would take over both existing technical assistance and defense support programs. As Soviet diplomats are wont to say, it was not accidental that the IDAB recommendations of March 1957 greatly resembled the Owen-Trezise proposal. The latter had worked closely with the IDAB staff which was headed by Alfred Reifman, a State Department economist; and it was not accidental that Millikan and I were in close touch with Bowie and Owen as well as the IDAB, although it should be underlined that they were all strong-minded men quite capable of formulating their own views.

As deliberations moved forward in the State Department in the late winter of 1956–1957, under the supervision of Herter, the fund became the central issue; and a good many conflicting views and interests came into play. These are clearly traced out by Edgerton and need not be rehearsed here.[72] The upshot, on March 15, was Herter's approval of a development loan fund.

The prospects for a large increase in total aid appropriations to support such a fund were, however, firmly deflated two days earlier. Eisenhower, at a press conference, was asked: "Well, is there any intention to increase the economic aid, as Mr. Eric Johnston recommended?" He replied: "Not in any great amount over what we have already recommended." Behind this response was Eisenhower's curious approval of Humphrey's denunciation of the president's budget message of 1957 as involving tax burdens that would lead to "a depression that will curl your hair." Eisenhower, defending Humphrey, had urged Congress to find ways to cut the budget. It was not an optimum setting in which to launch a grand new initiative in development aid.

On the other hand, after Johnston's Senate testimony on the morning of April 3, Fulbright told the State Department's liaison officer, Philip Claxton (who worked closely with Owen and Tresize), that he could support the Johnston proposal. Dulles met that afternoon to consider the testimony he was scheduled to deliver five days later before the Senate Special Committee, having been told by Herter of Claxton's conversation with Fulbright. He decided to support the fund and saw Eisenhower on April 4 with Herter. The upshot was Eisenhower's agreement to shift some defense support funds to a new development fund. Once Eisenhower's agreement was obtained, Dulles, with one exception, apparently informed none of his cabinet colleagues, most of them dissident. He did tell Hollister, who was his subordinate in charge of foreign aid, on Friday, April 5; but Eisenhower was already in Gettysburg for the weekend and inaccessible. On Sunday, April 7 Dulles prepared his testimony, delivering it the next morning.

I turn now to the economic-development aspect of the program.

We believe that all economic development, including that which goes to countries with which we have common defense, should be considered together. We also believe that more emphasis should be placed on long-term development assistance.

It is true that our economic aid cannot be more than a marginal addition to any country's development efforts. This addition can, however, be significant and even determining. It can break foreign exchange bottlenecks and it can be a key factor in stimulating a country to a more effective development program of its own. If our development aid is to have this effect, however, we must do two things: (i) break away from the cycle of annual authorizations and appropriations, and (ii) eliminate advance allocations by countries.

Economic development is a continuing process, not an annual event. Present annual appropriations have resulted in procedures which do not allow either us or the receiving countries to make the most efficient use of the resources which we are providing.

The best way to achieve this greater efficiency is, we believe, the establishment of an economic development fund to provide assistance through loans on terms more favorable than are possible through existing institutions. To be effective, such a fund would need continuing authority and a capital authorization sufficient for several years, to be renewed when needed.

Such a fund could extend aid for specific programs or projects submitted by applicant countries. Each request for a loan from the fund should meet certain criteria, including a showing (i) that financing cannot be obtained from other sources; (ii) that the project is technically feasible; (iii) that it gives reasonable promise of direct or indirect contribution to a nation's increased productivity. . . .

On the assumption that economic development is hereafter made through loans and not through grants, this would, I surmise, require a development fund able to make loans which, not for fiscal year 1958, but over the future, might come to reach $750 million a year. The procedures we suggest should permit substantial savings in terms of lesser administrative costs and an ability to accomplish more with less expenditure. On the other hand, the needs may become more compelling.

In addition, there is the continuing limited requirement, to which I have referred, for grant aid to meet contingencies and imperative needs which cannot realistically be met by loans. Also, of course, there are the technical-assistance programs now running at about $150 million a year.

In conclusion I recall the report of the Foreign Relations Committee of last June in relation to the mutual security program. The committee report said:

". . . the next few years may be more difficult in some respects than the last few. The problems are becoming subtler and more complex. The mutual security program must be adapted to meet the new circumstances."

We believe that the proposals I have outlined this morning are "adapted to meet the new circumstances." They are based upon the high-quality studies you have commissioned and those made by and for the executive branch. Many of these agree to a remarkable extent, not only on the value to us of our military and economic aid to others, but also on changes in the form of our mutual security program which would make it more effective in promoting our national interests.

We accept responsibility for our proposals, but do not claim sole credit for them. We regard them as being derived equally from the work of the Congress and from the efforts of the executive branch. We believe that their broad outline is sound. We recognize that there are various ways by which this outline can be carried out.[73]

Dulles' testimony, his evident commitment to new aid principles, and his prior understanding with Eisenhower created a new situation. But the dissidents were not wholly defeated. The battle came to center not on the fund, but on multi-year financing which would bypass the Congressional appropriations committees. Dulles was at a NATO meeting in Paris during the most intense phase of the counterattack; and Herter appeared to be losing ground to Humphrey. On May 7, Dulles, back from Paris, confronted Humphrey and accepted a compromise: the administration would request appropriations for the first year of the fund and, at the same time, ask for an additional two years of borrowing authority. This deal was cut without consultation with Eisenhower; but the president, refreshed by a two week vacation, threw himself with vigor into the battle for the new approach to foreign aid, including a nationally televised address on May 21 wholly devoted to the subject.

Clearly, a corner had been turned in policy conception, institutionally, and in the balance of power within the administration. And the turn in the road was consolidated bureaucratically at the end of the year with Dillon's becoming chairman of the loan committee of the DLF.

But the initial upshot was modest. The Senate supported the DLF as presented by the administration; but the resistance in the House was considerable. Its members had not shared, like the Senate, in bringing the DLF to life; the House, as the ultimate constitutional appropriating body, was more sensitive to even a limited bypassing of the appropriations process; and then there was Otto Passman, who, as chairman of the subcommittee on foreign operations, enjoyed greatly his quasi-regal authority over foreign aid. He ultimately took the position that unless the DLF was limited to a one-year appropriation there would be no appropriation for the first year and, indeed, appropriations would be withheld from all other aid categories. The blackmail worked, but a step had been taken. The DLF was clearly not the grand long-term commitment of an additional $2 billion a year as the American component of a global program of $3.5 billion envisaged in CENIS' *A Proposal* and C. D. Jackson's *World Economic Plan*. But it was the pilot project Jackson had reluctantly concluded was the only realistic way to move forward, given the curious mixture of attitudes at the top of the Eisenhower administration.

Jackson promptly recognized that Dulles had created a new situation. On April 11, he wrote to Eisenhower noting Dulles' "most rewarding" statement before the Senate committee on the 8th. He suggested that the president be "publicly and strongly identified with this proposal," and that the "large national citizen's organizations" be mobilized as a method for both "grassroots education" and political support. On April 18, Eisenhower agreed but said the organization should not have "a progressional—or White House—character." On April 9, Jackson, having been drawn by Sherman Adams and Herter into the design of a presidential speech as well as the mobilization of citizens' groups, strongly objected in a letter to Eisenhower to dealing with both the budget and mutual security in the same address: ". . . it will inevitably link in the public mind a nasty political fight—the budget—with an imaginative, positive, 'happy' program." On April 30, Eisenhower replied in a rather vivid letter which, after discussing the linkage, agreed to two speeches, if necessary; but he did make the linkage, in his own way, quite effectively, and much in the spirit of his April 30 letter to Jackson. The occasion was his May 21 Address to the American People on the Need for Mutual Security in Waging the Peace:

> We live at a time when our plainest task is to put first things first. Of all our current domestic concerns—lower taxes, bigger dams, deeper harbors, higher pensions, better housing—not one of these will matter if our nation is in peril. For all that we cherish and justly desire—for ourselves or for our children—the securing of peace is the first requisite.
>
> We live in a time when the cost of peace is high.

Yet the price of war is higher and is paid in different coin—with the lives of our youth and the devastation of our cities.

The road to this disaster could easily be paved with the good intentions of those blindly striving to save the money that must be spent as the price of peace.

It is no accident that those who have most intimately lived with the horrors of war are generally the most earnest supporters of these programs to secure peace.

To cripple our programs for Mutual Security in the false name of "economy" can mean nothing less than a weakening of our nation.

To try to save money at the risk of such damage is neither conservative nor constructive.

It is reckless.

It could mean the loss of peace. It could mean the loss of freedom. It could mean the loss of both.

I know that you would not wish your government to take such a reckless gamble.

I do not intend that your government take that gamble.

I am convinced of the necessity of these programs of Mutual Security—for the very safety of our nation. For upon them critically depends all that we hold most dear—the heritage of freedom from our fathers, the peace and well-being of the sons who will come after us.[74]

Eisenhower asked for $500 million for the DLF, by switching funds already requested, plus authority for $750 million for each of the two succeeding years. Congress granted him $300 million for one year only; and the total aid appropriation came to $2.8 billion as opposed to the $3.4 billion requested. Congress acquiesced in the DLF, the Senate with reasonable enthusiasm; but neither house was in what might be called a generous mood.

Against the background of the story traced out in this chapter a central question is evident: Why was Dulles prepared in 1957 to confront Humphrey and to throw his weight behind a development aid proposal when he was not prepared to do so in the three previous years? One can not answer with confidence that kind of question about the balances at work in another man's mind. But I would guess that these four circumstances mainly explain the change:

(a) Dulles was committed to presenting proposals to a Senate committee of considerable power, clearly demanding substantial change in the foreign aid program, clearly leaning to Eric Johnston's view rather than that of the Fairless committee. Inescapable commitments of this kind are, quite often, a forcing mechanism in policy-making, concentrating the minds of political leaders wonderfully, like Dr. Samuel Johnson's impending gallows. Dulles would have been in an awkward position indeed taking, say, George Humphrey's or Fairless' position on April 8, 1957, before the Senate Foreign Relations Committee; and besides, he did not believe in it. Thus, Fulbright's support for the Johnston proposal gave Dulles an opportunity he seized.

(b) There was, also, ready-to-hand a well-staffed, concrete proposal available within the State Department, backed by a highly trusted aide, Robert Bowie.

(c) The proposal was capable of being launched on a relatively modest scale by switching the allocation of foreign aid funds already submitted to the Congress—the condition for acquiring Eisenhower's support.

(d) Christian Herter, rather than Herbert Hoover, Jr., was the undersecretary of state charged with overseeing the day-to-day process of formulating the State Department's foreign aid position.

The real, if limited, success of the venture also required that the intellectual architects of the DLF within the State Department—Owen, Trezise, and their co-conspirators—be formidably competent, energetic, and dedicated bureaucratic infighters.

Thus, Dulles was at last permitted to move in a direction he had wished to move for at least three years.

The last months of 1957 were colored, of course, by the psychological, diplomatic, and political forces set in motion by the launching on October 4 of the first Soviet satellite. On October 31, Dulles sent a memorandum to Eisenhower expressing concern that "Sputnik will lead Congress to be liberal with military appropriations, perhaps even with the military aspects of mutual security, but will offset this by cutting down on the economic aid. This seems to us of at least equal importance." [75] He suggested that this point might be introduced into presidential speeches.

Dulles' anxiety was shared at just this time—and his perspective supported—from an unlikely quarter: Adlai Stevenson. Stevenson was asked to consult with Dulles in formulating a post-Sputnik policy in general and, specifically, on a position for Eisenhower to take at a NATO Heads of Government meeting scheduled for mid-December in Paris. [76]

In a session on November 6, 1957, with members of the State Department and outside consultants (but not yet Stevenson), the official Memorandum of Discussion reports:

> The Secretary said that the prospect was that we would get more money for outer space than we need and that we would then lose the war which really counts—which is the economic war. [77]

Both Nelson Rockefeller and Stassen, who were present, urged that, in the former's phrase, "We should institutionalize our economic effort in support of the uncommitted areas," including such regional groupings as the Colombo Plan. Stassen cited the OEEC as the appropriate instrument for this purpose.

NATO was a narrowly military grouping. It had, as it has today, difficulty in finding concert on political problems outside the NATO area. Moreover, it was seen around the world as a military enterprise from which neutral nations wished to keep their distance. The OEEC, derived from the Marshall Plan organization, was evidently a possible instrument for mobilizing a concerted aid policy; but it excluded Japan, which, from about 1955, had not only fully recovered from the war but had moved into an extraordinary surge of growth which made it a potential donor rather than recipient of foreign aid.

Stevenson asked if I were prepared to help him in his task as consultant on the NATO meeting, which I was pleased to do.[78] We easily agreed that in addition to whatever new military measures or improved methods of political consultation might be canvassed, the U.S. should press hard at the forthcoming NATO meeting for a new, enlarged and concerted program of development aid. This view was incorporated in a fifteen-page memorandum to Dulles from Stevenson of November 29, after a week's hard work in the State Department where Stevenson was in close touch with all the relevant staffs. Stevenson suggested the OEEC as the appropriate coordinating mechanism. On December 4, Dulles asked Stevenson to develop his ideas on alliance economic policy in more detail, which Stevenson did in a second memorandum of December 5 which began rather tartly as follows:

> You asked yesterday for some further explanation of the proposals set forth in my Memorandum No. 1 of November 29 for a more effective and dramatic Western economic effort in the cold war.
>
> The suggested U.S. position that has gone forward to Ambassador Burgess is all right as far as it goes, but it does not go anywhere—beyond expression of "interest in an enlargement of the resources available to the less developed areas." The *action* portions which I suggested have been deleted.
>
> I have urged that we
>
> (1) Announce that we are asking Congress for a substantial increase of our foreign development funds;
>
> (2) Call upon the other NATO countries to make increased resources available for underdeveloped countries;
>
> (3) Propose a special meeting of the OEEC to be held in January to (a) determine a scale of effort for foreign economic development; and (b) improve coordination among the participating countries.[79]

He then argued his case in tight, substantive style for five further single-spaced pages.

On December 3 I had written as follows to Stevenson:

> As you move down to the wire in preparation of papers and in your own decisions, here is the sharp edge of the issue which, we gather, may make the difference between success and failure in the economic initiative.
>
> The British will be extremely skeptical of any move other than a verbal move in the field of economic development until they are clear that Washington is serious. Specifically, they will not want to commit themselves to an OEEC meeting until they see that the Administration is willing to contemplate legislation on India (or the Economic Development Fund) which looks more than one year ahead. Ideally, what is needed is a Congressional statement of intent, as in the case of the Marshall Plan, which looks four years ahead. They will also want assurances that a vague American commitment in Paris is not backed away from, leaving London holding the bag; since they do not have the excuse of Congress. They will probably press, therefore, for some effort at emergency legislation on India.
>
> As the issue is diplomatically confronted, the India question will, I suspect, bulk larger and larger because of the heavy pressure it now exerts on sterling balances.
>
> Given the national interest in getting the economic development business put before the country on an effective priority basis, this British point of view is worth meeting; but it can probably be bargained against some enlarged British contribution to the common military or economic effort.
>
> From what we hear, your advice to Dulles last Friday was absolutely correct: it will be impossible to get a serious European effort without prior evidence of a serious American effort. From here on we're not going to get anything for nothing.

But the fact was that Eisenhower, despite the sensitivity of Dulles, Herter, Dillon and others to the importance of the issue, was in no mood for a "serious" concerted development effort, and the Europeans were not about to take the lead. The American delegation raised the problem in Paris in general terms; but it was alone, as Stevenson reported in a letter to me of December 23 after a de-briefing by Dulles:

> Foster Dulles called me this morning, and among other things said that the only NATO country that talked about economic development at all at Paris was the United States. I got the impression that we have a lot of work to do with our Allies if there is going to be any progress toward coordination, let alone enlargement. But I quite agree that we should go on talking about it, and all the more so!

Only a prior, major surge in U.S. development aid policy might have made concerted action at the summit meeting possible; Eisenhower was not prepared to initiate such a change; and, besides, time was short.

There may have been one constructive long-term result of Stevenson's exercise. It may well have heightened a consciousness in the U.S. government of the need to transform the OEEC into a coordinating instrument for development assistance. That transformation was achieved, under the leadership of Douglas Dillon, by December 1960 when the OEEC was converted into the Organization for Economic Cooperation and Development (OECD), whose Development Assistance Committee (DAC) has subsequently monitored and, to a degree, fostered coordinate action in support of the developing countries.

9. The Foundations for Development Aid Are Laid, 1958-1960

In the history of development aid, 1958 was an important year. As Chapter 1 details, Kennedy and Cooper got their resolution through the Senate and girded for a second round in 1959. Of more immediate importance, the World Bank presided over a path-breaking *ad hoc* short term consortium that bought time for the failing Indian Second Five Year Plan. The DLF survived a second congressional year and began to operate in concert with other sources of development assistance. An initiative by Senator Mike Monroney in 1956 led, via a Senate Resolution passed in July 1958, to the creation in 1960 of the International Development Association (IDA), a soft-loan window in the World Bank. In a speech of August 13 before the United Nations General Assembly, Eisenhower offered U.S. support for a regional development program in the Middle East; and in "a sweeping change in United States policy toward Latin America,"[80] Eisenhower announced on August 27 U.S. willingness to participate in the creation of what was to become the Inter-American Development Bank (IADB).

Before seeking to explain this burst of institutional creativity in the field of development policy in 1958, it should be noted that virtually none of this new enterprise was reflected in current U.S. budgetary outlays or in the aid dispositions of the Congress. In what was now a dreary, repetitious exercise, the administration asked for about $4 billion in military and economic aid; the Congress pushed it back to just about the level of the previous year ($3.3 billion), of which 68 percent was military aid and defense support. When I gave testimony before the Senate Foreign Relations Committee on February 27, 1958, in support of development aid in general and for India, in particular, Fulbright evoked vividly the recalcitrant mood of the Congress as well as an honest but not wholly germane response from his witness:

> *Senator Fulbright.* . . . You have had a year now to reflect upon the failure of the Congress to adopt a long-term program of funds for loans for economic development, the program which this committee recommended almost in the precise form which you recommended. Are you optimistic, in view of the experience of the last year, that your ideas will be followed by this Congress?

> *Mr. Rostow.* I have had to pose, sir, as an expert on many things, but I would not pretend to judge the mood of Congress or the political forces at work in the country. . . .

> *Senator Fulbright.* . . . You have indicated an understanding of the problem. Do you have any reason to believe that this Congress will respond to your proposals? I see no reason to believe there will be any more response now than there was last year. This matter was examined in great detail. This committee spent practically a year examining the foreign aid program from every point of view. As I said, the committee really, to a great extent, agreed with your proposals, and so did the Senate. But the matter got nowhere; the proposal was completely emasculated.

> *Mr. Rostow.* Yes.

> *Senator Fulbright.* Now, it is obvious that we are greatly concerned, but I don't think the United States will now have such a program as you recommend. . . . I do not know why you hesitate to give your own personal opinion. Do you feel optimistic about it, or not? That is all I am asking.

> *Mr. Rostow.* I will tell you why—

Senator Fulbright. Do you have a feeling, either one way or the other? I don't know why you should hesitate. I don't want to push you.

Mr. Rostow. I will tell you why I hesitate. It is not that I fear to give you a judgment. It is because, as a citizen who is interested in these matters, I am in a fight.

Senator Fulbright. Yes.

Mr. Rostow. I may be the smallest fellow in the fight, but when I am in a fight I don't generally ask as my first question: What are the odds? Am I going to succeed or fail? I ask: What is the problem, and what can I do before the options are closed? That is why I came back at you; because the books are not yet closed on how the Senate responds, or [how] the Nation's leaders and the public as a whole respond.

Senator Fulbright. Well, I withdraw the question. Perhaps it is premature to ask it. I think your thinking about what is involved here is extremely interesting.[81]

The chronic dissidence about foreign aid in the House was heightened in 1958 by the state of the economy: a sharp rise in unemployment to 6.8 percent for the year; a rapidly rising federal deficit; and the emergence, for the first time in the postwar years, of anxiety about the U.S. balance of payments as the balance on current account shifted unfavorably by $4 billion. For most politicians seeking re-election in November this was not a setting in which it was judged helpful to have to defend a vote for a large increase in foreign aid. Why and how, then, did an administration which, excepting the DLF, had exhibited for four years (1954–1957) little effective will to innovate in development policy move forward in four areas in 1958, each of which carried with it large potential future claims on the federal budget as well as quite radical shifts in the direction of foreign aid?

The answer in each of the four cases differs, but they had these things in common:

(a) 1958 was a year of multiple crises heightening strategic as well as diplomatic concern about the trends at work in the developing regions.

(b) The team at work in the executive branch beneath Eisenhower was either eager to move forward in development policy (e.g. Herter and Dillon) or willing if the case was strong (Anderson). Moreover, Humphrey, Hoover, and Dodge had gone; and Dulles, by and large, viewed benignly the changes which went forward.

(c) Despite Fulbright's apparent discouragement about the congressional process in February, the Senate, on balance, remained pro-development aid and supportive of its innovators: Fulbright himself, Monroney, Kennedy, and Cooper, as well as the staff of the Senate Foreign Relations Committee.

(d) As noted earlier, the initiatives could be taken without increasing current appropriations.

Of these factors, the sense of gathering crisis in the developing regions was, I would guess, the most important single force at work. It was least explicit in the successful passage of the Monroney Resolution on July 23, 1958, which laid the basis for IDA.[82]

Monroney's initial concept arose from his attendance at a meeting of the Inter-Parliamentary Union in Bangkok late in 1956. While there he was struck by four facts: the attractiveness of Soviet aid policy among developing countries as experienced by some of his colleagues from those countries; the virtues of multilateral as opposed to bilateral U.S. aid; the existence of local currency (so-called counterpart) funds, notably those derived from the sale of U.S. surplus grain under P.L. 480, which had been in operation since 1954; and the inadequacy of World Bank hard loans in meeting the investment needs of developing countries. He hit on the idea of converting the counterpart funds into a pool for productive investment. Superficially, it appeared a quite painless way for the American taxpayer to increase development assistance.

He was only to discover later that the capacity of these funds to substitute for new soft loans from abroad was rather limited.

On his return from Thailand in December 1956, he discussed the idea with both Fulbright and with Eugene Black, who had been a vigorous and increasingly effective president of the World Bank since he took over in 1949.

Nothing much happened to the idea in 1957, as it became clear that the local currencies generated by P.L. 480 loans were not only depleted but committed for other purposes specified by law. In 1958 the idea picked up momentum as its central feature was converted from counterpart funds to "long term loans available at a low rate of interest and repayable in local currencies to supplement World Bank loans." That element in the proposal gathered the critical support of Black. Herter was broadly sympathetic, although the State Department was concerned that Monroney's initiative might inhibit the expansion of the DLF. Dulles, moreover, felt strongly that the U.S. should maintain a substantial degree of bilateral control over its development funds for political purposes. Finally, Monroney's continued emphasis on the use of local currencies gave quite a lot of trouble as Robert Anderson and Dillon explained in Senate hearings the limitations of this instrument for the purpose envisaged. The hearings on March 18–20, 1958, were quite stormy and the outcome of Monroney's initiative was clearly in doubt.

Quiet diplomacy, in which Dillon played a key role, finally yielded Senate Resolution 264, which passed 62–25 on July 23, not without some last-minute fireworks. The text of the basic compromise given in the Notes reflects clearly the critical shift from local currencies to low-interest long-term loans to be financed by governmental contributions on a multilateral basis.[83] By the end of 1958 the IDA concept had been accepted by Eisenhower and entered international negotiation.

The other three development initiatives were clearly linked

to situations of heightened anxiety or crisis. The launching of the Kennedy-Cooper resolution on March 25 related explicitly, as we have seen (p. 5, above), to Indian difficulties with the Second Five Year Plan against the background of the apparently exuberant success of Mao's Great Leap Forward of 1958. In May the Indian government felt impelled to reduce its planned scale of investment by about 15 percent as it searched for supplementary sources of foreign aid.[84]

The Inter-American Development Bank (IADB) was detonated into life—and, indeed, a new phase in U.S. policy toward Latin America was launched—by a more dramatic event. On May 8, 1958, Vice-President Nixon was roughed up by a mob in Lima; on May 13, he had an even more difficult time in Caracas. Eisenhower alerted naval and Marine forces in the Caribbean against the possibility that Nixon would have to be rescued by force of arms. With Castro moving toward power in Cuba, the administration became convinced that Communism was a clear and present danger in the hemisphere; although it was not until the end of 1958 that Castro's tilt to Communism was fully appreciated in Washington.[85]

In the wake of Nixon's vicissitudes in Latin America, President Kubitschek of Brazil addressed a letter to Eisenhower calling for a restoration of "Pan American ideals in all their aspects and implications" which, he said, had "suffered serious impairment." The administration understood that what Kubitschek had in mind was, above all, the need for a more forthcoming policy of U.S. economic support for Latin America, which had experienced a 34 percent deterioration in the terms of trade (excluding petroleum) between 1951 and 1958 and a deceleration in economic growth. In fiscal year 1958, U.S. economic aid commitments to Latin America were only $88 million out of a total of $1.46 billion; and as late as September 1957 the U.S. continued its long-standing opposition to the concept of an Inter-American Bank which was pressed forward with vigor at an OAS meeting in Buenos Aires. But in the wake of Nixon's troubles, ideas which had been advocated for some years by Milton Eisenhower, Nelson Rockefeller, and some who currently held posts in the administration, received a more favorable hearing than they had earlier. In June 1958, in a reversal of previous policy, the administration participated in the first of a number of commodity study groups which led in September to an agreement designed to stabilize coffee prices; in July, the U.S. government decided to support the IDB, a decision formally announced on August 12, 1958.

1958 was also marked by back-to-back crises in the Middle East and the Formosa Straits, running, respectively, from May to August and from August to October. The latter generated no new initiatives in development policy, the former did: Eisenhower's proposal for a Middle East regional development plan. Although that proposal was not taken up, it is useful to examine its origin because it illustrates even more fully than the difficulties in India and Latin America the complexity of the setting in which the priority for development policy rose in the late 1950s.

The American landing in Lebanon on the morning of July 15, 1958, was rooted in the Middle East Resolution signed by Eisenhower on March 9, 1957. After the Suez crisis, Eisenhower concluded that: "The existing vacuum in the Middle East must be filled by the United States before it is filled by Russia."[86] A new basis had to be found to protect "Western rights" and disabuse Moscow and others of the notion that the West was in permanent disarray and the United States neutralized in that area.

The Middle East Resolution authorized American cooperation with and assistance to any nation or group of nations in the Middle East "in the development of economic strength dedicated to the maintenance of national independence." To that end, it authorized upon request programs of military assistance and military aid against armed aggression from any nation "controlled by international Communism." The problem for the United States in the Middle East during the mid

1950s was the difficulty in defining the phrases "armed aggression" and "controlled by international Communism."

Moscow and Washington were operating in a situation with its own churning dynamics that involved a number of elements: the Arab struggle with Israel; the rise of a new generation of Arab radical leaders; Nasser's effort to encourage the rise of such leaders (notably in Syria, Saudi Arabia, Iraq, and Jordan) and the nationalist resistance to Nasser's domination; the Bedouin-Palestinian schism in Jordan; the Moslem-Christian schism in Lebanon; and the tensions between the Arabs and the non-Arab Moslems in Turkey and Iran. In this turbulent modernizing region Moscow and Washington were dealing with situations where their control over events was dilute, and where national and regional objectives were, in the end, paramount.

The Middle East crisis of 1958 climaxed a series of lesser crises which took place over the previous year and a half. Arab radicals, inspired if not wholly controlled from Cairo and Damascus, pressed ardently against the moderate governments in Beirut and Amman, as well as against the Saudis and the pro-Western government in Baghdad.

In May 1958 Lebanon went before the United Nations Security Council to accuse Egypt and Syria of arming the rebels and instigating revolt on the issue of a second term for President Camille Chamoun. The question of sending American armed forces to Lebanon was raised at this time. By early July the situation had eased somewhat, but the amphibious forces of the United States Sixth Fleet, which had been ordered to the eastern Mediterranean at this time, remained close by.

On July 14, 1958, however, both the new Arab Union of Jordan and Iraq and the Baghdad Pact were broken. The Hashemite monarch of Iraq was overthrown and murdered, along with the Crown Prince and the Prime Minister, Neuri es-Said. The revolution was led by young military officers, Nasserite and anti-Western; but there was no firm evidence of Cairo's hand in the enterprise, let alone Moscow's. The acute

146

anxieties of Jordan and Lebanon led Hussein and Chamoun to request British and American armed intervention to protect their independence under the Middle East Resolution of 1957. United States seaborne forces began to move unopposed across the Lebanese beaches the day after the coup in Iraq. On July 17 British paratroopers moved into Jordan, where a plot against Hussein had failed.

It is the cumulative buildup of tension and trouble in the Middle East which explains Eisenhower's instant response to the Iraqi coup of July 14th: "That morning I gathered in my office a group of advisers to make sure that no facet of the situation was overlooked. Because of my long study of the problem, this was one meeting in which my mind was practically made up regarding the general line of action we should take, even before we met."[87]

Eisenhower's decision to move on July 15, before the meaning of the Iraqi coup could be fully assessed, was based on an instinctive judgment that the Middle East was getting out of hand, rather than on precise evidence that "armed aggression" from a nation "controlled by international Communism" had occurred or was about to occur.

Robert Murphy, a senior foreign service officer, was promptly launched into the Middle East along with the Marines. His mission was to comfort a harassed and ill Chamoun; to commit him to the early election of a successor; and to explain to the new leader in Baghdad, Abdul Kassim, and to Nasser the limited objectives of the American initiative.

The operation stabilized the Middle East for some time. There was no U.S. move against the new government of Iraq, as Moscow and Peking feared. American influence was not used to keep Chamoun in power, as he may have hoped. Nevertheless, the Anglo-American landings strengthened Jordanian, Lebanese, and Saudi confidence in their ability to survive against radical nationalists backed by Moscow and Cairo. The military operations provided a demonstration that, in the face of nuclear blackmail, the United States was prepared to move military forces in defense of its interests. That demonstration increased the degree of independence even radical Arab nationalists felt they could assert against Moscow.

With Peking pressing its flank, Moscow had to react. It did so by demanding a high-level meeting of heads of state. It hoped to bring Britain and the United States to the bar as opponents of nationalism. As during the Suez crisis, the threat of missiles and "volunteers" was also invoked, but in ways which did not commit Moscow to act. Moscow resisted Peking's pressure for what it regarded as an excessive reaction. A series of exchanges between Eisenhower and Khrushchev on the forum in which the matter should be debated led finally to the convening of the United Nations General Assembly, which Eisenhower addressed on August 13. By this time the Middle East was relatively calm, the presidential election in Lebanon having taken place at the end of July.

Dulles initially urged a narrow focusing on the question of indirect aggression. He left Washington for a conference in Latin America, to return late on August 8; but before leaving town he had asked C. D. Jackson and me to come to Washington to develop materials for Eisenhower's speech before the United Nations. Our inclination was to put the question of indirect aggression in a larger context of the rise of radical Arab nationalism and to focus on the possibility of regional development in the Middle East. In addition, we wanted to counteract the image in the Middle East and elsewhere evoked by Moscow's use of nuclear threat during the Suez crisis.

On Friday morning, August 8, we were installed in a large State Department office normally used by ambassadors on leave in Washington. We assembled our thoughts and drew ideas from many parts on the bureaucracy, including Lewis Strauss and his AEC's water-desalting crusaders and the State Department policy planning staff. We talked at length with Vice-President Nixon, who appeared to agree with the line we were about to take; but who also told us that his influence in the White House was virtually nonexistent. Jackson and I worked together most of the night, aided in the frenetic effort by Henry Owen of the policy planning staff. Jackson was able to hand a draft to Dulles during breakfast at Dulles' home on August 9. With a nod of approval in principle, the draft was then given to those bearing operational responsibility in the government. At the Treasury, Robert Anderson made sure that resources, including a diversion of oil revenues, would be available for Middle East development if the Arab world responded. The document moved forward, after the usual redrafting, to Eisenhower, its essential structure unchanged.

In the delivered speech before the United Nations, Eisenhower reaffirmed and extended the American commitment to the Baghdad Pact in the wake of Iraq's probable defection. He thus isolated the problems of the Arab world from those of the non-Arab Moslems to the north and foreclosed a possible Soviet move to neutralize the whole of the Middle East. Second, he sought United Nations support for continued Lebanese independence under the less Western-oriented but presumably stable government that emerged from the 1958 crisis. Third, he suggested a United Nations standby force that would represent an alternative to the direct application of British and American power in the region. Fourth, he proposed that Israel and the Arab states agree on a moratorium in arms purchases that might reduce mutual fears and, conceivably, set the stage for a definitive settlement. Fifth, he offered substantial economic assistance to the Arab world, including a diversion of a margin of Western oil company revenues for regional economic development. The whole program was framed by the demonstration that the United States and Britain were not prepared to abandon the World War II truce lines in the face of Soviet missile and "volunteer" threats.

The broad objective of the speech was not merely to reaffirm American opposition to direct and indirect aggression but also to hold up a vision of American support for a constructive expression of Arab nationalism—and the nationalism of others in the developing world.

In the preface to Book 3 of *Waging Peace*, Eisenhower quotes this passage from his August 13 speech:

> The world that is being made on our planet is to be a world of many mature nations. As one after another of these new nations moves through the difficult transition to modernization and learns the methods of growth, from this travail new levels of prosperity and productivity will emerge.
>
> This world of individual nations is not going to be controlled by any one power or group of powers. This world is not going to be committed to any one ideology.
>
> Please believe me when I say that the dream of world domination by one power or of world conformity is an impossible dream.

So far as doctrine was concerned, the need to deal with Arab radicalism accelerated the shift in Eisenhower's initial stance toward the developing world. His August 13 speech acknowledged, in effect, that what the United States was prepared to do for radical Arabs in their most disruptive mood, the United States must be prepared to do in Latin America, Asia, and Africa as well. The criterion that economic aid should be an instrument of support only for those joined with the United States in military alliance against the Communist bloc was, evidently, gone. The objective of economic assistance as a means for supporting the emergence of independent states, and for focusing their ardent nationalism increasingly on the modernization of their societies, had been enunciated under circumstances likely to commit the United States over a long future. In the context of American economic foreign policy since the Korean War, this was a radical departure.

But the churning ambitions, conflicts, and anxieties of Middle Eastern political and diplomatic life did not permit a united, positive regional response to Eisenhower's August 13 offer; and, indeed, of the major countries of the area only Turkey and, for a time, Iran were able to concentrate a high proportion of their energies on the tasks of national development. Nevertheless, the environment in which Kennedy, Cooper, and others of like mind carried forward their assorted development crusades in 1959 was somewhat different—and a bit more congenial—than that which prevailed a year earlier. And for this fact the crises in India, Latin America, and the Middle East were primarily responsible.

10. The Kennedy-Cooper Resolution Succeeds, 1958-1961

Against the multi-dimensional background sketched out in Chapters 2–9 we return now to the Kennedy-Cooper enterprise which we left at the close of Chapter 1 with passage in the Senate on June 6, 1958, rejection in conference on June 17. As the two senators looked forward to resuming their effort in the next session of Congress, they continued to keep the issue alive by arguing their case in the media and urging that existing resources and mechanisms be used to provide immediate assistance and permit India to avoid a drastic cutback in the objectives of the already reduced Second Five Year Plan. For example, they wrote a letter to the *New York Times*, published on July 29, 1958 (see Appendix H), contesting an editorial which had viewed India's industrial objectives as excessive and risking the danger of inflation. They urged that the DLF be fully funded to permit additional resources for India, reiterating their specific proposal for "a free-nation mission to India, drawing on men such as John McCloy and Sir Oliver Franks" and the general proposition that, in view of "the growing and ominous economic effort which Communist China has mounted, . . . the Atlantic Community, Japan, and the Colombo Plan merge their thinking on this over-shadowing problem in Asia."

Meanwhile, the World Bank moved effectively onto the scene in August. The Bank's president, Eugene Black, called a meeting, attended by five countries, to deal with India's immediate foreign exchange crisis. Here is how the Bank's historians describe the occasion:

> The first consortium, the one for India, was not organized initially for the purpose of mobilizing and coordinating external financing for India's five-year development plans. Rather, it was originally conceived as a temporary rescue operation that came into being in 1958, after it had become apparent that India's rapidly shrinking holdings of foreign exchange would be wholly insufficient to finance the second five-year plan, which was then under way. Until 1961, the meetings were officially referred to as "meetings on India's foreign exchange situation." B. K. Nehru, who was appointed India's commissioner-general for economic affairs in Washington to lead the operations from the Indian side, describes the task as India saw it.*

> It was decided that this immediate rescue operation should not be handled through diplomatic channels in order to avoid any political flavour being brought into it but should be regarded as a simple banking operation. The World Bank was our international banker. We were to go to it and place our difficulties before it, tell it that we wanted a large loan and ask it to raise the finance for us from whatever sources it thought proper in a manner similar to what a commercial concern would do *vis-à-vis* its own bankers, if it got into financial difficulties. . . .

> It was . . . demanded by me and agreed to by him [Mr. Black] that we would not directly ask any government to help us and we would not even be present at any meetings the World Bank might arrange of governments who it thought would be willing to finance us. Mr. Black demanded and I agreed that we would explain to governments what our difficulties were, but that would be the limit of our activity.

> The first meeting of what subsequently became the Aid-

*B. K. Nehru, "The Way We Looked for Money Abroad," in Vadilal Dagli (ed.), *Two Decades of Indo-U.S. Relations* (Bombay: Vora and Company, 1969), pp. 20–21.

> India Consortium was held in Washington in August 1958
> and agreed to give us to the last cent the money we said we
> would need which was over a billion dollars. There were no
> political conditions attached nor any economic ones beyond
> our undertaking to complete the (reduced) Plan as pre-
> sented to the World Bank.[88]

On August 29, 1958, the *New York Times* could report that
the Bank, the United States, Britain, West Germany, Japan and
Canada had generated "the largest multi-nation economic aid
plan ever arranged for an under-developed country": $350
million in immediate emergency assistance plus, less firmly,
the prospect of an additional $600 million over the period
running up to the end of 1961.

When Kennedy and Cooper returned to their self-imposed
task in 1959, a good deal had changed—quite aside from the
time-buying initiative of the World Bank. First, the Democrats
had won a major victory in the Congressional elections of
November 1958, gaining thirteen seats in the Senate, forty-
eight in the House of Representatives. From the point of view
of foreign aid politics, the departure from Congress of a good
many opponents of development aid was more important than
the statistical outcome. In the Senate, for example, Knowland
had retired to run unsuccessfully for governor in California.
His successor (Claire Engel), like the successors to William
Jenner (Vance Hartke) and Edward Martin (Hugh Scott),
were also figures more sympathetic to foreign aid. Of the ten
defeated Republican senators, nine were replaced by men
less conservative on the foreign aid issue. The Congressional
landslide also had the effect of appearing to increase the likelihood of Democratic victory in the presidential elections of
1960, and thus somewhat heightened the stature in Washington of Kennedy, who was clearly one of the possible candidates after his not unexpected, but nevertheless overwhelming re-election to the Senate with 73.6 percent of the total
vote.

Second, and more narrowly, Kennedy and Cooper were

strengthened by the recruitment of two members of the House of Representatives who joined in presenting a fresh version of their concurrent resolution: Chester Bowles, one of the earliest American crusaders on behalf of Indian economic development, and Chester Merrow, a Republican from New Hampshire.

Third, the World Bank was now a central actor in the drama and Kennedy was in close touch with both Black and one of the Bank's vice-presidents, Burke Knapp. The World Bank emerged as an operational substitute for the OEEC as the possible sponsor of an international mission to India.

Fourth, the acute foreign exchange crisis and the pessimism in New Delhi about India's prospects had considerably eased. A memorandum of B. K. Nehru to his staff of June 1969 indicates that the *ad hoc* assistance organized in August 1958 by the World Bank, a bumper harvest, and the discovery of oil in western India mainly account for the change. (The collapse of Mao's Great Leap Forward and the growing tension between Moscow and Peking would have further heightened the mood if they were fully understood at the time.) Thought in India turned increasingly to the design for the Third Five Year Plan to cover the period 1961–1966.

Finally, the case for large scale, sustained economic assistance to India, if not quite the conventional wisdom in Washington, was much more widely accepted than a year earlier, in part because it had been demonstrated at the World Bank meeting in August 1958 that other countries were prepared to join the United States in aid to India on a significant scale; in part because of the expanding activities of the DLF, the movement toward IDA and IADB, and the altered stance of the Eisenhower administration towards development lending as reflected in its August 13, 1958, offer of a Middle East regional development plan. The older emphasis on military aid and support plus private international investment had been breached on many fronts. In particular, the emergence of the DLF and the possibility that IDA offered as a soft loan window at the World Bank were of critical importance, because they were precisely the kind of financial institutions required to sustain support for India's development.

Nevertheless, as Frederick Holborn pointed out to Senator Kennedy early in 1959, even India's short-run problems were not at an end (see Appendix I). India confronted a heavy repayment burden on international loans already contracted; a good deal of emergency aid had to be allocated to meet unpaid bills and existing shortages rather than to finance new projects; her export prices were declining; and the pressure of rising population on food supply was still acute. Holborn concluded: "All last year Indians were told to wait until 1959—now it is here."

All this was reflected in the presentations to the Senate by Kennedy and Cooper of their revised concurrent resolution on February 19, 1959.* Bowles briefly presented the resolution in the House on the same day, on behalf of himself and Merrow.

Kennedy's speech was entitled "The Economic Gap" which he contrasted with the missile gap:

> The attention of the Congress and the American people in recent weeks has been turned—and properly so—to the forthcoming "missile gap." I have spoken on this floor previously about this "gap" and the dangers it presents—I intend to do so again—but I want to speak today about a gap which constitutes an equally clear and present danger to our security.
>
> *Unlike the missile gap, the gap to which I refer will not reach the point of critical danger in 1961. That point has been reached now.*
>
> *Unlike the missile gap, the gap to which I refer is not even on the surface being reduced by the combined efforts*

---

*The full text of those presentations is to be found in *The Congressional Record*, 86th Congress, First Session, Vol. 102, Part 2, pp. 2737–2740.

of our executive and legislative branches. It is, on the contrary, consistently ignored and steadily widening.

Unlike the missile gap, the gap to which I refer gives rise to no speculation as to whether the Russians will exploit it to their advantage and to our detriment. They are exploiting it now.

I am talking about the economic gap—the gap in living standards and income and hope for the future—the gap between the developed and the underdeveloped worlds—between, roughly speaking, the top half of our globe and the bottom half—between the stable, industrialized nations of the north, whether they are friends or foes, and the overpopulated, under-invested nations of the south, whether they are friends or neutrals.

It is this gap which presents us with our most critical challenge today. It is this gap which is altering the face of the globe, our strategy, our security and our alliances, more than any current military challenge. *And it is this economic challenge to which we have responded most sporadically, most timidly and most inadequately.*

After making once again the case for the importance of India, Kennedy argued that 1958 was "their"—the Communists'—"round"; 1959 should be "our round":

During the past year India has had a national growth rate of only 3% and 2% of this is largely dissipated by population increases. Two years ago India was reaching a national growth rate of nearly 5%, but the cutbacks in her Plan and bad harvests have blighted this achievement.

In short, to nations in a hurry to emerge from the rut of underdevelopment, Communist China offers a potential model. 1958 was their "round." As their trade and aid offensive mounted, as their own example proved more attractive, our trade and aid programs faltered and our economy stood still—with our recession cutting the price received for commodities the underdeveloped nations must sell, while our inflation continued to boost the prices they paid for our machinery.

But 1959 could and should be our "round," our year. We

have, in this Congress, in these next few months, a moment
of opportunity which may never come again. If we act now,
on the right scale, in the right way, we may reverse the ever-
widening gap—we may diminish the threat of a Communist
takeover, and increase the chances of a peaceful evolution
in India and other uncommitted, less developed areas. This
year, 1959, could be the year of their economic downfall—
or the year of their economic "take-off," enabling them to
get ahead of their exploding population, to stabilize their
economies and to build a base for continuing development
and growth. Whichever answer emerges will shape for a generation to come the destiny of the world and the security of
our nation. And which answer emerges is in large measure
for this Congress to decide.

Kennedy then focused sharply on the need to expand the resources available in the DLF, the major potential U.S. source of
long-term low interest loans: "When this body decides the future of the Development Loan Fund this year, it will also in
large measure be deciding the future of India." He went on to
urge an international mission to India citing Escott Reid of
Canada (as well as McCloy and Franks) as illustrative of the
stature required, reflecting the rather generous role of Canada in the August 1958 World Bank barn-raising for India as
well as Reid's personal advocacy of aid for India; and he
looked to the emergence of "a donor's club, under the sponsorship of the World Bank" rather than the OEEC.[89]

The proposed concurrent resolution now read as follows:

Whereas the continued vitality and success of the Republic of India is a matter of common free world interest,
politically because of her four hundred million people and
vast land area; strategically because of her commanding
geographic location; economically because of her organized
national development effort; and morally because of her
heartening commitment to the goals, values, and institutions
of democracy: Now, therefore, be it

> *Resolved by the Senate (The House of Representatives Concurring)*, That it is the sense of Congress that the United States Government should invite other friendly and democratic nations to join in a mission to consult with India on the detailed possibilities for joint action to assure the fulfillment of India's second five-year plan and the effective design of its third plan. And that the Secretary of State report to the Congress on the feasibility of such a mission after consultation with interested governments and with the Republic of India.

The shift of emphasis to the emerging Third Indian Five Year Plan is evident.

Again Cooper spoke more briefly in support, making the case in general terms and citing the role of Eisenhower, Dulles, Herter and Dillon in working, over the previous year, "with other countries to provide substantial aid to India's economic development."

On May 4–5, 1959, as foreign aid legislation moved forward in the Congress, a rather remarkable event occurred in Washington—a "Conference on India and the United States—1959." It was sponsored by a bipartisan citizens' group, the Committee for International Economic Growth (CIEG). Its chairman was Eric Johnston, who had played a significant role in the emergence of the DLF in 1957 (see above, pp. 126–127). A year earlier the CIEG had mobilized an impressive array of speakers at a Washington conference in general support of development assistance, among them President Eisenhower, former President Truman, Vice-President Nixon, Allen Dulles, James Killian, Dean Acheson, and Adlai Stevenson, as well as a distinguished baseball player of the time, Stan Musial, and the actress Myrna Loy. The 1959 conference was less glamorous, narrower, and more professional. Indian as well as American officials participated, as well as American businessmen, academics, and Barbara Ward. As noted earlier, she had written a widely-read twenty-page special supplement on India for the January 22, 1955, issue of the London *Economist* and was an effective and indefatigable crusader for aid to India and the developing nations generally.

Behind the conference lay not merely a convergence of India's needs and U.S. interests, as they came increasingly to be defined, but also the emergence of a corps of Americans (and others) who had entered during the 1950s into the study of India's problems with such patent objectivity, human sympathy, and enthusiasm that, as I. G. Patel was later to write, "we should be privileged to count them as honorary citizens of this ancient land."[90]

While things were moving forward in Washington, Kennedy, conscious of the importance in U.S. politics of aid contributions by other nations, engaged in a bit of lobbying overseas. I had worked with him on the project, along with other members of CENIS, since November 1957 (see above, p. 71). In September 1958 I left on a year's sabbatical to Cambridge, England, but I kept in touch with Kennedy, both directly and through Holborn; and, in particular, I discussed the project with British Treasury and Foreign Office officials and journalists. My central theme was this:

> . . . what emerges from the Congress in the coming session may well depend substantially on what, at the right time, appears to be the scale and willingness of European nations, Canada, and Japan to enlarge and, especially, to extend the time period of their commitments to aid the underdeveloped areas. And I suggested that Britain might have a role to play—in both the Commonwealth and the OEEC, in exploring what those contingent commitments might be.[91]

I kept in touch with B. K. Nehru when he was in England. (The letter in Appendix M reflects these activities.) Kennedy also sent Holborn to Europe in December 1958 to assess prospects on the spot. We conferred at some length in Cambridge. In May 1960, while in Germany on academic business, I sought to stir up the German Foreign Office in Bonn.

The German officials courteously heard me out at a lunch in a hotel overlooking the Rhine, but it was a moment when they were more immediately concerned with the quadripartite negotiations on Germany then underway. In Paris I also saw Monnet, whose Action Committee in support of European unity was already advocating a greatly enlarged European support for the developing countries. Monnet immediately saw in the Kennedy-Cooper resolution a way not only of helping India, but also of tightening the bonds across the Atlantic by engagement in common enterprise. He wrote to Kennedy on June 10, 1959, forwarding the latest Action Committee documents.

On the whole, things fell into place rather well in 1959 for the Kennedy-Cooper enterprise. In March, Kennedy talked to Dillon at the latter's request on both the India resolutions and the amendments to the Battle Act, and in a subsequent letter to Dillon of March 21 Kennedy asked if there was a form for the India resolution that might meet State Department objections. Those objections centered on two points: the fact that Pakistan was excluded; and the judgment that a mission dispatched by a Congressional committee was preferable to one made up of even distinguished private citizens from different countries. Holborn, in a memorandum to Kennedy of April 6, 1959, argued that if the resolution were broadened to include Pakistan the State Department might accede in time to launching the international mission:

> Our resolution after all is intended to be a pilot venture in
> international consultation at a high level. The purposes of
> such a mission and a Congressional Committee would not be
> the same. Congressmen cannot talk as frankly to the Indians
> about the shape of the Third Plan as could the senior states-
> men who would go to India with the International Mission.
> Moreover, one of the purposes of the International Mission
> would be to try to encourage other nations to raise their
> sights and to move along with an increased American effort.

> If we continue to talk about it in these terms I think that there is a possibility of support by the State Department.[92]

Holborn proved to be correct. Differences with the State Department were resolved after a letter from Macomber to Fulbright of May 4 (Appendix K) indicated that the administration might support the resolution if its terms were modified to embrace all of South Asia. Kennedy and Cooper agreed to the change, and the revised resolution was presented to the Senate Foreign Relations Committee, with Bowles appearing from the House, on July 14. Executive sessions were held on July 21 and July 23. A representative of the Treasury expressed cautious administration support, characterizing the revised resolution as "a purely exploratory measure and a useful one."

At this time it also became clear that the World Bank would be the best sponsor of the mission, especially if its plans for IDA came to fruition (see Holborn-Kennedy memorandum of July 13, 1959, in Appendix L).

B. K. Nehru reports, in a letter to me of August 5, 1982, the final drafting of the resolution in early September 1959. "He [Kennedy] asked me if I would help in amending the Resolution. I say it must have been September because Morarji Desai was then in town which he usually was only for the Bank-Fund meetings. Max Millikan and Paul Rosenstein Rodan were also in town and after consulting Morarji we (principally I. G. [Patel] and Max) worked on the Resolution and sent it back to Kennedy through I. G. and Holborn."

On September 10, 1959, at the instigation of Lyndon Johnson, the amended resolution was agreed to in the Senate by voice vote, without dissent. Its text, with excisions and additions (in italics), is reproduced on pp. 164–165.

In the early autumn, a not trivial obstacle emerged: the Indian government appeared to resist the idea of the international mission. Indians had, of course, followed the Kennedy-Cooper enterprise from the beginning and with implicit support. But as it moved toward reality, the problems it might raise, as well as solve, became more vivid. After all, there was something odd about the legislature of one country generating a resolution that an international mission be sent to another, even if the latter was rather hard pressed.

The issue was resolved early in October when Morarji Desai, the Indian finance minister who was then in the United States, agreed that India would receive the mission early in 1960, on the assumption that it would visit other countries as well. As we shall see, Indian nervousness was not wholly dissipated until the mission's work was completed.

As 1959 drew toward its close, the attention of those concerned with this matter shifted towards the membership, exact status, and sponsorship of the international mission. The concurrent resolution had called for an initiative by the president in consultation with "other free and democratic nations." This was resisted on the grounds that it might commit the U.S. government too deeply; and, besides, the diplomatic procedure might be cumbersome since the object was to appoint high-level personages, not members of governments. There was some thought of the World Bank's directly organizing the mission, but this was judged to endanger the independence of the assessment sought, given the Bank's already deep involvement with India. Despite his increasingly evident decision to seek the Democratic nomination in 1960, Kennedy followed these matters in detail and helped sort them out in increasingly close collaboration with Dillon. The remaining problems (see Appendix N) were resolved with some elegance by having Eugene Black, president of the Bank, "suggest" in his personal capacity that three distinguished men, "as independent private individuals," undertake the mission. They were Hermann Abs, chairman of the Deutsche Bank of Frankfurt; Sir Oliver Franks, chairman of Lloyd's Bank, London (but also a philosopher of distinction as well as a former ambassador to the United States); and Allan Sproul, former president of the New York Federal Reserve Bank.[93]

Calendar No. 591

86TH CONGRESS
1ST SESSION

S. CON. RES. 11

[Report No. 594]

IN THE SENATE OF THE UNITED STATES

FEBRUARY 19, 1959

Mr. KENNEDY (for himself and Mr. COOPER) submitted the following concurrent
resolution; which was referred to the Committee on Foreign Relations

JULY 28, 1959

Reported by Mr. KENNEDY, with amendments

[Amend the preamble; strike out all after the resolving clause and insert the part printed
in italic]

CONCURRENT RESOLUTION

Whereas the continued vitality and success of the ~~Republic of
India is a matter~~ *Governments of South Asia are matters* of
common ~~free world~~ interest *to free nations*, politically because of ~~her four hundred~~ *their five hundred and twenty-five*
million people and vast land area; strategically because of
~~her commanding~~ *their vital* geographic location; economically because of ~~her organized~~ *their resources and their*
national development ~~effort~~ *efforts*; and morally because of
~~her heartening commitment to the goals, values, and institutions of democracy~~ *the great necessity that they continue
to make progress and succeed in their earnest efforts to improve the lot of their peoples*: Now, therefore, be it

1   *Resolved by the Senate (the House of Representatives*

2   *concurring),* ~~That it is the sense of Congress that the United~~

3   ~~States Government should invite other friendly and demo-~~

V

Their appointment was announced on December 19, 1959
(see Appendix M for press comment). Their report, after a six
weeks' visit to India and Pakistan, took the form of a letter
dated March 19, 1960, from New Delhi, addressed to Black,
later published as *Banker's Mission to India and Pakistan,
February–March, 1960*, by the World Bank (Appendix N).

The report, which owed a great deal to Frank's leader-

1 ~~cratic nations to joint in a mission to consult with India on~~
2 ~~the detailed possibilities for joint action to assure the fulfill-~~
3 ~~ment of India's second five-year plan and the effective~~
4 ~~design of its third plan. And that the Secretary of State~~
5 ~~report to the Congress on the feasibility of such a mission~~
6 ~~after consultation with interested governments and with~~
7 ~~the Republic of India.~~

8 *That it is the sense of the Congress (a) that the President of*
9 *the United States of America should explore with other free*
10 *and democratic nations and appropriate international organi-*
11 *zations the desirability and feasibility of establishing an inter-*
12 *national mission to consult with the Governments of countries*
13 *in the area of South Asia on their needs in connection with*
14 *the fulfillment of currently planned and anticipated develop-*
15 *ment programs over the next five years and to consider and*
16 *recommend ways and means of jointly assisting in the imple-*
17 *mentation of those plans in cooperation with the Governments*
18 *of South Asia, and (b) that if the international mission is*
19 *established, the President of the United States of America*
20 *should report to the Congress on such recommendations as*
21 *are made by the mission.*

Amend the title so as to read: "Concurrent resolution to
invite friendly and democratic nations to consult with countries of South Asia."

ship and lucid drafting, dramatized the reality of poverty in
the two countries, the pressure of rapid population increase,
the seriousness of the development efforts undertaken by the
governments, the modesty of their targets, and the need for
long-term, low interest, official loans as well as private capital
imports. It touched in temperate, well-modulated language
on a number of sensitive points: the requirement for mutual
understanding of the political imperatives operating on borrower as well as lender; the need for higher priority for agriculture and for nurturing a diversified private sector in the

borrowing countries; and the need for a liberal trade policy in the lending countries to permit additional foreign exchange to be earned. Read in retrospect, this brief, unpretentious but unambiguous report deserved I. G. Patel's high praise: ". . . one of the most heart-warming documents in the annals of international relations."[94] It also performed precisely the function Kennedy and Cooper had envisaged: it rendered politically respectable long-term development aid to India.

The reaction of Indian officials is well captured in a letter of March 21, 1960, from Harry G. Curran (the Bank's resident representative in India) to Eugene Black:

> The Government of India awaited the arrival of the Wise Men with rather mixed feelings. They hoped and believed the Mission would prove helpful to them—and were very appreciative of your friendly initiative in organising it—but they were a little nervous about its composition. Franks, they believed, had an exceptional understanding of the problems confronting developing countries; but they were less sure of Abs and Sproul. They had fears of a hard German banker closely associated with private industry and the export trade, and a rigid old Federal Reserve conservative. In the event they were agreeably surprised.
>
> Franks more than fulfilled their expectations. They sensed at once that he was fundamentally sympathetic to their aspirations, and were fascinated by his dynamic personality and quick mind and elegance of phrase. Abs also impressed them very favourably—a massive impression of power and quick grasp of fact. Although he didn't say very much, it was a genial silence with a twinkle in the eye, and when he spoke it was very much to the point. Sproul also they liked—they thought him a kindly older man, anxious to understand and less rigid than they had feared.
>
> The Wise Men themselves were I believe favourably impressed by what they heard and saw, and by the Third Plan as it was exposed to them. You will know their general conclusions from their letter. . . . There remain no doubt ques-

tion marks in their minds—*e.g.*, whether the proclaimed drive for food production will be effective; whether the deficit financing in the Third Plan can be kept down to the intended relatively modest level; the need for a more positive effort to increase exports; the desirability of more positive Government action and declared intention to attract private foreign investment; whether even this large Third Plan can keep pace with the rising population. But on the whole I believe they were satisfied that the G.O.I. had achieved a good deal since independence, and that the Third Plan was a serious and not unrealistic attempt to continue what remains to be done. As regards the much discussed Public v. Private Sector argument, I believe the Wise Men were convinced that India was not moving towards a Socialist State in which private enterprise would be squeezed out of existence, but that on the contrary, the evidence suggested that the Government's approach to problems (although this was perhaps not openly admitted) was becoming more pragmatic, that private industry was undoubtedly expanding rapidly, and that in as far as its expansion was hampered, it was more by bureaucratic complexities (for which the Indians have a natural bent!) than by ideological intent.

The Mission's progress was therefore smooth, the relations with the Government very friendly and everyone parted on excellent terms.

There was however some disappointment that there was not an opportunity for more frank discussion on the conclusions reached by the Wise Men. Franks and Abs would, I believe, have welcomed this—and would also have liked to take advantage of the chance to make a number of points to the Government which they would not have wished to express publicly or even to have included in an official letter to you. Sproul however was strongly opposed to any discussion of their conclusions. As you will know from his cable to you, he was much concerned about what he would have to face on his return to the U.S., and, with visions no doubt of Congressional committees breathing over one shoulder and the press over the other, took the view that their conclusions must remain confidential until you had considered them and decided what should be made public. It proved impossible to move him from this position; and so although all three were very friendly in their last talks with the Prime Minister and Finance Minister, and Franks turned on all his eloquence and charm to say not much in as nice a way as possible, the G.O.I. await with great interest to hear from you what in fact the conclusions of the Mission are.

In the wake of the report, the World Bank dispatched a technical study mission to India, headed by Michael Hoffman; and in the autumn of 1960 the two-phase rhythm of the India and Pakistan consortia formally began: a session of economic analysis followed in the spring by a pledging session. The Third India Five Year Plan was reviewed in Paris in September 1960; and in April 1961 the first pledging session took place. By that time Kennedy was, of course, president; and he had the satisfaction of rounding out the effort launched in March 1958 by committing the United States to make a major contribution at the first pledging session of the India consortium in April—a constructive act that gave Kennedy some comfort, coming as it did amidst the painful process of cleaning up the mess in the wake of the Bay of Pigs failure. The U.S. was prepared to lend $500 million to India for each of the first two years of the Third Plan if the other members of the consortium would match the American figure. They failed to do so in April, but they came close enough in a special meeting in May for the Third India Five Year Plan to be launched with a fairly solid and reasonably adequate base of international support. As Kennedy's aide with responsibility to follow this among other matters, I was able to send him a memorandum on June 1, 1961:

> Herewith a report on the second Consortium meeting on India, which represents a major success. There is no doubt that your boldness in putting up the $500 million [for fiscal year 1962] has jacked up everyone's contributions. We all agree this should help us on the Hill. Those dealing with the Hill have already been alerted as to the result.

The India consortium was under way and the Pakistan consortium as well; but, of course, economic and social development in the subcontinent did not unfold smoothly. Over the next twenty years the two countries confronted many vicissitudes as they made their way forward carrying the burdens of excessive rates of population increase and vast, low-productivity rural sectors. Moreover, economic and social development does not take place in a vacuum. The two nations confronted political crises, including conflict with each other and the division of Pakistan into two states. Nor did the sense of convergent interests between Washington and New Delhi which marked the late 1950s and early 1960s prove stable; and the common-law marriage between India and the consortium, presided over by the World Bank, was not always smooth and easy. But it survived, played on the whole a constructive role on the world scene, and created a model for at least sixteen similar arrangements over the next decade.

11. The Institutionalization and Vicissitudes of Development Aid, 1961-1984

The focus of this book is the Kennedy-Cooper initiative of 1958–1959 and its place in the turning point in U.S. and international development policy toward the close of the 1950s. This is not an effort to write a full history of development aid—a subject I commend to some hardier soul. Nevertheless, it may be useful to provide in this chapter a brief sketch of how development aid was consolidated and institutionalized in the course of the 1960s and to suggest the major phases of its subsequent evolution down to the early 1980s. A summary of this kind may be useful before turning, in the final chapter, to reflections, with the benefit of hindsight, on some of the issues embedded in the story of development policy during the 1950s.

Kennedy, as president, did not delay long before translating his views on development aid, generated while he was in the Senate, into executive initiatives. On March 1, 1961, he sent to the Congress a message on the Peace Corps established by executive order that day; on March 13, he launched the Alliance for Progress in an address to the assembled Diplomatic Corps of the Latin American Republics; and on March 22 he sent to the Congress a special message on foreign aid embracing the concept of the Development Decade. Acknowledging a continuity with Truman and Eisenhower—and thereby reaching out for bipartisan support—Kennedy nevertheless opened and closed his message with rhetoric of a distinct and positive cast:

This nation must begin any discussion of "foreign aid" in 1961 with the recognitions of three facts:

1. Existing foreign aid programs and concepts are largely unsatisfactory and unsuited for our needs and for the needs of the underdeveloped world as it enters the Sixties.

2. The economic collapse of those free but less-developed nations which now stand poised between sustained growth and economic chaos would be disastrous to our national security, harmful to our comparative prosperity and offensive to our conscience.

3. There exists, in the 1960s, an historic opportunity for a major economic assistance effort by the free industrialized nations to move more than half the people of the less-developed nations into self-sustained economic growth, while the rest move substantially closer to the day when they, too, will no longer have to depend on outside assistance. . . .

I believe the program which I have outlined is both a reasonable and sensible method of meeting those obligations as economically and effectively as possible. I strongly urge its enactment by the Congress, in full awareness of the many eyes upon us—the eyes of other industrialized nations, awaiting our leadership for a stronger united effort—the eyes of our adversaries, awaiting the weakening of our resolve in this new area of international struggle—the eyes of the poorer peoples of the world, looking for hope and help, and needing an incentive to set realistic long-range goals—and, finally, the eyes of the American people, who are fully aware of their obligations to the sick, the poor and the hungry, wherever they may live. Thus, without regard to party lines, we shall take this step not as Republicans or as Democrats but as leaders of the Free World. It will both befit and benefit us to take this step boldly. For we are launching a Decade of Development on which will depend, substantially, the kind of world in which we and our children shall live.[95]

Specifically, Kennedy sought to shift the existing aid program in the following directions:

(a) a unification of technical assistance, development lending, Public Law 480, and other scattered activities;

(b) a concentration on national development plans as opposed to specific projects, with priority for nations making serious and coherent self-help efforts "to reach the stage of self-sustaining growth";

(c) a multilateral approach, designed to draw other industrialized nations systematically into the effort on a larger scale; and

(d) authority from the Congress for long-term (five year) authorization and borrowing authority to make dollar-repayable loans.

As noted earlier (pp. xiii–xiv), Eisenhower's final aid request of the Congress was high: some $800 million more than the sum actually voted in the previous year. For the first year, Kennedy therefore stayed with Eisenhower's request for a $4 billion economic and military authorization, but proposed to shift allocations toward development loans, repayable in dollars over long periods.

Even this aid increase appeared difficult to get from a Congress more conservative than that elected in 1958. Sorensen's low-key first draft of the aid message was geared to the rather gloomy prospects on the Hill. Kennedy evidently wished to aim somewhat higher. He had Sorensen send the draft to me for revision. My suggestions were radical and extensive but wholly consonant with Kennedy's views as I had known them over the previous three years. And, when Kennedy approved the new directions suggested by me (and, perhaps, by others), Sorensen, quite typically, carried forward in a more heroic direction with verve and elegance.

In 1961 Kennedy moved the foreign aid program some distance toward the goals he had formulated in the late 1950s; although its momentum was damped by initial administrative problems and then, in 1963, by increased congressional resistance in the post-Cuba missile crisis letdown of anxiety about the Cold War. As we shall see, other forces operating later in the 1960s further diminished U.S. support for development aid.

Nevertheless, Kennedy achieved a good deal. He got from Congress the authority to make long-term commitments; although he did not get the borrowing authority for aid lending he sought. The latter would have been a bold innovation, relieving development lending (not grants) from the annual appropriations cycle. It might have helped sustain the level of American capital flows to the developing world in the later 1960s. But it was rejected as "back-door financing" and a dilution of congressional power over the purse strings. He completed the initiative he undertook as a senator, launching the India and Pakistan consortia arrangements in the World Bank with a strong U.S. contribution, inducing proportionate contributions from others. This not only strengthened development programs affecting the lives of some 40 percent of the people in the non-Communist portion of the developing world, but also set a pattern for multilateralism which was rapidly extended in the 1960s. He launched the Alliance for Progress as well as the Peace Corps. When the American contribution to development is measured as a whole (including the World Bank, IDA, the IADB, etc.), the lift in resources made available in the early 1960s is quite impressive: an increase of one-third. And there is a major element reflected in the data on U.S. development aid (see Table 10, above) which reaches beyond Kennedy's time. His strong advocacy of international support for serious development efforts helped induce other nations to expand their contributions, a trend which continued as the 1960s wore on. In 1960 the United States supplied 58 percent of official development assistance. Kennedy's lift in the American effort was not promptly matched, and by 1963 the figure was 62 percent. In 1968 the expanding contributions of others (notably Canada, Germany, Italy, Japan, the Netherlands, and Sweden), combined with growing con-

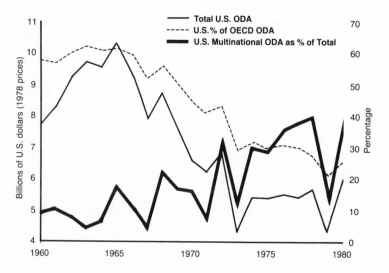

CHART 3. U.S. Official Development Assistance (ODA), 1960–1980

gressional resistance, had brought the American proportion of an enlarged total down to 56 percent.

As Table 10 and Chart 3 (based on Table 10) show, U.S. official development assistance, in terms of current dollars, peaked in 1963 and declined thereafter until the expansion required by both accelerated inflation and the needs of developing countries in the wake of the quadrupling of international oil prices in 1973–1974.

Table 11 summarizes the evolution of U.S. and total OECD official development assistance in real terms and as proportions of GNP.

This is not an appropriate occasion to trace out in detail all the forces which yielded the results set out in Tables 10 and 11. Broadly speaking, factors operated over this period on what might be called the supply and the demand sides of the development assistance market.

TABLE 11. Official Development Assistance, U.S. and Total OECD: Selected Years, 1960–1980

Year	United States ODA			Total OECD ODA	
	In Billions of $ U.S., 1978	Percentage U.S. GNP	Percentage Total, OECD	In Billions of $ U.S., 1978	Percentage OECD GNP
1960	5.9	.53	58	13.1	.51
1965	8.0	.58	62	16.7	.49
1970	5.2	.32	45	14.9	.34
1975	4.9	.27	26	17.9	.36
1980	6.0	.27	27	22.2	.37

Source: *World Development Report 1981* (World Bank) Table 16, pp. 164–165, except first column in which U.S. ODA is corrected by U.S. GNP deflation. OECD ODA is corrected by a collective deflation described on p. 188 of *World Development Report 1981*.

On the side of supply, the Johnson years were a defensive period in the story of American assistance to the developing world. The outcome of the Cuba missile crisis induced a sense that the world was a less dangerous place. Congress felt under less pressure to sustain foreign aid, the developing nations more free to assert strongly their national interests. The Indian-Pakistani war of 1965 led to immediate reductions in aid to both countries and, to a degree, cast a shadow over the whole process of development lending. Similarly, the war in Southeast Asia, increasing in intensity from July 1965, diverted congressional attention from and reduced congressional will to sustain development aid at previous levels. Increasing U.S. balance of payments problems set up forces pressing in the same direction.

In this setting President Johnson fought both to hold the line and to alter the direction of the aid programs. First, he assumed leadership in focusing attention on the food-population balance. A series of studies within the government in 1964–1965 made clear that, if existing trends in population and food production persisted, the world would face before 1980 a true Malthusian crisis. Population increases of over 2 percent and increased urban demand were not fully matched by increases in food production; production in the developing world was expanding mainly by increases in acreage rather than in yields; acreage that could be brought into production was limited in a number of key countries; and history suggested that a surge in yields awaited a higher level of development in general. A good part of humanity seemed caught in a desperate trap. Net grain imports into the developing countries rose from 19 to 36 million tons between 1960 and 1966.

Johnson decided to use his margin of influence and leverage actively to encourage an increase in agricultural productivity and an expansion in population control policies in the developing world. The authority of AID to support family planning programs was expanded short of the financing of contraceptive devices themselves and the equipment to make them.

Johnson was aided by both a disaster and new technology. The disaster was two successive droughts in India. The new technology was the emergence of new high-productivity strains of wheat and rice from protracted research by international teams conducted in Mexico and the Philippines, respectively.

The Indian drought provided the occasion for a sharp change in priorities within India. Meanwhile, despite the heavy budgetary costs involved, Johnson mobilized in those years a fifth of the American wheat crop for India, and some 600 ships, in the largest maritime assemblage since the Allied Forces crossed the English Channel on D-Day. For a period of two years, more than 60 million Indians were sustained entirely by American food shipments.

The upshot was a revolution in agricultural productivity in critical parts of the developing world. In Asia, for example, the area planted with new seeds increased from 200 acres in 1964–1965 to 38 million in 1968–1969. The revolution posed problems as well as new possibilities; but the new seeds and the investment required to make them efficient bought some valuable time and yielded by the 1980s an India which, for the time being, was self-sufficient in food supplies.

A second distinctive feature of Johnson's policy was the priority he attached to the dimensions of development that bore directly on the life of human beings: education and health, as well as food and population control. This impulse clearly arose from his own early experience in Texas which had generated a sense of outrage at the unnecessary wastage of human beings born into the world and not provided with all the food and medical services they needed, all the education they could absorb. From fiscal year 1966, AID shifted to a new emphasis on education and health as well as agriculture and population control.

Third, Johnson pressed hard and systematically to move economic assistance to the developing world onto a multilateral basis in which others would do more, the United States less, on the principle of "partnership and fair shares." This was linked to his thrust toward regionalism, the subject of the next volume in this series. The Asian Development Bank (ADB) was built around proportionate contributions, rooted in principles of equity; and the role of the Latin American and European nations and Japan in the IADB expanded. The International Development Association of the World Bank (IDA) was also attractive for this reason. Johnson made special efforts to bring Japan into Asian development efforts on a basis of equality of contribution to the capital of the ADB, and 30 percent to The Hague consortium in support of Indonesian development after Sukarno's overthrow.

Fourth, Johnson gave special attention to Latin American development. Here his experience and judgment converged with a commitment to carry forward his predecessor's policies. It was both a difficult and a propitious period for renewed effort. It was difficult because the first few years of experience had revealed that there were no miracles that Washington could perform to bring about accelerated economic and social progress; the job would have to be primarily Latin American. It was propitious because most Latin American leaders had come to accept this fact and, with Kennedy's support, set up the Inter-American Committee on the Alliance for Progress (CIAP) at a meeting in Sao Paulo on November 11–16, 1963. This new instrument of the OAS, whose vitality faded by the end of the 1960s, provided, for a time, the possibility of Latin American leadership in the Alliance. CIAP included only one North American member, dramatizing the appropriate junior-partner status of the United States. Its annual country-by-country review process yielded an increasingly thorough and sophisticated process of mutual evaluation of self-help and legitimate external assistance. The Congress acted to require U.S. aid to Latin America to be guided by CIAP recommendations.

The upshot was a considerable increase in official lending

to Latin America, which persisted through the Johnson administration: a rise from $981 million in 1963 to $1.7 billion in 1968. By the end of the Johnson administration, Latin American growth as a whole was moving forward at rates beyond the 2.5 percent per capita target set in 1961 at Punta del Este, although the performance of some individual countries remained erratic (Table 12).

Johnson's aid policy—like his policy toward the developing regions in general—was shaped by his acute awareness that they were, despite all their vicissitudes, gathering strength and were increasingly determined to shape their own destiny on the world scene. This process was accompanied by an equally important rise of economic strength in Western Europe and Japan relative to the United States. In a world of diffusing power, he sought, therefore, to reduce the role of U.S. bilateral aid and transfer responsibility and authority to multinational institutions. Thus, in 1964 the proportion of U.S. ODA contributed via multilateral institutions was 6 percent; by 1970 the figure had risen to 16 percent. The trend was general. For the members of the DAC as a whole, the equivalent figures were 6 percent and 14 percent. By 1975 the U.S. figure had risen to 35 percent, the DAC to 23 percent.

On the side of demand the period between 1961 and 1973 saw several countries move forward in their development

TABLE 12. Rate of Growth of Latin American Gross Domestic Product per Capita (%), 1965–1970

1965	2.5
1966	1.5
1967	1.4
1968	3.3
1969	3.7
1970	3.8

Source: Organization of American States.

179

sufficiently to justify marked reductions in ODA; for example, South Korea, Taiwan, Thailand, Turkey, and Greece. On the other hand, radical alterations in the political situation in Brazil and Indonesia, accompanied by increased domestic attention to development, increased the effective demand for foreign aid. And, as noted earlier, Latin America, taken as a whole, also proved capable of absorbing productively an increased flow of development assistance.

In the late 1960s and early 1970s a new intellectual strand entered the debate over development aid: an emphasis on "basic human needs." It conformed to Johnson's priority in U.S. foreign aid for food, health care, and education; but it had quite different roots.

The "basic human needs" strategy represented a revolt against the perceived inadequacies of development doctrines and policies of the 1960s in general and, quite specifically, against the report of the Pearson Commission: *Partners in Development: Report of the Commission on International Development* (1969). That report, financed by the World Bank, was an effort to dramatize the need for continuing and even enlarged development assistance at a time when political support in the advanced industrial countries was weakening. A good many analysts and commentators felt, however, that its recommendations were too modest and conventional.

The Pearson Commission recommended that an average growth target for the developing countries of 6 percent be set for the 1970s; official development assistance be targeted at 0.7 percent of GNP for the advanced industrial countries with 20 percent allocated through multilateral agencies; and that the terms of ODA be limited to 2 percent interest (with 25–40 year maturity). The quantitative target percentage of GNP was twice the current level. In that sense, the Pearson Commission report was quite ambitious.

The report was reviewed at an international conference organized by Columbia University and held at Williamsburg and New York, February 15–21, 1970.[96] These gatherings yielded

180

a document called the Columbia Declaration which included these passages:

> In incomes, living standards, economic and political power, one-third of the world has in recent decades been pulling steadily ahead, leaving the remainder of mankind in relative poverty, in many cases to live without clean water, education, basic medical facilities or adequate housing. Yet with modern technology and existing productive capacity, none of this need continue if mankind would develop the will and organization to use the resources at hand.
>
> . . . new objective criteria for effective development assistance are required. An overall minimum growth rate for all countries is, no doubt, a desirable objective. But it is essential also to develop targets designed to achieve a minimum average per capita income of $400 to be reached by all countries not later than the end of the century. Criteria are also needed which focus on the living standards of the bottom quarter of each country's population. We also suggest setting up of a special fund devoted specifically to the fulfillment of social objectives in the areas of education, health, family planning, rural and urban works, housing, and other related social programs.
>
> . . . None of us underestimates the need for major change in political, social and economic policies and institutions within the developing countries. Without them, international efforts will be to no avail. Performance criteria should increasingly focus on income distribution, land and tax reform, ineffective trade and exchange rate policies, size of military expenditures, and the promotion of social justice.
>
> . . . A frank report by the developing countries would have revealed a more pessimistic picture, especially when attention is directed: to the losses from changes in terms of trade which often exceed annual gains from aid; to the prospect of growing numbers of unemployed; to the inequities in the distribution of aid under bilateral political influences; to the weaknesses in the existing institutional framework of aid; and to the growing strength of the multinational corporations which often distort the pattern of national development.

The Pearson Report emphasizes a partnership between the developed and developing countries which too often is simply an illusion. . . .

. . . There is an urgent need to strengthen the multilateral international framework in the fields of trade, aid, and relations between rich and poor nations. This must cover the United Nations as well as other international and regional institutions. Such strengthening necessarily involves the channeling of increased and independent finance and moves toward compulsory contributions by member countries. International power must increasingly be shared democratically; and this objective can only be attained by strengthening the role of institutions in which the developing economies have a representative vote.[97]

The "basic human needs" doctrine was not ignored in the 1970s. The World Bank, for example, under Robert McNamara's direction, allocated increased resources for social purposes and conducted sophisticated analyses of the relationship of poverty and excessively skewed income distribution to aggregate and sectoral growth rates. A great deal of both poverty and abnormally skewed income distribution was, in fact, linked to excessive rates of population increase and inadequate attention of governments to agriculture and to the modernization of rural life. Inadequate tax collection and the diversion of government funds to a variety of dubious subsidies (thus constraining allocations for health, education, and other important social purposes) also played a role.

Where birth rates were rapidly declining and agricultural productivity and the modernization of rural life taken seriously, the lowest 20 percent of the population received proportions of total income comparable to distribution patterns in advanced industrial countries; e.g., South Korea and Taiwan.

Despite these deeper forces which largely determined the social outcome in developing nations, the rise of the "basic human needs" doctrine undoubtedly led to some reallocation of national and international development resources and, perhaps equally important, to intensified analyses of the anatomy of poverty in developing countries.

But the fact is that during the 1970s the governments of the advanced industrial countries rejected not only the high objectives and demands of the Columbia Declaration but also the targets of the Pearson Commission report. The proportion of collective OECD GNP allocated to ODA remained, essentially, static: it was .34 percent in both 1970 and 1979.

The Nixon administration started off with a positive effort to expand development assistance. It increased by almost 25 percent between fiscal year 1969 and fiscal year 1971, the bulk of which, following the trend during the Johnson administration, represented increased contributions to multilateral lending institutions (the World Bank, Inter-American Bank, and the Asian Development Bank).[98] These initiatives were crosscut in August 1971 by the measures undertaken to deal with the acute U.S. balance of payments crisis which had emerged in the second quarter of that year. These included a 10 percent cut in foreign aid which dropped sharply by 1973.

Then came the global grain shortage of 1972–1973 and the quadrupling of international oil prices in 1973–1974. These phenomena yielded a phase of enlarged requirements for foreign exchange support among developing countries, notably those importing oil, if growth rates were not to be sharply reduced. The more advanced of these countries, with access to private capital markets, increased their private borrowing. The needs of the less advantaged were, to a degree, met by a rise in ODA. Between 1973 and 1975, U.S. ODA, for example, rose by 44 percent at a time when prices rose by 20 percent; but private lending to developing countries almost doubled, to a level more than twice that of U.S. ODA. The pattern for the DAC countries as a whole was similar. The members of OPEC also contributed resources to ease some of the pressures generated by the rise in the oil price. Between 1972 and the peak in 1975, OECD ODA rose 21 percent in real terms. As the real price of oil declined slightly in 1976–1977, external assistance to the developing countries leveled off. With the second oil price convulsion of 1978–1979, the pattern roughly repeated, with a rise in OECD ODA, in real terms, of 12.2 percent between 1977 and 1980. For the United States, the real increase in ODA over those years was 19.8 percent.

In short, the international development assistance system did respond, to a degree, to the special burdens imposed on the oil-importing developing nations by the two oil shocks of the 1970s.

Meanwhile, starting in 1974, a protracted North-South debate and negotiation proceeded in the United Nations and elsewhere, centered on the concept of a New International Economic Order (NIEO). Calls for a NIEO antedate the quadrupling of the oil price; but that event set the initial tone of the negotiations. It did so by inducing the political leaders of the South to believe that a time had come when their command over the flow of raw materials necessary to the more industrialized North provided the leverage to exact important concessions which would enlarge the North-to-South flow of foreign exchange and technology. Many of those who took the kind of view incorporated in the Columbia Declaration felt that, at last, they had found the lever to bring their doctrines to life.

For many intellectuals and politicians in the developing world, the success of OPEC in asserting its power in the autumn of 1973 was a memorable and heartening event. Here were nations—mostly small, in some cases poor, in all cases not fully modernized—using their control over a basic raw material to shake the foundations of the rich and comfortable societies which had based their post-1945 prosperity on cheap energy. Hitherto weaker states successfully asserted their capacity to divert more resources to themselves. At last, they could feel that the unfair allocation of the benefits that their raw materials had provided in the past was redressed. Whether that allocation was, in fact, fair or unfair is a complex, debatable question; but OPEC's action was a demonstration of power through a disciplined cooperation the developing nations had never before been able to generate.

The impulse to emulate OPEC by political pressure, where producers' cartels were not a realistic option, was heightened by another fact. The progress in modernization made in a good many developing nations in the 1950s and 1960s had yielded a generation quite as capable of sophisticated analysis of the world scene as those who provided the staff work for OPEC. Leaders of that generation felt themselves much more nearly the technical equals of their opposite numbers in the North than had the pioneers of development in the previous generation. They were quite right.

And so they went on the offense in 1974. It was tactically as well as psychologically understandable that they should do so. On the one hand, the North was shaken by the rise in the oil price and looked weak and uncertain after two decades of majestic, confident growth; on the other hand, the world economy, for part of the year at least, was experiencing high raw material prices. The foreign exchange position of a good many producers of raw materials, other than oil, was strong as a result of the several previous years of global economic expansion.

If one reviews the major international conferences of 1974, one might guess that North-South relations had already polarized and that the world faced inevitably a protracted neomercantilist struggle. There were the acrimonious United Nations General Assembly debate of April 1974, the population meeting at Bucharest, the food conference at Rome, and the sterile session on the law of the seas at Caracas. In all of them, the air was filled with rhetoric about imperialism; with claims for the unilateral transfer of resources from the rich to the poor; and with the ardent assertion of national sovereignty by the less developed nations, combined with equally ardent demands that the more developed states surrender sovereignty and behave in terms of the requirements of the international community. In the face of this verbal and political onslaught, the more developed nations mainly reacted defensively.

The special United Nations session of September 1975 was, in tone and substance, markedly less contentious than those of 1974. Three factors appear to account for the change. First, the United States arrived with rhetoric of reconciliation and a working agenda for North-South cooperation. Although the American commitment of resources was limited, the rhetoric, the headings for action, and the assumption of leadership were useful. Second, and perhaps more important, the OECD recession over the previous year had badly damaged prospects in many parts of the developing world, demonstrating in a rather painful way the reality of North-South interdependence. In 1974, close to the peak of the previous boom, there had been much talk from the South about the North's excessive consumption of raw materials; in 1975 the South was concerned about foreign exchange losses from declining raw material sales and prices. Third, the damage done the developing world by OPEC's oil price increase was better understood and the somewhat artificial 1974 unity of the developing nations was thereby strained despite the formal maintenance of a common front against the industrial North.

A package of resolutions emerged from this session on September 16, 1975, which covered four main headings: a variety of measures to enlarge the foreign exchange earning capacity of developing countries through international trade; increased aid; the accelerated transfer of technology; and measures to accelerate agricultural production in the developing nations and to provide international grain stocks as a hedge against poor harvests in developing nations.

This agenda was pursued for the better part of two years in the Conference on International Economic Cooperation and Development in Paris. The tone of the negotiations was temperate; but the new realism, in Maurice Williams' phrase, yielded only meager results: a promise to raise a special $1 billion fund to aid the most hard pressed developing nations;

a commitment to consider at a later time the creation and financing of buffer stocks and commodity price stabilization; a commitment to consider debt rollovers on a case-by-case basis; and the offer of long-term support for transport and communication development in Africa.

The North was willing to do something about the worst manifestations of disarray in the developing world (the aid fund and selective debt rollovers); but the grand vision of a new international economic order incorporated in the resolution of September 16, 1975, had all but disappeared.

This happened for three reasons: the South lacked the power to enforce its will on the North; politicians in the North lacked a political base to meet even the legitimate claims of the South, due to the state of the northern economies; and the ideological mood of 1974 yielded an agenda that was neither politically viable nor addressed effectively to the issues which might have led to cooperation rather than confrontation. In addition, the effort to deal with economic issues, in global fora, dominated by foreign office officials rather than representatives of the ministries which bore direct responsibility for domestic economic problems, virtually guaranteed that the results would consist of ambiguous resolutions rather than actions which would enlarge the flow of resources from North to South.

As the NIEO negotiations demonstrated their sterility in the course of 1977, Robert McNamara, president of the World Bank, sought to recreate a consensus on the basis of which a new phase of North-South cooperation for development might be mounted. He appointed an independent commission on international development issues consisting of seventeen distinguished public figures, ten from developing nations, seven from advanced industrial countries, chaired by Willy Brandt. After almost two years of work, supported by an able international secretariat, the commission published its report (*North-South*) in 1980.

North-South is an eclectic amalgam of many perspectives

on the North-South relationship, all geared to the central recommendation of a massive increase in the transfer of resources to the developing nations. The report opens with a
strong moral appeal written by the commission's chairman.
The special requirements of the poorer developing countries
are dramatized. The requirements for enlarged investment in
certain key resource sectors are analyzed; *e.g.*, agriculture,
energy, raw materials, pollution control. The report argues
that investment opportunities are lacking in the advanced industrial world and large resource transfers to the South would
stimulate employment in the export industries of the North.
The NIEO program was reflected at a number of points, including the recommendation that the power of the developing nations in the multilateral financial institutions be increased. The final recommendation of *North-South* was that
"A Summit of World Leaders" be convoked to "change the international climate and enlarge the prospects for a global
agreement." This was the only *North-South* recommendation
initially agreed among the major governments; thus, the Cancún meeting of October 1981.

It is fair to say that, from 1974 through 1981, the effort to
induce an enlargement in development assistance by multilateral North-South negotiations had failed. The North, be-
devilled by a process of stagflation it could not master, with
serious social as well as political consequences, was not in a
mood to divert large additional flows of resources to the
South; and its various spokesmen found little difficulty in rebutting a good many of the arguments presented in United
Nations fora and *North-South* in advocacy of such a diversion.

While these high level efforts were going forward with in-
different results, a quite different, narrower functional approach to North—South cooperation was emerging. It took its
start with certain palpable facts of virtually universal concern:

1. The cost of current oil imports was straining the balance
of payments of many oil—importing developing countries;
the prospects for aggregate oil production from existing ex-

porters were for decline over the period 1980–2000; oil consumption requirements were rising rapidly in most developing countries; therefore, programs to expand domestic oil production and substitutes for oil, as well as programs of conservation, were urgent in the developing countries, including current oil exporters.

2. The rate of increase in the demand for food was outpacing the rate of increase of domestic production in many developing countries requiring increased reliance on food imports. In addition, high proportions of the children in many developing countries were not provided with diets adequate to guarantee the full development of their physical and mental capacities. Therefore, an acceleration of domestic agricultural production and productivity was urgent, as well as intensified efforts to reduce birth rates.

3. A failure to resolve the conflict between nationalist insistence on the control of raw materials in developing countries with the requirements for confidence in an adequate rate of return on foreign investment was leading to a distortion of investment flows away from certain developing countries to the cost of those countries and the international community. This situation, widely recognized by analysts of the South as well as the North, led to recommendations to heighten efforts to reconcile the legitimate imperatives in conflict, reconciliations which had proved possible in a number of cases on a bilateral basis.

4. Gross degradation of the environment—notably, accelerated deforestation and soil erosion—was occurring in a number of developing regions with dangerous degenerative results. An increasing appreciation of this situation led to recommendations for North-South collaboration to halt and reverse the process.

These sectoral insights led me to the concept of a sustained partnership effort, focused around solution to those key problems, which would have the following characteristics:

1. The work would be conducted, to the maximum pos-

sible, on a regional basis. Sectoral investment planning of the kind required would be, simply, impossible with some 150 countries around the table.

2. With the World Bank cooperating in all regions, leadership would be assumed by the Inter-American, the African, and the Asian development banks. Although Europe would naturally play a special role in Africa, the U.S. in the Western Hemisphere, the U.S. and Japan in Asia, all the major advanced industrial countries would participate in the three regional ventures.

3. Perhaps most important, the governments would be represented, in each functional area, by those who bore direct operating responsibility for the relevant sector at hand.[99]

If successful, the upshot would be a shift of priorities and domestic resources within developing countries to solve these problems, and a radically increased flow of external capital and technical assistance. This approach would, of course, also recognize the need for enlarged external aid for poor countries, often small, which have proved to be particularly vulnerable to the turbulent environment of the world economy since 1972; and it would recognize as well that certain trade issues are best negotiated at a global level.

The logic of a sectoral, functional approach began to emerge pragmatically as public officials contemplated both the sterility of the NIEO negotiations and the character of the constraints on growth in the developing regions. It was clearly reflected, for example, in "Hemispheric Cooperation and Integral Development," the report of a group of experts appointed by the secretary general of the OAS.[100] The World Bank moved in this direction with its proposal for a special energy facility to expand its capacity to assist developing countries in meeting their enormous needs for investment in the energy sector. As noted earlier, embedded in *North-South* were chapters reflecting this approach, although they were overwhelmed by the overriding theme: the need for a massive increase in the transfer of resources. And, at Cancún,

Reagan proposed as one of his five principles to guide "a positive program of action for development": "Guiding our assistance toward the development of self-sustaining productive activities, particularly in food and energy."[101] Reagan also left open the possibility of pursuing the development dialogue in regional as well as global institutions.

But, clearly, the United States government was not prepared actively to lead in this direction; and no other government promptly took up the option Reagan laid on the table, discouraged, perhaps, by the fact that the bulk of Reagan's intervention was devoted to an insistence that the solutions to problems of development were to be sought through private enterprise rather than public policy.

The Reagan administration began, in fact, with a lucid, ideological bias against official development assistance. Its basic position was almost identical to that of the Eisenhower administration in its early years; namely, that liberal international trading arrangements and private capital flows would provide for virtually all the economic needs of the developing countries. Concessional aid should be provided primarily "to help those poorer countries which, for reasons beyond their control, have not been able to improve their standards of living. The rationale for aid to countries whose low economic performance results more from inappropriate domestic policies than from external factors needs to be reexamined."[102] All this was what I. G. Patel has called "the new fundamentalism."[103]

In this spirit, the Reagan administration conducted in 1981 a major review of the World Bank and the regional development banks. While respectful of their competence and achievements, this report urged greater attention to loan "quality" rather than "quantity"; accelerated "graduation" of developing nations from soft to hard World Bank loans and from the latter to private capital markets; a shift from multilateral to bilateral aid; and pressure on countries requiring concessional aid to improve their domestic economic performance and, in particular, to generate an increase in privately produced output. A review of these matters by a new administration was wholly in order; and, taken by themselves, there was nothing outlandish in these recommendations. But these lines of policy, clearly linked to the domestic economic doctrines and policies of the Reagan administration, confronted three problems.

First, the attempt to reconcile a policy of monetarist gradualism, to reduce the inflation rate, with a supply-side stimulus to private investment and a movement toward a balanced budget, failed in the administration's first two years. Monetarism yielded not a subsidence of inflation accompanied by a strong expansion of the economy but a sharp recession, marked by extremely high real rates of interest, radical declines in investment and productivity, and a grotesque expansion of the federal deficit about half of which was due to the recession.

The recession, spreading as it did to Western Europe and Japan, had four distinct damaging effects on developing countries:

(a) it reduced the volume of exports flowing from South to North;

(b) it reduced the prices of those exports;

(c) it strengthened protectionist pressures in the North; and

(d) it set up a conflict between legitimate claims to deal with heightened social problems in the North and legitimate claims for development assistance from the South.

In addition, high interest rates in the OECD capital markets, stemming from U.S. policy, brought extraordinary pressures to bear on the balance of payments position of many developing countries. Their momentum in the 1970s had been maintained in substantial part by borrowing abroad from private sources. For example, 85 percent of the capital flow to Latin America in 1981 was in the form of private loans; but, in that year, a net capital inflow of $20 billion was outweighed by annual interest charges which had accumulated to the level of $22 billion. Although private banks are under strong compulsions to roll over rather than to call debts to governments when the alternative may be severe international financial crisis, there were signs in 1982 that the private banks were anxious to reduce their exposure at just the time when the multiple effects of domestic U.S. economic policy were weakening the balance of payments positions of developing countries. These were not circumstances when the Reagan administration's homilies on the virtues of private enterprise and private international borrowing quite met the case.

Second, the Reagan administration confronted, in the Caribbean and Central America, economic, social, and, in some cases, strategic crises which required extraordinary measures of external assistance. As developing countries go, those most severely affected were not particularly poor in terms of real income per capita. But, in general, they lacked the domestic resources to adjust in a resilient way to the pressures imposed by high oil import prices and the U.S.-induced global recession. Moreover, some lacked adequate access to private capital markets. They required and, in an *ad hoc* decision, were granted special concessional assistance in a cooperative venture in which the United States was joined by Colombia, Venezuela, Mexico, and Canada. The process recalls a bit the manner in which the Eisenhower administration was led by strategic crises to alter its initial canons for foreign aid.

Third, a doctrinaire insistence on heightened reliance on private foreign investment (and increased reliance on private investment within developing countries) did not mesh well with the resource-related agenda inescapably confronted by the developing regions. With respect to energy, for example, it is quite true that a great deal of the development of conventional oil and natural gas in developing regions can be partially financed and technologically assisted through private foreign investment; but, evidently, where, for whatever reasons, countries have developed government corporations to develop their oil and natural gas resources, they are not about to dismantle these institutions to meet the requirements of a particular U.S. administration. Perhaps more important, there is an inescapable government role (and role for ODA) in cases where:

(a) Capital requirements are beyond the capacity of domestic and foreign private firms; *e.g.*, large hydroelectric dams and power stations.

(b) Long periods of gestation and uncertainty about cost and the efficiency of new technologies are involved; *e.g.*, synthetic plants.

(c) Large infrastructure investments must accompany the development of new energy resources; *e.g.*, coal mines in areas distant from existing centers of economic activity.

There were similar problems with the task of accelerating agricultural production and productivity in developing regions—an objective increasingly accepted in principle. Fair market pricing for agricultural products would surely help in countries where such prices were artificially restrained on behalf of urban populations; but the modernization of rural life often requires irrigation works, enlarged rural credits, and investments in education, health, and transport facilities beyond the capacity of the private sectors to manage. There was an additional legitimate claim on public resources, national and international, to retrieve arable land where it had been permitted to erode and to launch programs of reforestation. Thus, a dogmatic and indiscriminate faith in private enterprise initially inhibited the Reagan administration from acting effectively in the developing regions even with respect to problems where it perceived that solutions were in the interest of the United States.

In 1982–1983 the Reagan administration, like many of its predecessors, was confronted with a major, unanticipated problem for which its doctrines provided no satisfactory response. The large borrowings of certain key developing countries in the 1970s, which permitted the maintenance of reasonably high rates of real growth despite the slowdown of the advanced industrial countries, became unmanageable. The virtual stagnation of the United States, Western Europe and Japan in the period 1979–1982, combined with the pathologically high real interest rates induced by U.S. monetary policy starting in October 1979, was the proximate cause of the crisis. The decline in the real (and then nominal) price of oil added certain oil exporters to the list of nations unable to meet interest and principal repayments. After a period of initial shock and reticence, the Reagan administration joined other advanced industrial countries in expanding the resources available to the IMF to roll over debts which would otherwise have gone into default with dangerous consequences for major private banks and the international financial system as a whole. The scale of the required roll-overs transcended even the expanded resources of the IMF. Complex consortia embracing the IMF, the central banks, and the private banking systems of the advanced industrial countries had to be created, case by case. The cost of the roll-overs was a series of commitments to austerity by the borrowing countries which not only threatened the stability of their often fragile social and political structures, but also induced a decline in exports from the advanced industrial countries, for the proportion of total exports going to developing countries had risen in a striking way during the 1970s reaching close to 40 percent for the United States.

The Reagan administration may well go down in history as the largest provider of foreign aid to developing countries since 1945; but its time-buying roll-over crisis loans, required in good part because of its domestic economic policies of 1981–1982, did not, in fact, constitute a foreign aid policy.

12. Some Reflections

This examination of the Kennedy-Cooper resolution in its larger setting poses a range of issues which justify a few final reflections.

First, there is the resolution itself, in its 1958 and 1959 versions. In supporting enlarged aid to India in those years, Kennedy was, as we have emphasized, by no means alone; but there was a special character to the way he went about the job.

He could easily have joined those who simply argued, in general terms, that U.S. aid for India should be increased. They formed a considerable body of influential, if still minority, opinion in 1958–1959. He insisted on going further and responding to the harder question: what could he, as a senator of modest influence, do concretely to bring about this result in the political setting which existed in the critical two years? He perceived that the key might lie not only in a bipartisan effort but also in creating a situation where the expansion in American aid was part of an international effort; that currents of opinion and policy in Western Europe might make this feasible; and that a positive report from a small, prestigious international mission to the subcontinent might serve as the catalyst, helping tip the balance in both the executive branch and the Congress as well as in European policy.

In pursuing this shrewd insight, Kennedy was forced to operate over a wide front: to organize knowledgeable staff work; to assure he was in step with the Indian government; to engage the Western Europeans; to achieve acquiescence, at least, from the executive branch; to generate support from the press; and, of course, to carry his colleagues in the Senate and develop as much support in the House of Representatives as possible. And, as the World Bank emerged in the second half of 1958 as the likely operational agent for executing the proposal, he had to deal with that institution. Kennedy, as senator, did not command a large professional staff knowledgeable in foreign affairs. Indeed, his ties to the academic community were, at the time, rather thin. Members of the phalanx of intellectuals that had been attracted to Adlai Stevenson during his two campaigns either hankered for a third Stevenson effort in 1960 or were politically uncommitted. Kennedy sought out and found in CENIS a group whose ardent commitment was to enlarged development aid rather than to party or political personality. He understood this clearly and used us well, not only as a source of information, ideas, and drafts but also to help align the Indians, the Western European governments, elements in the executive branch, and the press.

In this effort Frederick Holborn was extremely helpful to Kennedy. He maintained day-to-day ties not only to CENIS but also to sympathetic figures in the executive branch, the diplomatic community (including the World Bank), and the press. He followed closely relevant developments in key congressional committees; and he undertook an exploratory trip to Western Europe in December 1958. As a part time aide to Kennedy from mid 1957 (full time from February 1958), Holborn's working agenda transcended, of course, the carrying forward of the Kennedy-Cooper resolution. But the various dimensions of that task fitted well the range of functions to which Kennedy assigned him; and his close and easy working relations with CENIS assured that we all kept in step.

In the end, however, the success of the Kennedy-Cooper effort hinged on neither Holborn nor CENIS. It flowed from other elements in the equation; the heightened sense of anxiety in Washington in the wake of Sputnik; the transient image of Mao's success with the Great Leap Forward; and the arrival of Herter, Dillon, and Robert Anderson on the Washington scene in the wake of the departure of Herbert Hoover, Jr. and George Humphrey. Two other personalities were important to a favorable outcome: Eugene Black who, at the World Bank, seized the initiative on aid for India in the foreign exchange crisis of 1958 and became the natural sponsoring agent for the Wisemen rather than the OEEC; and Oliver Franks who, in effect, led the mission to India and Pakistan early in 1960 and shaped its report.

Kennedy did not lose interest in the project after the 1959 version of the resolution passed the Senate and the World Bank assumed responsibility for the three-man international mission. He followed events closely and kept in touch with Black. In the wake of Kennedy's January 1960 announcement that he would make a run for the Democratic presidential nomination, his energies and those of his staff were, perforce, focused overwhelmingly on that enterprise. Nevertheless, he continued to intervene helpfully in the unfolding process of executing the Resolution. Kennedy understood, as senator as well as president, that the effective making of policy required much more than rhetoric or even legislation; it demanded follow-through and compulsive attention to detail.

Although the Kennedy-Cooper resolution was only one piece in a large mosaic, it remains worth study as a rare example of a successful policy initiative launched from the legislative branch of government.

A second matter posed by this tale is, simply, a question: Why was Eisenhower so slow to throw his full weight behind an enlargement of development aid? The source material now available, incorporated in Chapters 6–9, leaves no doubt that as early as the spring of 1954 Eisenhower and Dulles had concluded that the effective conduct of U.S. foreign policy, in the face of forces generated in the developing regions and their quite effective exploitation by the Soviet Union, required the mobilization of additional resources for economic assistance to nations not linked to the U.S. by military pacts. But they did not begin to move effectively in this direction until they decided to support the DLF in 1957 and then only by switching aid resources from other accounts. In 1958 they responded to crisis circumstances in Latin America, India, and the Middle East and acquiesced in the concept of IDA. None of these actions taken in 1957–1958 required an immediate substantial increase in budgetary appropriations for foreign aid, but all carried substantial longer-term budgetary implications. There is no doubt that the substantive turning point in U.S. foreign aid policy occurred in Eisenhower's second term. The puzzlement is why, when the need for this reorientation in policy was understood by Eisenhower as early as 1954, was action so long delayed and then undertaken in response to crises or the initiatives of others—the Senate, Kubitschek, the World Bank.

The answer lies, I believe, in the convergence of three factors; first, the resistance to the idea of a large increase in development aid Eisenhower confronted within his own administration, in the Congress, and in public opinion. Eisenhower's letter to Jackson of August 16, 1954 (see above, pp. 100–102), is a serious document. As he formulated the problem, the question was, how do you make a speech "inspiring as to purpose and [one which would] avoid alarming as to cost." Eisenhower had succeeded in making just such speeches in 1953 in the wake of Stalin's death and in proposing Atoms for Peace. He was to do the same in 1955 with his Open Skies proposal in Geneva. But with development aid he knew an inspiring purpose had to be accompanied by fairly large and specific numbers to be effective.

Of the resistances to such a substantive initiative Eisenhower perceived, the one that troubled him most, I suspect, lay within his official family. George Humphrey, in particular, was a man he valued. He got on easily with him, shared, in part of his mind, much of his fiscal outlook, and respected the power of the Taftite political base in the Congress he broadly represented. On the other hand Eisenhower knew that his view of the world, as well as his responsibilities, differed from Humphrey's. Robert Bowie recalls Eisenhower turning on Humphrey at a meeting around the Cabinet table, when the latter was complaining about the excessive role of the Indian government in the economy, and saying: "George, if you faced their problems you would do the same thing." But Eisenhower was unwilling to take Humphrey up on the mountain and say: "This is what we have to do and I need your help to do it."

This inhibition reflects a second factor in the equation and flowed from Eisenhower's administrative style both as commanding general and president. He sought consensus in his staff—or compromise—before acting. Thus, when Jackson in 1954 asked for a command decision from Eisenhower on the World Economic Plan, the president's wholly typical response was to ask Jackson to come back to Washington to bring about consensus: ". . . unless there is one person in the setup who is really concerned about these things and pulls the others together, things just simply don't get done. . . ." (see above, p. 100). Eisenhower did not accept the notion that the concerned person who must pull the others together and get the job done is the president. Dulles decided that without the president's unambiguous prior commitment he could not perform the pulling together on this issue in the political context of the period. He was thus left in some anguish to cope as best he could with the unresolved conflicts over development aid within the executive branch; finally perceiving and acting decisively on the DLF in 1957, exploiting the small window of opportunity provided to him by the course of events.

The third factor at work was, I suspect, Eisenhower's own ambivalence about the budgetary implications of enlarged development aid. I cited earlier the astonishment of Eisenhower's own citizen-lobbyists, stirred into action by the White

House under Eric Johnston's leadership, when we called on Eisenhower on April 8, 1958, after mounting a rather glamorous two-day conference in Washington in support of foreign aid. Eisenhower's theme was: "Where are we going to get the money from?" (see above, p. 126). In terms of the nation's resources, foreign aid was never a large item; and even the maximum proposals for its expansion did not threaten to make it so. As noted earlier, under the pressure of events Eisenhower acted, in his second term, in ways which set in motion later substantial requirements for additional foreign aid appropriations; and his final budget, laid before the Congress after the election of 1960, included a proposed increase in development aid larger than any he proposed during his own period of responsibility (see above, pp. xiii–xiv). One can, therefore, argue that Eisenhower's anxiety about generating the resources required related more to the opposition he might face in his own camp rather than to a concern for the possible strain on the nation's resources. But there may have been an element of authentic ambivalence within him on this point.

Whatever the elements that determined Eisenhower's stance, the operational fact, as summarized by Robert Bowie (in a conversation while I was writing this book), is clear: "The president was simply not prepared to give development aid the necessary priority." The upshot was a costly delay.

Given the central theme of this series of essays—ideas and action—it is worth commenting explicitly on the light this story throws on that relationship. In one sense, it is an account of the triumph of one set of ideas over another. In 1953–1954 U.S. economic policy was dominated by the straightforward doctrine of the Randall Report incorporated in Eisenhower's message to Congress of March 30, 1954:

> Aid—which we wish to curtail;
> [Private] Investment—which we wish to encourage;
> Convertibility—which we wish to facilitate;
> Trade—which we wish to expand.

As the Eisenhower administration came to a close, World Bank consortia for India and Pakistan were emerging, a soft-loan window of the World Bank (IDA) existed, the IDB had been created, and the DLF was expanding its operations as part of the U.S. aid program. And on January 20, 1961, a president determined to make expanded development aid a central feature of his foreign policy was inaugurated.

Lacking a single executive focus for decision, the process of linking ideas and action occurred in a rather curious triangular way. The ideas were generated in universities and research institutions of which CENIS was a significant example but by no means unique. These ideas flowed in two important directions: to sympathetic members of Congress and their staffs; and to sympathetic members of the executive branch at both high and working levels. They flowed also to the World Bank and other international institutions, and, of course, to other academics and interested laymen in the United States and abroad.

Those working in the public service were by no means merely passive recipients and a transmission belt for the ideas generated outside; and the ideas that flowed to them, while based on intellectual concepts, were at least quasi-operational in form. CENIS, for example, felt that part of its duty was to understand the political context of action well enough to present its notions in ways which working politicians and bureaucrats could recognize as potentially realistic. There was thus an interacting osmotic process between those conducting research and generating ideas and those charged to act.

The triangle was closed by the quiet, faintly conspiratorial collaboration between sympathetic members of the Congress (and their staffs) with sympathetic officials of the executive branch (and their staffs).

The triangular process was framed by considerable propaganda activity conducted by both political and academic figures: books, articles, and letters to assorted editors; speeches and symposia; appearances before congressional committees;

etc. This protracted effort, conducted from 1954 to, say, Kennedy's election, was a kind of substitute for the clear presidential command decision Jackson sought from Eisenhower in 1954 and was refused.

Looking back at the intellectual struggle for development aid of the 1950s and at the political figures who joined early in the campaign, I would underline a chastening fact. The path-breaking victories won in the form of IDA, the IDB, the India and Pakistan consortia, the Alliance for Progress, and the Decade of Development did not come about because, at last, we persuaded the opposition that we were right. They came about because a series of crises emerged in the developing regions which forced on responsible politicians an acute awareness of the political and strategic danger of not assisting the process of development in Latin America, Africa, the Middle East, and Asia. It was Vice-President Nixon's difficulties in Lima and Caracas in May 1958 (promptly and skillfully exploited by President Kubitschek) that shifted the balance of power within the Eisenhower administration towards support for the IDB and other positive responses to Latin America's development needs long urged upon it; and Castro's emergence in 1959 as a working ally of Moscow was not irrelevant to easy Congressional acceptance of the Alliance for Progress. Similarly, the somewhat romantic image of economic and social progress in the P.R.C., during Mao's Great Leap Forward, assisted Kennedy, Cooper, and Black, via the Banker's Mission to India and Pakistan of early 1960, in setting in motion the World Bank consortia for those countries. Again, the Lebanon-Jordan crisis of August 1958 led President Eisenhower to propose a generous plan for regional development in the Middle East which, unfortunately, was not taken up. In fact, the whole critical period when the long-run foundations for development assistance were laid was framed by the protracted anxieties, in the United States and elsewhere, that followed the Soviet launching of the first satellite in October 1957. The story of the transition to large-scale sustained development aid is, thus, a vivid illustration of Jean Monnet's dictum: ". . . people only accept change when they are faced with necessity and only recognize necessity when a crisis is upon them." [104]

Nevertheless, the work of the development crusaders was not irrelevant. When governments in the advanced industrial world were forced by events to turn to the tasks of development, there existed a body of thought and doctrine, based on research, debate, and some practical experience, which permitted reasonably sensible courses of action to be fashioned quickly. And, perhaps most important of all, development thought and doctrine had been thrashed out between economists of the North and South. This lively process proceeded not only in universities, but also on the occasion of research and aid missions to developing countries and within the secretariats of the World Bank, the United Nations, and the regional economic commissions. It was, clearly, a two-way process of mutual education. The existence of this common framework of reference, often underpinned by close personal ties, rendered North-South collaboration much easier than it would otherwise have been once the institutional framework for development assistance was built and put to work in the late 1950s and early 1960s.

A fourth matter worth comment relates to a point made in Chapter 11. The arrival at the White House of John Kennedy, with his whole-hearted and deeply rooted acceptance of the doctrines of the development crusaders of the 1950s, did not launch a long era of expanded development assistance and amicable North-South relations.

There was, it is true, a brief interval of relative harmony with India and Latin America on which some still look back with nostalgia. So far as India was concerned, three factors account for this transient passage: the consolidation of the World Bank consortium arrangements behind the Third Five Year Plan; the prompt U.S. logistical support for the beleaguered Indian forces at the time of the border clash with

China late in 1962; and Kennedy's respect for Nehru and the human ties that developed between Indian and U.S. officials symbolized by Mrs. Kennedy's visit to India. These strands in the U.S.-Indian relation were not trivial. But beneath the surface there were, quite naturally, fundamental unresolved differences in perspective. By far the most important was the clash between the U.S. interest in a settlement between India and Pakistan and Nehru's determination to offer no concession whatsoever on Kashmir. From an Indian point of view (and sometimes the point of view of the U.S. ambassador in India), the continuing U.S. insistence on maintaining friendly relations with Pakistan, including some elements of military assistance, complicated relations with India. Of lesser importance were India's relations with the Soviet Union and the gap between the private and publically stated views of Indian officials on Southeast Asia. But it was the incapacity of India and Pakistan to resolve their problems that was, above any other factor, to complicate U.S. relations with India in the post-Kennedy years. Kennedy, although skeptical that an outsider could be effective, did all he could do to induce an India-Pakistan agreement; but he failed.[105]

Despite the complications of the Bay of Pigs, three rather similar factors yielded a transient interval of relative harmony in U.S. relations with Latin America: the launching of the Alliance for Progress; the extraordinary unforced hemispheric consensus that Khrushchev's missiles in Cuba were unacceptable; and Kennedy's charismatic appeal to Latin Americans. Again, beneath the surface, even in Kennedy's time, there were abiding unresolved problems that indicated U.S.-Latin American relationships were, in fact, suffused with latent elements of friction. There was, for example, the unwillingness of the Latin American countries located at some distance from the Caribbean to accept the domestic political tension of joining those closer (most notably, Venezuela) in combined efforts to limit Cuba's capacity for troublemaking across borders. This was the central issue at the January 1962 Punta del Este conference. And there were recurrent problems for Kennedy in the instability of domestic politics in Latin America yielding more military regimes than the common hemispheric aspirations for democracy would decree.

And beyond India and Latin America, Kennedy's wholehearted support for development assistance did not prove to be a panacea. He had difficulties with, among others, Sukarno, Nkrumah, and, after a promising start, Nasser.

The reason for those difficulties goes to the heart of what development aid could and could not accomplish in the context of U.S. foreign policy as a whole. Politicians in developing countries faced, like politicians everywhere else, difficult choices. The endemic raw material of politics was nationalism—in fact, a reactive nationalism—reacting against the memory of past intrusions, current intrusions, or feared intrusions from more advanced nations.[106] A reactive nationalism has been, in fact, the most powerful single force driving forward (and, at times, backward) the process of modernization.

But nationalism can be turned in any one of several directions. It can be turned outward to right real or believed past humiliations suffered on the world scene, or to exploit real or believed opportunities for national aggrandizement which appear for the first time as realistic possibilities once the new modern state is established and the economy develops some momentum. Nationalism can be held inward and focused on the political consolidation of the victory won by the national over the regionally based power; or it can be turned to the tasks of economic, social, and political modernization which have been obstructed by the old regionally based, usually aristocratic societal structure, by the former colonial power, or by both in coalition.

Once modern nationhood is established, different elements in the coalition press to mobilize the newly triumphant nationalist political sentiment in different directions: the soldiers, say, abroad; the professional politicians, to the triumph of the center over the region; the merchants, to economic development; the intellectuals, to social, political and legal reform.

The cast of policy at home and abroad of newly created or newly modernized states hinges greatly, then, on the balance of power within the coalition which emerges and the balance in which the various alternative objectives of nationalism are pursued. Quite often the critical balance is determined not by a clearly definable, stable coalition but by the character of the leader who happens to emerge out of the dynamics of early post-colonial politics.

In such settings—say, Indonesia, Ghana, and Egypt of the 1960s—where passionate domestic politics enjoyed an evident primacy, and external ambitions or anxieties sometimes outranked economic progress at home, development assistance could play only a limited role. It could strengthen the hand of those who, for their own reasons, sought to move their countries forward in a serious sustained effort at economic and social development. What it could not do is to force, say, a Sukarno, an Nhrumah, or a Nasser to concentrate his political energies and economic resources on development as opposed to other objectives to which he accorded, for his own reasons, a higher priority. Nor, evidently, could the existence of a flow of development aid guarantee that politics in developing countries would automatically assume democratic forms.

Some such insight into the nature of the political process in the developing countries is required to understand why the story of foreign aid in the 1960s and 1970s is crosscut at many points by disruptive crises and other circumstances which, for a time, lowered the legitimate claim of some developing countries for assistance and discouraged the donors.

In this setting the major achievement of the 1960s—and Kennedy's in particular—was to institutionalize a substantially larger share of development aid around serious, internationally recognized criteria, so that collaboration for development could proceed, damped, in part at least, from the oscillations in the mood of donors induced by the erratic course of North-South relations or changes in their own domestic and foreign policy preoccupations.

Given the image of economic and ideological competition between India and China which played so significant a role in the debates on aid for India in 1958–1959, it is worth reflecting briefly on that dimension of the story with the benefit of hindsight.

In first approximation, the actual evolution of events, as compared to the conventional wisdom of the time, is a splendid example of irony in history. The apparently close alliance of the U.S.S.R. and P.R.C. of 1958–1959 has given way to exacerbated confrontation while India has sustained reasonably amicable relations with both the U.S.S.R. and the West; Mao's economic doctrines and policies, so politically impressive to some in the 1950s, led the P.R.C. into a dead end from which China's rulers are painfully seeking to extricate themselves, moving towards some version of a mixed economy with an important role for private incentives and, perhaps, a private sector. Meanwhile India's mixed economy moves forward in a pattern of reasonably stable, if modest, progress, though it is also burdened by an excessive "state bourgeoisie." With respect to agriculture, the dramatic measures of collectivization in the P.R.C. of the 1950s proved, as elsewhere, inhibiting. They left China in the early 1980s heavily dependent on food imports, whereas India has, for the time, achieved self-sufficiency, although at a relatively low average nutritional level. By 1984 China had drawn a basic lesson from its relative experience, having launched a new system of agriculture based on family incentives and responsibilities.

As the CENIS studies of Communist China in the 1950s indicate, it was by no means impossible to predict that Mao's economic policies were wrong-headed and the Sino-Soviet tie potentially unstable; but none of us would have dared predict that things would look quite the way they do as of 1984.

So far as economic development is concerned, the central

fact is that both countries confronted—and still confront—an extremely difficult task: the modernization of a vast, low productivity agriculture under conditions of decelerating but still high rates of population increase. The problems of modernizing rural life and of excessive rates of population increase are critical challenges for virtually all contemporary developing nations. It is the extraordinary scale of the Chinese and Indian problems that deserve special comment.

Industrial development is inherently easier than agricultural development. Capital and technology must, of course, be mobilized as well as private or public entrepreneurs, engineers, managers, a working force of appropriate skills, transport and other infrastructures. But, to a degree, capital, technology, engineers and, in some cases, entrepreneurs can be imported. Physically, industrial plants are concentrated in space. One localized effort, in which all the required elements are brought together, can yield a significant percentage increase in national output in a given industrial sector. Against the background of cumulative initiatives that began in mid nineteenth-century India and at about the turn of the century in China, these two countries, as noted earlier (pp. 30–31), command substantial industrial establishments of increasing technological sophistication.

Progress in agriculture and in birth control is a quite different process. Tens of thousands of villages and millions of families are involved. In agriculture, adequate price incentives can affect the decisions of many farmers, and in birth control, mass communications can help carry the word. But, in fact, the diffusion of new agricultural technologies and of new attitudes toward family size is slow business. Basically, this is why India and China, two of the most technologically advanced developing countries, still have low per capita real incomes and have experienced relatively low average rates of growth in real income per capita as compared to many smaller developing countries at equivalent or lower levels of technological sophistication.

Although the simple conventional image of a potentially decisive test of democracy in India versus Communist dictatorship in China as political instruments for economic and social progress was drastically altered by developments in China and in Sino-Soviet relations, in a larger sense the test of Communist versus non-Communist methods in Asia did take place over the past quarter-century. As of 1984 the Communists clearly have not won. Indeed, it is evident that the current rulers of the P.R.C. have been impressed by and sought to learn from some of the cases of remarkable success in non-Communist Asia, including Taiwan.

As for India, its prospects never generated the romantic visions stirred by Mao's policies of the 1950s. A brilliant review of the state of the Indian economy in the London *Economist* (March 28, 1981) begins:

> India has always been a fashionable object of gloom. Since independence, each decade has thrown up a new threat to the country's foundations. In the 1940s, it was communal violence—understandably, after perhaps half a million people had been killed in six weeks. In the 1950s, secession was supposedly in the air as the neatly drafted constitutional clauses governing relations between Delhi and the (now 22) states started to crack under the strain of regional and linguistic rivalries. In the 1960s, the 'life-boat' theory of a planet doomed by Malthusian shortages cast India as the natural candidate for being chucked overboard, the better to save the others. In the 1970s Mrs. Gandhi's emergency seemed to confirm long-standing doubts that India could be governed democratically.
> On all four counts the pessimists have been wrong.[107]

Nevertheless, India confronts severe problems, notably in the industrial sector. Oddly enough, they bear a family relationship to a key problem the current leaders of the P.R.C. are trying to overcome: over-reliance on bureaucratic control over the economy. In the case of the P.R.C. this problem is a heritage of Communist doctrine and the imperatives of Communist politics, against the background of the much older heritage of the mandarin central bureaucracy. In the Indian case, there is the inheritance from the British of a large civil service whose role was strengthened by the autarchical bias of early planning designs as well as by the anti-capitalist biases of some of India's leaders reflecting, perhaps, their sympathetic associations with British Labour Party leaders and intellectuals. In addition, as noted earlier, non-economic forces of these kinds were strengthened by the need to allocate scarce foreign exchange.

Whatever the origins of the problem, virtually all hands now agree, including the Indian government, that a state bourgeoisie with vested interests in the perpetuation of its own power and authority has emerged, whose heavy administrative hand and substantive biases have radically throttled back the rate of growth in the industrial sector and produced some serious distortions in the balance of the Indian economy. On the other hand, the trauma of the food crisis of 1965–1967 and, perhaps, a salutary nationalist reaction to the severe pressures applied by President Johnson, in the context of U.S. aid, to elevate the priority of agricultural production, have resulted in precisely the result Johnson sought: a surge of output and the maintenance in recent years of substantial grain stocks and, even, a low level of net grain exports. In India the diffusion of the Green Revolution has clearly bought valuable time, although the deceleration of the rate of population increase has probably been less than in China, and Indian self-sufficiency in food is not yet guaranteed for the long pull.

There is still another problem shared by the two giants of the developing world: an inadequate linkage of their scientific and technological capacity to many key sectors of their economies. In military production, atomic energy, and space activities effective linkages have, by and large, been developed. And, in varying degree, this has happened or is happening in agriculture. Chinese intellectual life was, of course, severely set back by the impact of the Cultural Revolution; but the basic problem in both countries appears to be in the failure to create close osmotic ties between elite scientific research institutes and the conventional industrial sectors. (The failure is not unlike that of the American motor vehicle, steel, and machine tool industries to build the kind of linkages to the research and development community which have maintained the vitality of the chemical, electronic, and aerospace sectors.) As the world economy moves on from the technologies of steel, metalworking, and the basic industrial chemicals to the microchip, genetics, the laser, robots, and new industrial materials—all of which are or are likely soon to be highly relevant to economies at the stage of the Indian and Chinese—this failure of institutional linkage could prove costly.

Looking back on the terms in which the China-India comparison was viewed in 1958–1959 one simple fact does emerge: with the exception of Mrs. Gandhi's brief emergency period, Indian democracy has survived. Given the extraordinary character of the subcontinent—its scale, low real income levels, multiplicity of languages and racial strains, the complexity of relations between the center and the states—this is, in my view, the greatest of the "miracles" in the developing world of the past three decades. The fact that Indian planning and administration were excessively intrusive—a circumstance perceived by P. T. Bauer (and others) in the 1950s—did not put Indian political life on the road to serfdom.

Up to this point, the story of foreign aid has been told from a partisan point of view; that is, the author's frankly acknowledged biases and involvement have been permitted to shape the analysis, defining heroes and villains, successes and setbacks. But it is time now to ask skeptically two questions, the answers to which have been thus far assumed: Were Soviet aid policies in the developing world, in the 1950s, as significant a challenge as Eisenhower, Dulles and others judged them to be? And, more fundamental, looking back from the 1980s, were the long range programs of development aid launched by the advanced industrial countries in the 1950s worth the effort?

Like all counter-factual questions in history these are difficult to answer with a high degree of confidence. This is peculiarly true of the question of Soviet aid because Soviet and U.S. policies, in this domain as in others, was interactive; that is, the Soviet aid and trade policies launched after Stalin's death were, in part, a response to Point Four and subsequent U.S. initiatives of the early 1950s just as later U.S. aid policies responded, in part, to the believed challenge of Soviet policies in India and elsewhere. It is, therefore, impossible to predict what policies Moscow would have pursued if the United States, along with Western Europe and Japan, had not launched the policies it did starting in the late 1950s. There are, nevertheless, a few observations that can be made with reasonable confidence.

First, as noted earlier (pp. 17–18), the bulk of Moscow's economic aid to non-Communist countries in the 1950s was concentrated at a relatively few points of serious strategic interest to the Soviet Union. For example, as of February 1, 1958, 87 percent of Soviet bloc economic aid went to Afghanistan, Egypt, India, Indonesia, and Syria. In ten other countries it kept its hand in with small or modest loans or grants.

In response to its own progressively widening strategic and political efforts in the developing world the list of major Soviet aid efforts increased with the passage of time. But as Table 13 shows, over the whole period 1954–1979, 63 percent of total economic aid went to nine countries, with only Indonesia and Egypt (1975–1979) dropped from the 1958 list. The lesser degree of concentration represents quite substantial Soviet efforts in Tunisia, Turkey, Iran, a number of sub-Saharan countries, and Latin America. The role in development aid of the Communist governments of Eastern Eu-

TABLE 13. U.S.S.R.: Economic Aid Agreements with Major Non-Communist LDC Clients, 1955–1979[1]
(millions of U.S. dollars)

	1955–64	1965–74	1975–79	Total
Total	3,805	6,255	8,120	18,190
Middle East	1,450	2,520	3,895	7,870
Egypt	1,000	440	0	1,440
Iran	65	725	375	1,165
Iraq	185	370	150	705
Syria	100	360	310	770
Other	100	625	3,060	3,790
North Africa	250	300	2,365	2,920
Algeria	230	195	290	715
Morocco	0	100	2,000	2,100
Other	20	5	75	105
South Asia	1,440	2,355	1,185	4,980
Afghanistan	530	300	450	1,290
India	810	1,130	340	2,280
Pakistan	40	655	225	920
Other	60	270	170	490
Sub-Saharan Africa	490	380	335	1,200
Latin America	30	595	340	965
East Asia	150	110	NEGL	260

[1] Because of rounding, components may not add to the totals shown.

Source: National Foreign Assessment Center, *Communist Aid Activities in Non-Communist Less Developed Countries, 1979 and 1954–1979*, Washington, D.C., October 1980 (ER-80-10318U), p. 7.

rope expanded over this quarter-century. The strategic character of the Communist program is suggested by the fact that, for the whole period 1954–1979, military aid agreements to non-Communist countries totaled $52.8 billion; economic aid agreements, $33.0. OECD official aid over the same period approximated $190 billion.

The Communist aid effort in the non-Communist developing world has evidently been serious, long-term in character, and backed by an impressive flow of resources. But what would it have been if the OECD shift to development aid had not occurred in the late 1950s? One can only guess at an answer. One clue is that the Communist effort has been notably enterprising, alert to Western vulnerabilities, energetic in its exploitation, and undiscouraged by the need to write off failures from time to time; *e.g.*, in Indonesia and Egypt. It is therefore reasonable to assume that if the United States and other advanced countries had not responded to, say, Indian and Latin American needs in the late 1950s, the Soviet Union might well have done so with greater vigor; and that Moscow's political and strategic influence and authority in the developing regions would probably be considerably greater than it is at present.

There is, however, a significant caveat to be made on this point. The driving political force in the developing regions is, palpably, nationalism. To estimate that enlarged Soviet economic aid, without an answering U.S. effort, would have increased Moscow's influence in the developing regions is not to conclude that many more countries would have been brought directly under Soviet control. In fact, military assistance has been a more powerful lever in that respect than economic aid because of the dependence on spare parts and replacements it creates. Even then, several countries have broken out of that dependence when their national objectives clashed starkly with those of the U.S.S.R.; *e.g.*, Egypt and Indonesia.

Put another way, the fact that the U.S. did commit itself seriously to programs of development aid did not increase the number of U.S. military and political allies; but it probably did create a better balance between U.S. and Soviet political influence than would have otherwise existed. Beyond that one can not safely go.

This brings us to a larger question: Has development lending been a good thing? Are the lives of men, women, and children in the developing regions better than they would have been if, say, the doctrines of the chairman of the Randall Commission had prevailed and the advanced industrial countries had confined themselves to technical assistance or no aid whatsoever in their relations with the developing regions?

First, some background facts. Supported by external aid, the aggregate average performance of the developing regions in the 1960s and 1970s approximated or exceeded our earlier hopes, falling in the range of 4.5–5.5 percent per annum, yielding an average increase in GNP per capita of 1.6 percent for low-income countries, 3.8 percent for those in the World Bank's middle-income range (generally, what I define as the drive to technological maturity). The former figure approximated the nineteenth century performance of the presently advanced industrial countries during take-off (1.7 percent); the latter substantially exceeded the earlier performance during the drive to technological maturity (2.1 percent).[108] And these aggregate growth rates were strongly reflected in such basic social indicators as length of life and level of education: by World Bank calculations life expectancy increased from 42 to 57 in low-income countries between 1960 and 1979, from 53 to 61 in middle-income countries; population per physician more than halved in both categories; adult literacy rose from 27 to 43 percent in low-income countries; between 1960 and 1976, from 53 to 72 percent in middle-income countries; the numbers enrolled in secondary schools and higher education about doubled in both categories. As we all know, there is a long way to go; but sustained economic growth in the third quarter of the twentieth century was not a statistical artifact nor a process insulated from the life of the average citizen.[109]

I would share, then, I. G. Patel's summation:

> I for one do not . . . believe that this record of growth is vitiated to any significant degree by growing inequalities in

incomes. While those glib of tongue may repeat the cliché of the rich getting richer and the poor getting poorer, and while the first part of this statement is almost universally true, I doubt if there are many countries where the second part of the charge is even remotely valid. The poor may seem poorer to eyes which are getting accustomed to plenty, and this is perhaps as it should be. But impatience with what could and should be should not lead to the denigration of the good that has already taken place. Even Europe and North America never achieved in the heyday of capitalism and imperialism before the first world war the kind of rates of growth they have witnessed in the past twenty or thirty years. The socialist world, despite signs of stress, has also maintained its share in total world GDP [Gross Domestic Product] around 15 or 16% of the total, so that they too on an average have not lagged behind in the race for economic progress. The credit for this record of performance everywhere must go primarily to national effort. But international co-operation has certainly been an essential and important ingredient.[110]

What about Patel's final sentence? Granted that there has been substantial economic and social progress in the developing regions, uneven as it is among countries and, often, within countries, the relevant question here is whether development aid contributed significantly to this outcome. As in the case of Soviet aid policies no such counter-factual question in history can be firmly answered. One simply cannot trace out all the substantial consequences of removing one significant variable from the equation. Any attempt to answer the question is, therefore, inherently arbitrary, impressionistic, and personal.

It is possible to argue that development is, in the end, primarily a matter of self-help, and aid, while not trivial, clearly not decisive. Total investment in the developing regions has been generated overwhelmingly from domestic resources— say, 90 percent; and net official development assistance may now account for only about 6 percent of total gross investment. But in certain cases the availability of development aid clearly bought time for nations to find their feet and go forward on their own; and the flows of development assistance from abroad encouraged private investment and stimulated domestic investment, public and private, in certain important sectors. External capital carried with it certain supplementary advantages: it provided scarce foreign exchange; it often carried with it the transfer of new technologies, entrepreneurship, and technical upgrading of the working force; and it focussed attention and resources on specific projects, regions and targets of opportunity that might not otherwise have been addressed so promptly—if at all. In other cases, however, it may have postponed, at some cost, confrontation with reality. I am inclined to think, for example, that some, at least, of the P.L. 480 loans and grants in the 1950s and 1960s were counter-productive. They carried with them the illusion that U.S. grain surpluses, beyond the capacity of commercial markets to absorb, were a permanent feature of the world economy. They may well have slowed up the adoption of effective agricultural policies in certain developing countries.[111] Any knowledgeable observer of the scene can cite both individual loans and country loan programs that yielded, to put it mildly, disappointing results. Like the private sector, the world of ODA—official development assistance—has had its Edsels.

It has also been argued that without development aid, with its encouragement of planning, the economies of the developing countries would have been less centralized, more reliant on the price system and the bracing winds of competitive private enterprise. This I disbelieve. The odds are that the strains on their balance of payments would have pushed developing countries toward even more authoritarian solutions, and they would now be more dominated than they are by compulsive central planning mechanisms, less open to the disciplines of domestic and international price competition.

218

But I am skeptical that any kind of satisfactory approximation of an answer can be established by argument, one way or another, in these more or less economic terms. I would judge the decisive considerations to be three; and they are all political.

1. The existence of institutionalized development aid elevated the stature of the men and women in the governments in developing countries who were seriously committed to economic and social development and capable of formulating the case for assistance in terms of internationally recognized standards. After all, external resources are, in the short run, extremely important to hard-pressed governments in developing regions; and those capable of negotiating successfully for such resources become important national assets. From close observation of many developing countries, I have no doubt that the domestic priority of development was thus heightened.[112]

2. In an inherently divisive world, with ample capacity to generate international violence, institutionalized development aid has been perhaps the strongest tempering force, quietly at work, giving some operational meaning to the notion of a human community with serious elements of common interest.

3. The existence of institutionalized development aid helped damp, to a significant degree, the domestic conflicts inherent in the modernization process in those countries which pursued reasonably balanced, purposeful, and sustained development programs; and that, rather than the prompt adoption of the institutions of Western democracy, was a critical part of the case for foreign aid.

A word now about foreign aid and the Cold War. As we have seen, various Cold War crises served as the catalyst which altered the political balance in the struggle of the 1950s for enlarged development assistance. But that fact had its costs. The flow of aid has, to a degree, remained responsive, in both its direction and scale, to the intensity of the

Cold War dimension in policy toward the developing regions. But it is also true, to a degree, that development aid was institutionalized, notably through the enterprise of the World Bank in the regimes of Eugene Black, George Woods, and Robert McNamara, and through the regional development banks. It is no small thing that, by World Bank calculations, official development assistance was expected to approximate $29 billion in 1981 from the members of the OECD, and perhaps $5 billion from OPEC. Aid from Communist governments to non-Communist developing countries approximated $2.6 billion in 1979. There are those who believe these sums are too low, too high, and/or misdirected or misused in one manner or another. Foreign aid has never been a subject that lent itself to easy consensus or complacency. Nevertheless, it is a unique historical phenomenon that the advanced industrial countries have recognized an interest in the economic fate of the developing countries worth the regular allocation of something like .35 percent of GNP.[113]

As I. G. Patel has written: "The whole concept of international economic co-operation is of such recent origin and so novel that it has perhaps not registered itself strongly on the consciousness of ordinary people anywhere. And yet, the achievements in this field are so impressive by any realistic standards that it would be foolish to overlook them and positively harmful not to preserve them and indeed to build further upon them."[114]

But still, the seriousness of the larger northern governments about development has tended to fluctuate with the scale and locus of conflicts in the South. And this has reduced one of the advantages we believed would flow from the kind of steady long-term approach some of us advocated in the 1950s; that is, it reduced the possibility of heading off crises that might otherwise occur. Moreover, aid granted in the midst of crisis is generally less efficient, dollar for dollar, than aid granted steadily in support of ongoing development programs.

My final reflection concerns a still larger issue: is regular growth still a legitimate objective for the developing regions? Do global resource limitations decree that the old devil, diminishing returns, will soon generate a global crisis unless the developing regions and the advanced industrial countries level off promptly, adopt new, less materialistic criteria for the good life, and even things out within the human family by drastic redistribution of income and wealth within national societies and among nations? This was, of course, the theme of *The Limits to Growth*.[115] That study was subjected to the careful criticism its radical conclusion deserved; and the flaws revealed in the analysis diminished the inevitability of its apocalyptic judgment, as the authors came to acknowledge.

But quite aside from the potentialities for continuing to fend off diminishing returns through man's ingenuity—as we have done for two centuries—there is no evidence that *The Limits to Growth* prescription is politically, socially, and psychologically viable. On the contrary, the thrust for higher real incomes by less advantaged groups and nations is one of the most powerful forces operating on the world scene; and so is the determination of advantaged nations and social groups to sustain and even improve their material status. Thus far the tensions generated by these ambitions have been softened because the pie to be divided was expanding. It is one thing to quarrel about fair shares when all are gaining in real income; the struggle for fair shares is a more dour matter in the face of a static or low growth rate in real income per capita.

But trees do not grow to the sky. It is wholly possible, even certain, that, with the passage of time, man's perceptions of affluence will change; or change will be forced upon him. More than two decades ago, in writing *The Stages of Economic Growth*, I raised the question of what would happen in the richer societies when "diminishing relative marginal utility sets in, on a mass basis, for real income itself." The problem was much discussed in the 1960s. A margin of the more affluent young went into revolt against the values of material progress and the consequences of those values as they perceived them. They sought nonmaterial objectives. And a no-growth strand exists in the politics of most advanced industrial countries. But it is not a majority view. The fact is that, among both the early- and latecomers to industrialization, we must count on a protracted period of effort to continue to grow. Right or wrong, the odds are that the effort will be made; and serious policy-making should be based on that probability. As a black colleague of mine once said, the disadvantaged of this world are about to buy tickets for the show; they are quite unmoved by the affluent emerging from the theater and pronouncing the show bad; they are determined to find out for themselves.

That determination underlines the urgency of the kind of North-South functional cooperation outlined in Chapter 11. The problems of energy, food, raw materials and the environment that we confront in the world economy may not decree an end to industrial growth after, say, a run of 250 years from the late eighteenth century. But those problems are real and still degenerative; that is, they will worsen with the passage of time unless national and international policies change.

In the end, those policies should reflect the universal stake, shared equally between the North and South—and, I would add, East and West—in a continuity of industrial civilization which would permit us to level off in population and, later, in real income per capita when we are so minded, not by bitter Malthusian or other resource-related crises. The most primitive self-interest should, then, bring nations and peoples close to accepting the injunction of the poet after whom I happen to be named, to which I have often returned:

> One thought ever at the fore—
> That in the Divine Ship, the World,
> breasting Time and Space,
> All peoples of the globe together sail,
> sail the same voyage,
> Are bound to the same destination.

Appendix A

The State Department Opposes the Kennedy-Cooper Resolution, May 1, 1958

[*Note*: This polite but ultimately chilling State Department letter, expressing the desirability of avoiding "resolutions limited to individual countries," incorporates the position around which a good deal of the opposition to the Kennedy-Cooper resolution rallied in 1958, and forced a modification of the resolution in 1959. (Source: Papers of John F. Kennedy, Pre-Presidential Papers, Senate Files, Holborn Subject File, "India, 3/29/58—9/6/60" folder, box 562.)]

DEPARTMENT OF STATE
Washington

May 1, 1958

Dear Senator Green:

I refer to my interim reply of March 28 to your request for the Department of State's comments on Senate Concurrent Resolution 74 "To express the sense of Congress on the importance of the economic development of India" and wish at this time to give you the Department of State's observations on this resolution.

The Department of State welcomes this evidence of the growing recognition of the importance of India and its successful development through democratic techniques. We are in wholehearted agreement that the economic progress of India is, like that of many other countries, essential to the accomplishment of United States foreign objectives.

India has, as you know, embarked on a Second Five-Year-Plan designed to provide a sound basis for long-term growth. The Indian development effort is being carried forward with vigor and determination and within a democratic framework. We are especially gratified with the major and growing role which is being played in this effort by private business.

India has had to curtail the Second Five-Year-Plan for lack of foreign exchange resources. For these reasons the United States Government is taking several important measures to provide development financing for India. The Export-Import Bank and the Development Loan Fund are extending lines of credit of $150 million and $75 million respectively. Substantial shipments of United States agricultural commodities are going forward under PL 480.

These measures help to meet only the immediate Indian problem. Continuing programs will be needed to achieve development objectives in our foreign policy interests not only in India but in many other countries.

The concept expressed in the resolution of enlisting the cooperation of other Free World countries in mutual endeavors to secure Free World objectives is also one which the Department of State endorses wholeheartedly. Every effort is being made to encourage such cooperative activity for the best interests of all.

Thus, the Department endorses and welcomes the concepts embodied in the resolution of the importance to us of the economic development of India and the desirability of enlisting the cooperation of other Free World countries. We wish to note additionally that these objectives apply equally to many other Free World countries. As a general rule, therefore, the Department believes it desirable to avoid resolutions limited to individual countries.

I trust these comments will be helpful to you and your Committee.

Sincerely yours,

William B. Macomber, Jr.
Assistant Secretary

Appendix B

*The Arguments against the Kennedy-Cooper
Resolution on the Senate Floor, June 6, 1958*

[*Note*: This is a radically edited-down version of the vigorous debate of
June 6 and the vote on the Kennedy-Cooper resolution. Editing is designed to capture both the arguments adduced and something of the flavor of the opposition; that is, support for Bridges' amendment. The full
text of the debate is to be found in the Congressional Record, 85th Congress, Second Session, Vol. 104, Part 8, pp. 10396–10414.]

Mr. BRIDGES. Mr. President, my amendment proposes to strike
from the committee bill section 2, the sense-of-Congress provision
regarding India's second 5-year plan. . . .

If the committee amendment is adopted, India will be the only
nation—of the more than 60 nations the United States is aiding—
which will be mentioned in the statement of policy in the entire
act.

To me, this would be a mistake on the part of the Congress. . . .

As the committee bill is drafted, for example, the expression of
Congressional interest in the Western Hemisphere is relegated to
the tail end of the bill. Such discrimination against the nations of the
Western Hemisphere, most of whom have been our friendly allies
far longer than India, is shocking to me. . . .

In many respects, I think it is unfortunate the committee has confronted the Senate with this issue. The danger of generating ill will
is inherent in the proposal. . . .

Mr. THYE. The Senator from New Hampshire has made a very
valid point. We might find ourselves highly embarrassed among

other nations next year if they said, "You will have to include us specifically in the construction of the bill; otherwise we will not believe you to be acting in good faith relative to us." Is not that what the Senator from New Hampshire is contending?

Mr. FLANDERS. After talking with scores of people in India, my conviction was that the first 5-year plan was well conceived, well carried out, and benefited the country.

I shall not develop my objections to the second 5-year plan, in connection with which we are asked to assist India to complete successfully her current program for economic development. But fundamentally it seeks to install labor-saving processes in a labor-surplus country. That would make for disorganization and unemployment and for disaster in India. So under no circumstances would I vote for such a proposal.

What India needs is more and better food, better clothing, better shelter, and better education for individuals.

The first 5-year plan was directed toward that objective. The second 5-year plan is directed toward industrial development—to see how many tons of steel can be manufactured there, to see how high production statistics can go. It is based directly on the program of the Soviet Government and the Red Chinese Government. . . .

So I have two reasons for wanting to get rid of the section. One is the reason which has been expressed, the singling out of India, in the face of the feeling of the South American countries, for instance, that they are being neglected. The second reason is that it seems to me the section does not recognize the nature of the support we can give to India which will be most helpful to the Indian people.

• • •

Mr. MALONE. Mr. President, I read a portion of the provision. I should like to ask the distinguished Senator from New Hampshire just what other nations join the United States in providing support for India or any other nation.

Just what other nations are assisting in furnishing this mutual aid to India?

Mr. BRIDGES. So far as I know, no other nation on earth is furnishing aid to India, certainly on the basis on which we are contributing. Perhaps some nations have made loans to India, but I am not familiar with them.

• • •

Mr. MALONE. I object to financing our competition. India is a great nation. I, too, visited India for a brief time. This is no reflection on Mr. Nehru, he regulates his own life; but my personal opinion is that he is a Communist and does not even know it. That is the way he operates. Whenever he has to make a statement, he is a neutral as between Russia and the United States. If a fight ever starts between the two countries, he will be on Russia's side, because he will have to be.

For 5,000 years India has had tremendous natural resources. Some of her mineral resources are perhaps greater than the United States has had. The standard of living of the Indian people has not been materially changed in that length of time.

Now, however, we have taken it upon ourselves to aid the whole world, by using our money, the cash of the taxpayers of America, and by dividing the markets of the workingmen and investors of America. It is our plan to bring the 500 million people of India up to our standard of living in the next few years.

• • •

Latest reports show there are more than 5 million unemployed in this country. Workers are fast being thrown out of employment in the textile industry in the New England states. No crockery manufacture is left in this country of any magnitude. The machine-tool industry is going down. In fact, we in this country cannot manufacture monkey wrenches in competition with $2 foreign labor. We give $4 billion a year to other nations so they may build plants to compete with our domestic production.

. . . . Mr. CASE of South Dakota. My general feeling [on foreign aid in general] is that we should be reducing the dollar amount involved. . . . At the present time, in view of the uncertain state of affairs, I am not in favor of abandoning the program, or anything like that. However, I think that starting a new or special program for a particular country would be a step in the wrong direction. . . .

. . . . Mr. ERVIN. Mr. President, the incorporation of this statement in the bill by the Committee on Foreign Relations was a serious mistake. I think it was a serious mistake from the standpoint of foreign policy. It proposes, in substance, that Congress make a pledge to one nation. But when we make a pledge of assistance to one nation, other nations will rise up and ask, "Why does the United States abstain from making a like pledge for our benefit?" . . . The pledge to

India will arouse antagonism against the United States by other nations. . . .

. . . . Mr. JENNER. Certainly this provision would be looked upon by the people of India, and certainly it would be represented by our State Department to future Congresses, as a moral commitment.

Why establish a precedent, as was suggested last night in connection with the amendment of the Senator from Massachusetts [Mr. KENNEDY].

Furthermore, I have not heard any Senator mention one of the countries that has proven vitally effective as our friend and has stood with us while the going was rough. While India has taken a position of neutralism, Pakistan has stood with us. Although the circumstances which apply to India are similar to those which apply to Pakistan, this provision refers only to India. . . .

. . . Mr. REVERCOMB. I join with the Senator in his great admiration for India. I admire the progress India has made and is making. But the Senator's own statement makes me feel that we may be singling out one nation over other nations which we may want to help. . . .

. . . Mr. DIRKSEN. . . . I thought that somewhere in the record there might be an embracing of the amendment by the Department of State. However, I notice at page 304 of the hearings, in connection with the discussion of the matter, the following statement by Mr. Rountree, of the State Department:

> "I am not sure that it is desirable to single out a particular country from many nations which do have urgent requirements for aid."

I have gone through the hearings, and Mr. Rountree, representing the Department of State, says, "I am not sure that it is desirable."

I do not know whether we are to determine the foreign policy, or whether it is to be directed by the Department of State. It may be that we have 97 Secretaries of State. However, I am always a little timid about venturing into this field. The distinguished Senator from Massachusetts, in effect, said, "Well, when we express the sense of the Senate, it is not a commitment." What is the sense of the Senate? Is it not the opinion of the Senate? Is it not the discernment of the Senate? Is it not the judgment of the Senate? Is it not the conviction of the Senate? What does the Committee on Foreign Relations say in its report? Let us look at page 7. I wish to read only a paragraph from the report:

> "The Indian second 5-year plan is now in a critical phase. The purpose of the amendment is to let the Indian people know that the Congress supports the efforts they are making. The amendment will also let the executive branch know that the Congress approves of steps to aid India. And most important, it will serve as a stimulus to American efforts to enlist other free countries in a united assault on India's economic problems.
>
> "The amendment is a statement of policy."

Either I can understand the English language or I cannot. This language has only one significance to me. I wish to be sure that it is incorporated in the RECORD.

We now go back to the amendment for a moment. It states that it is the sense of Congress that we provide assistance to India. I regard that as a moral commitment. How are we to provide the assistance? It says we are to provide the type that is necessary, the magnitude that is necessary, and for a duration that is necessary. It says adequate assistance. Someone else's ideas of adequate and mine may be entirely different.

However, I shall have to sit in the Committee on Appropriations when this matter comes along and pass on the question of adequacy. When the testimony comes, I may have one view; the Department of State may have other views. Once this language is written into the bill, they will point an accusing finger and say, "You will have betrayed a commitment of Congress to India if you fail to provide aid of a certain type, of a certain magnitude, for a certain period, and in an amount which is adequate."

For what purpose? To complete—that is what it says—to complete the current program. How far complete it? Successfully. That is what it says. I do not know whether I have ever encountered a moral commitment in my life, but if I have, this is it.

Let us not forget that there are two groups who will be reading the language. We will be reading it. We may say it is only a gesture. They will read it in Bombay, they will read it in New Delhi. They will read it in Calcutta. They will read it up in Kashmir. They will read it in Karachi. It will be for them also to say whether it was a commitment or not. It takes two, because it is a two-way street.

If it is the desire of the Senate to tie our hands now, very well. But I want to be on record this afternoon. While this is the 6th day of June, 1958, this matter will start cooling a little bit, and we will forget about the solemnity and about the importance of the language we write into the bill today. Therefore I wish to be sure that my hands are not completely tied before I make what I think is a proper protest.

I wish to add one thought before I conclude. The State Department and the President direct our foreign policy. I have seen no statement from the President on this point. I have seen no statement from the Secretary of State. He has repeatedly testified as to the importance and the significance of India in the whole world picture. . . .

. . . . The PRESIDING OFFICER.

The clerk will call the roll.

The legislative clerk called the roll.

The result was announced—yeas 35, nays 47, as follows:

YEAS-35

Anderson	Bricker	Case, S. Dak.
Beall	Bridges	Chavez
Bennett	Butler	Curtis
Bible	Capehart	Dirksen
Dworshak	Jordan	Russell
Eastland	Knowland	Stennis
Ervin	Kuchel	Talmadge
Frear	Langer	Thurmond
Goldwater	Lausche	Thye
Hoblitzell	Malone	Watkins
Hruska	Mundt	Williams
Jenner	Potter	

NAYS-47

Aiken	Carlson	Church
Allott	Carroll	Clark
Bush	Case, N.J.	Cooper

Douglas
Ellender
Flanders
Fulbright
Gore
Green
Hayden
Hennings
Hickenlooper
Hill
Holland
Humphrey
Jackson

Javits
Johnson, Tex.
Kefauver
Kennedy
Magnuson
Mansfield
Martin, Iowa
McClellan
McNamara
Monroney
Morse
Morton
Murray

Neuberger
Pastore
Payne
Proxmire
Purtell
Smathers
Smith, Maine
Smith, N.J.
Sparkman
Symington
Wiley
Young

NOT VOTING-14

Barrett
Byrd
Cotton
Ives
Johnston, S.C.

Kerr
Long
Martin, Pa.
O'Mahoney
Revercomb

Robertson
Saltonstall
Schoeppel
Yarborough

So Mr. BRIDGES' motion was rejected.

Appendix C

The Rise and Fall of the "Baldwin Plan"

[*Note*: This appendix is an account of the formulation in 1954 of the "Baldwin Plan" for enlarged aid to Asia, supported by John Foster Dulles and destroyed by Herbert Hoover, Jr. It was written by Charles F. Baldwin, later U.S. Ambassador to Malaysia, and made available for this book. It is a classic account of how the bureaucratic process can be used to drain virtually all substance from a potentially powerful initiative.]

In early June, 1954, the Economic Coordinator for the Far East* prepared and circulated to the Office Directors in the Bureau of Far Eastern Affairs a paper outlining certain economic aspects of the Far East situation which appeared to be particularly significant with respect to efforts to prevent the further spread of Communism in free Asia. Following a discussion of the adverse developments, from the standpoint of U.S. interests, which had occurred in Asia since World War II, the paper considered the relationship between elements of economic weakness in the free Asian countries, efforts to achieve greater political stability in those countries, and opportunities for the extension of Communist influence there. The paper concluded that there was a definite and important relationship—that persistent economic weakness particularly in the newly independent countries of Asia constitutes an open invitation for the spread of Communism and that, conversely, successful efforts to strengthen

*Baldwin's title at that time, later changed to Deputy Assistant Secretary for Far East Economic Affairs.

the economies of free Asian countries would enhance the ability of those countries to resist Communism. It was suggested in the paper that U.S. security interests would be served by increased efforts on the part of the U.S. to strengthen free Asian economies and to encourage greater economic cooperation among the free Asian countries.

These views expressed in the paper were approved by the three Office Directors of the Bureau.

Earlier in April, the Economic Coordinator had organized a departmental working party comprising representatives of FE, E, and EUR [the Far East, Economic, and European bureaus of the State Department] to study the question of Far Eastern regional cooperation. After receiving the responses of FE office directors to the views expressed in the paper mentioned above, he decided to expand the functions of this working party to include consideration of other means whereby the U.S. might contribute to a more rapid economic growth of the countries of free Asia. He decided also to include in the working party representatives of S/P and OIR [Policy Planning Staff and Office of Intelligence Research].

After the working party was thus expanded in membership and objective, Mr. Bowie, Director of the Policy Planning Staff, who was aware of its existence, informed the Economic Coordinator that the Secretary had recently asked whether U.S. actions in the economic field as a means of deterring Communism in Asia were sufficient. During the ensuing discussion the Secretary was notified of the departmental working party which had been organized by FE and he apparently instructed the Director of the Policy Planning Staff to take an active interest in its activities.

About the same time a few meetings were held with the Secretary to discuss the matter. As these meetings occurred before the Working Party submitted its report, only provisional reports of the progress of the study could be made to the Secretary. He appeared in those meetings to be aware of the relationship between economic weakness and Communist opportunities in Asia and to believe that positive future action by the U.S. would decrease economic weakness and would contribute to the defense of the area against Communism. He was, however, clearly uncertain as to the exact nature or the means by which this could be done and was obviously concerned with the possible impact of an expanded future U.S. aid program for Asia upon a Congress which had come to accept the belief that economic aid by the U.S. would continue to taper off.

The report by what came to be known as the "Asian Economic Working Group" was submitted to Assistant Secretaries Robertson, Byroade, Morton, and Waugh and to the Director of the Policy Planning Staff in a memorandum dated August 30. As an officer of the Foreign Operations Administration, Mr. McDiarmid had previously been added to the Working Group, a copy of the report was also submitted to Foreign Operations Director Stassen. In the Economic Coordinator's letter of transmittal it was emphasized that all the comments in the report rested on the assumption that the expanded economic aid program was contemplated by the Group only as a part, albeit an important part, of a balanced defense against Communism in Asia. It was further pointed out that the report was preliminary and subject to further elaboration.

The report made no recommendations. It did conclude that it should be U.S. policy to support efforts to ensure survival of non-Communist governments in Asia, even if those governments pursue so-called "neutralist" policies, in the face of a Communist strategy emphasizing subversion, agitation, and other political warfare tactics. It emphasized that, because of inadequate levels of investment, economic progress in the area had been slow. It expressed the opinion that our policy in Asia should give support to the positive goal of accelerated economic development which was espoused by so many Asians. The solution of Asian problems of poverty, economic instability, and other grievances arising out of economic stagnation which would be exploited to the maximum by the Communists, could, the Working Group believed, be materially facilitated by a new long-range program of assistance to the area, if the program were large enough to have a perceptible impact upon the people and governments there. The report recognized that such an expanded investment program to accelerate economic development would necessarily start slowly and gather momentum. It explained the difficulty, if not the impossibility, of estimating the amount of incremental investment which would be required to bring about in time a satisfactory and continuing rate of growth or of estimating the portion of the new investment required from external sources. It was emphasized, however, that unless the proportion of the incremental investment from domestic effort and resources was substantial, no amount of external aid in a given period would create the conditions necessary to assure a continuation of high levels of growth without further external aid. The objective, in the opinion of the report, should be to achieve a reasonably high rate of economic growth which would be self-sustaining and continuing, rather than a selected level of total investment, however high.

It was the considered opinion of the Working Group that the volume of external aid which would be required to achieve the desired results would have to be very considerably in excess of the amount of such aid extended to free Asia in recent years. After carefully disavowing any claim for accuracy of the estimate, the Group thought a total of external aid in an amount equivalent to $10 billion over a ten-year period might raise living standards in the recipient countries at least one per cent per capita per year, increase per capita GNP roughly 2.5 per cent per year and place free Asian economies on a self-sustaining basis. Of the total, it was estimated that about $7 billion would be required for India.

In the early years of the program special emphasis would need to be placed on technical assistance to break the bottleneck caused by the shortage of indigenous skills.

The future U.S. aid program, the report proposed, should emphasize the multilateral approach. Specifically suggested was a multilaterally endowed development fund which, operating under the aegis of a regional economic group (a more highly developed Colombo plan organization was suggested) would make loans for economic development purposes. Advantageous features of this method would be the active participation of the Asian countries and the blending of U.S. funds with contributions from other countries. The report urged that political or military commitments by recipient countries should not be required as a prerequisite to receiving future U.S. aid.

Several weeks after the Working Group report was given limited distribution, a meeting was called by the Director of the Policy Planning Staff to consider the report. Assistant Secretaries or their deputies and senior bureau economic officers were invited. Two sharply divergent viewpoints with respect to the report began to emerge at that time. One generally approved the report while the other questioned some of its basic proposals. Members of the latter group, for example, insisted that the mere mention of a sum of the magnitude suggested in the report would create antagonism in Congress and in other governmental agencies. They contended that acceptance of such a figure by the Congress or by the American people was out of the question. They questioned whether in fact the expenditure of that sum in the matter proposed would accomplish the purposes indicated. They raised the question of the effect of so large a program upon the future economic welfare of the U.S. They were particularly critical of the proposal that U.S. aid should be administered through an international organization and contended that adequate control of U.S. funds under such circumstances would be impossible.

The report was completed just before Secretary Dulles departed for Manila to attend the conference which produced the Manila Pact. He was given a copy of the report to take with him. Shortly after his return a meeting to discuss the report was held in his office. Mr. Dulles had not had an opportunity to study the report in detail but had looked over a summary of the report prepared for him. He appeared to be disturbed over the magnitude of the figure mentioned in the report and over the vagueness of the report with respect to expenditures which would be made and results which might be expected. He appeared, however, to be still convinced that more effective U.S. action in the economic field in Asia in the future would be necessary and important.

At about this time the National Security Council decided to form an Ad Hoc Inter-departmental committee to consider a number of NSC policy decisions in the economic field which pertained to free Asia. One of these required the U.S. to encourage the development of an Asian regional economic organization and to support, if necessary with substantial financial assistance, efforts of that organization to maintain the independence and freedom of the participating countries. The NSC had also decreed that technical and other economic assistance should be extended to these countries as a means of accelerating the rate of their economic growth and giving their people new hope with respect to present progress and future accomplishments. The responsibility of the new Ad Hoc Committee was to consider and recommend to the NSC appropriate courses of action to achieve these objectives of high-level, national policy.

After a certain passage of time, Secretary Dulles designated the

236

new Under Secretary of State, Herbert Hoover, Jr., as Chairman of the new Inter-departmental committee. Shortly after his designation, Mr. Hoover called another meeting of State Department officials at about the assistant secretary level, including the economic coordinator of FE, to discuss further the Working Group report of August 31 and to formulate a departmental position with respect to the activities of the recently created NSC Ad Hoc Committee. This meeting produced the same divergencies of opinion with respect to the Working Group report as had appeared at the previous departmental meeting. Accordingly, after lengthy discussion, Mr. Hoover requested a drafting committee comprising Messrs. Robertson, Baldwin, Nolting, and Kalijarvi to attempt to draft a memorandum which would be generally acceptable as a departmental position for the Ad Hoc Committee. The resulting paper recognized the need for a more effective program to strengthen non-Communist governments in Asia by economic and other means; recognized the importance of efforts to accelerate economic development in Asian countries; concluded that the amount and nature of future U.S. economic assistance to those countries should be left to further intensive study; and concluded further that multilateral consultation, planning of and programming of our economic aid to free Asia should be encouraged.

Several weeks elapsed between the presentation of this drafting committee report and the convening of the first meeting of the NSC Ad Hoc Committee on November 16. At that meeting of the representatives of the Departments of Treasury, Commerce, Agriculture, Defense; the FOA, the CIA, and the Bureau of the Budget made brief preliminary statements. The Treasury and Budget representatives appeared to be primarily concerned over the possibility that future U.S. economic assistance to Asia would be substantially greater in amount than in the past; the Defense Department did not object to the principle of increased economic aid so long as it did not interfere with appropriations for defense; the Commerce Department representatives favored the principle of future economic aid programs with some reservations; while the FOA and CIA representatives gave the greatest amount of unqualified support to the idea.

The principal positive action at this meeting was the announcement by the Chairman of his determination to organize a Working Group. Each member of the Ad Hoc Committee was asked to nominate to the Chairman a representative to serve on the Working Group. The economic coordinator for the Far East was named Chairman of the Working Group.

The first meeting of the Working Group was held Friday, November 19. Five sub-committees were established (South Asia, South East Asia, North Asia, Magnitude of U.S. Economic Assistance and Mechanism for Extending U.S. Assistance). The working Group submitted what it termed an interim report to the Chairman of the NSC Ad Hoc Committee on November 30. In the letter of transmittal the Chairman of the Working Group pointed out that the Group had been able to reach certain accurate conclusions, but had not been able to agree unanimously on such important a question as the general order of magnitude of future U.S. economic assistance or the manner in which such assistance should be extended and related to the activities of a regional economic group. The Chairman further emphasized the elements of the problem which made it impossible to estimate economic cause and effect in the under-developed Asian countries with the accuracy and precision which would be desirable in developing plans for future U.S. economic assistance. The interim report expressed the judgment of the Working Group that present economic conditions in Asia offered opportunities that could be exploited to Communist advantage; that improvement of economic conditions would constitute one means of opposing Communist efforts to extend their influence by means short of war; that significant economic improvement in free Asian countries required a program of basic economic development; and that increased U.S. economic assistance to those countries would accelerate their economic growth enough to make the additional assistance clearly justified by U.S. security interests. The report referred to the need of eliminating in Asia elements of economic weakness which create public discontent, hamper efforts to achieve internal stability, and increase vulnerability to Communist pressures. It expressed the opinion that one of the aims of the economic aid program for the area should be to encourage activities of an Asian regional economic organization. Because of the divergent views of members of the Group and their tendency to reflect the attitudes of their top superior officer the report reflected compromises on several basic issues. It was, therefore, not as strong and forceful a document as some members of the Group would have desired. If, how-

238

ever, the compromises had not been accepted there would have been no report.

In a letter of submittal to the Under Secretary, the Chairman of the Working Group requested instructions as to the wishes of the Ad Hoc Committee with respect to further work by the Working Group. There was no reply or comment either to the letter or to the Working Group Report, and in view of the absence of any indication that the Working Group should continue its activities no further meeting of the Group was held.

After the submittal of the Working Group report there was a period of several weeks duration during which high level activity on the question of an expanded economic aid program for free Asia appeared to be almost completely suspended. There was, however, no cessation of press articles and speculations, both in the United States and abroad about the matter. Due partly to the press comment, there was quite evidently a growing opinion in this country and abroad, including the countries of Asia, that the United States was giving serious consideration to an expanded program of economic aid for Asia. That assumption was strengthened by public references by the President and by the Secretary of State which at least suggested the likelihood of a new and expanded program of economic assistance. The contrast between this rising tide of public expectation and interest and the continued inactivity at the government level was striking. It was also disconcerting in view of the approaching requirements resulting from the inexorable routine of the Budget Bureau in preparing estimates of U.S. foreign aid for the coming fiscal year. The undesirability of delaying consideration and action on a matter of such importance had been emphasized months before in the report of the first State Department Working Group on the subject.

In early January, it became known that the Under Secretary (Herbert Hoover, Jr.) was in possession of a paper, reportedly prepared largely by him with some assistance from officers of the E area, which was designed as a proposed State Department position paper to be presented at the next meeting of the Ad Hoc Committee. That Committee had been continued in existence despite the fact that the President had recently appointed Mr. Joseph Dodge, Chairman of a new high level board known as the Council on Foreign Economic Policy. It apparently was Mr. Dodge's wish that the NSC Ad

Hoc Inter-Department Committee should conclude its consideration of the matter and submit its report to the NSC via the newly created Council on Foreign Economic Policy.

Two meetings of the Ad Hoc Committee were held on January 6. The State Department's position paper formed the basis of the Committee's consideration and, with some changes, it was adopted as the Report of the Ad Hoc Committee. Within three weeks that Report, with a few changes made during consideration of the report by the Dodge Council, had been adopted by the NSC.

Those who believed strongly in the need for the United States to assume dominant leadership in developing a strong economic counteroffensive in free Asia felt that the new policy fell far short of that goal. The policy statement recognized the need to strengthen the economies of free Asian countries and convince their people that adequate economic progress could be achieved by democratic methods, but there was little in the statement, in the opinion of its critics, to offer hope that U.S. policy with respect to economic aid for Asia would either be new, different, or effective enough to make a significant impact upon the Communist situation there. The tone of the policy statement seemed to be a curious combination of recognition of the need for more rapid Asian economic improvement and the fact that the U.S. should do something about it, on the one hand, and, on the other, a cautious and hesitant approach to the problem which seemed to reflect little or no enthusiasm for the idea on the part of the policy framers. The policy statement moreover contained numerous statements susceptible of different interpretations or unclear as to their precise meaning.

A summary of the approved policy statement is given below with observations in parentheses.

The objective of the economic assistance policy, given in the beginning of the paper, is to demonstrate the advantages of our free society and minimize the dangers of Communist influence through continued U.S. interest in greater economic strength and growth in the region and to demonstrate that the economic aspirations in the area could be met by adherence to free world rather than to the Communist system.

The "basic principles" presented in the paper include the following:

(a) Economic assistance is only one element of a program to

strengthen the forces of freedom; others are political, military, psychological and counter-subversive.

(b) U.S. assistance will be given on a bilateral or "selective natural group" basis. (The meaning of the quoted phrase is unclear.)

(c) Individual countries are to be aided with a view to obtaining a maximum long range effect on the area as a whole and short range programs should be reduced to a minimum. (In view of the fact that the policy statement does not propose elsewhere the means by which continuity could be achieved, and in view of the customary Congressional practice of appropriating only for the forthcoming fiscal year, this statement of principle loses most of its value.)

(d) Japan should be given special consideration.

(e) Each country individually must bear primary responsibility "for development" and the U.S. could not be expected to undertake such primary responsibility. (What provocation existed for such a statement is not clear; there is no reason to expect the U.S. to bear "primary responsibility" for the economic development of any Asian country.)

(f) The activities of private agencies should be encouraged whenever possible.

(g) Self-help opportunities should also be encouraged. (Nothing new here.)

(h) U.S. aid should be applied selectively in different countries and between countries of the area. (This appears to be completely meaningless and light is not thrown on it elsewhere in the paper.)

(i) The effectiveness of Soviet economic programs in Asia must be considered in determining the amount of U.S. aid.

(j) Control of aid funds should be maintained by the U.S. and such funds should to the maximum extent possible be made available on a repayment basis (including payment in local currency).

The paper then goes on to approve the strengthening of the Colombo Plan, perhaps through the establishment of a permanent secretariat, provided the initiative for such action comes from one of the Asian countries. This is as far as the policy statement goes toward any plan to achieve greater "multilateralization" of U.S. aid, such as through an economic development fund where dollars would be blended with other currencies but where the U.S. would retain adequate control of the dollars. The policy statement specifically provides that the U.S. should not participate in any new multilateral banking or currency institution in the area without NAC clearance.

The policy statement introduces the idea of supporting measures which would increase opportunities for intra- and inter-regional trade, and encourage the adoption of laws and policies which would stimulate the influx of private investment capital, and favors efforts to expand the U.S. market for products of the Asian area. It suggests various means of contributing to the economic strengthening of Japan.

The cautious tone was most apparent in such precautionary provisions in the policy statement as:

1. The aid policy and programs for Asia must be taken into consideration for their effect upon the U.S. economy and U.S. relations with other areas;

2. U.S. aid for Asia should be of the magnitude outlined in the President's budget message. (A curious and seemingly meaningless statement.)

3. U.S. financial contribution to Asian development "should be in realistic and reasonable amounts." (Also meaningless.)

4. U.S. efforts should not be a substitute for what other countries are doing or what they should do to speed up the region's development. (If this means anything, it is an indictment of ineptitude in planning and administering U.S. aid programs in the past; means of determining what other countries "should do" are not suggested.)

5. While the U.S. should make clear its continuing interest in continuing Asian development, it must make no promises of continuing financial contributions; those are dependent upon appropriations by the U.S. Congress. (A curious statement in view of the previous commitment to aid "individual countries with a view to achieving a maximum long-range effect on the area as a whole.")

6. Public pronouncements about U.S. aid should be consistent with anticipated results and avoid leading the people of Asia to expect more than can be accomplished by a given program. (This could mean almost anything.)

Except for the requirement of a review of previous and existing aid programs and a new look at the differences between the present categories of aid (such as "Direct Forces Support," "Defense Support," etc.), and for the rather half-hearted commitment to support the strengthening of the Colombo Plan, little that is new or different can be found in the policy paper. There is almost nothing in the citation of "Objectives," "Principles" and "Precautions" which has not guided previous aid programs for the Far East. Completely lacking in tone or substance is any determination to use aggressively and intelligently the weapon of economic assistance to hamper Communist plans and influence in Asia. The much discussed new program was "only a little more of the same."

It became generally known not long after the policy paper had been approved by the NSC and the President that the new policy had been formulated and adopted. Curiosity and speculation on the part of the press increased and the Department received increasing inquiries from foreign diplomatic missions in Washington. Little could be said, however, by Departmental officers because of the lack of any policy with respect to disclosure of the new policy. The situation was further confused and complicated by statements of high administrative officials which were curiously contradictory, an example being the naming, by Mr. Stassen in a public statement, of a figure for Asian aid which was almost double that which was mentioned publicly by Secretary of the Treasury Humphrey a few days later. This situation produced a caustic editorial in the *Washington Post* asking why, if the Administration had developed a new program of economic aid, it seemed to be intent on concealing that fact from the world and even acting as if such a program had not been developed. It was in this atmosphere that Secretary Dulles and his party departed for the Bangkok Conference in February.

Addendum written June 16, 1981.

I prepared the above before retiring in 1955. I tried to make it impersonal but the observant reader will probably conclude that the final report—prepared to meet Hoover's ideas—was a kind of "hatchet job" on the report of my committee. Completely omitted from this account is the ire which my committee's report apparently aroused in Herbert Hoover, Jr.— against me, as Chairman, and the other committee members for doing a job ordered by Secretary Dulles. As I was unable to obtain an appointment with Hoover, I felt the impact indirectly when the Deputy Under-Secretary, obviously apologetic and regretful, told me that, although I was on the so-called "future chief of mission list" I could not be offered a foreign post for which Hoover's approval would be necessary.

I responded appropriately when I was offered several other assignments, completed a tour of duty at the U.N. and submitted my resignation in a letter to Secretary Dulles in which I mentioned his failure to support a subordinate who was being unfairly penalized for carrying out orders. Mr. Dulles replied with a stereotyped expression of thanks for my services, and I retired never expecting to be again in the Foreign Service. As you know, President Kennedy decreed otherwise when he appointed me ambassador to Malaysia and enabled me to end my career in a rewarding manner.

C. F. Baldwin

Appendix D

Jackson's World Economic Plan and the
Princeton Meeting of May 15–16, 1954

[*Note*: This appendix, from the author's files, includes C. D. Jackson's formulation of a World Economic Plan; his telegram of invitation to the
Princeton meeting; and a list of those who participated. The World Economic Plan was, evidently, an elaboration of what he had proposed to
John Foster Dulles in their meeting of March 25, 1954.]

PERSONAL & CONFIDENTIAL
April 9, 1954

MEMORANDUM TO THE SECRETARY OF STATE

FROM: C. D. Jackson

After fourteen months in Washington, with a special portfolio in
what is known as the "cold war," it was only natural that I should
return to private life with certain ideas as to our assets and liabilities in this field, our successes and failures, and our unfilled
needs.

The free world and its leader, the United States, is under one serious handicap, about which very little can be done at this late date.
That is, that Communism and the Soviets have monopolized, and in
a very subtle way made their own, most of the benign words.

At the Berlin Conference, you will recall that Molotov never referred to the East German regime, or the Chinese Communist regime, or the puppet regimes of any of the satellites, without the ad-
jectival prefix "democratic and peace-loving." Theirs is Picasso's
"peace" dove. They are the sponsors of an endless variety of "peace"
petitions and campaigns.

Millions of people throughout the world know that these are Soviet absurdities—Soviet lies. And yet very subtly, through the endless repetition of these words and slogans, some part of what the Communists want to convey does rub off onto the subconsciousness of these same millions of people.

We on our side have had to make an unwilling contribution to this Soviet propaganda. Because Soviet expansion had gone so far and gathered so much momentum before we were willing to recognize the full gravity of the Soviet threat, our reaction had to be mainly a military reaction, either active as in Korea, or defensive as in NATO and EDC and our wide-ranging military assistance programs. Even in economic policy the attention of the world has been focused recently more on our restrictive East-West trade controls than on the elements of any constructive program.

Thus, while the Soviets were capitalizing on the repetition of the symbols of peace while actually waging war, we were forced to capitalize on the symbols of war while actually trying to preserve the peace.

One result of this military emphasis on our part has been that almost all of our long-term planning has been long-term military planning, with short-term economic planning thrown in when, as, and if. I don't think it is an exaggeration to say that the structure of our free world alliance is in grave danger of bogging down, even militarily, because we do not really have a long-term economic policy, outside of financial shoring up of military requirements.

I know that this is no new thought to you, but I wanted to state it because I feel that there is a particular urgency to this thought right now. The realization of this particular vacuum in our leadership has suddenly begun to gain tremendous momentum abroad, and if the realization is allowed to progress for many more months, we will be making the temptation of Russian economic and trade blandishments almost irresistible not only to many of our precariously balanced friends, but even to some of our very good friends.

Finally, the recent H-bomb developments have produced a real intellectual and emotional crisis throughout the world, and including our own country.

The curse was almost off the A-bomb—which was just about to be accepted as the newest conventional weapon—when the H-bomb went off, and people said to themselves, "This one we cannot live with; there must be some other way."

The "other way" we have not yet shown the world. And that is the purpose of this memorandum.

．．．

For many years, we have had a peaceful weapon which we attempted to use and on which we spent billions—namely, economic relief and reconstruction.

The Marshall Plan (ECA) was a stupendous undertaking in terms of billions of dollars. Its successors—MSA and now FOA and TCE—are tremendous undertakings.

The Marshall Plan for a period (note that I do not say "brief" period, although it actually was all too brief) captured world imagination. It is tragic that this impact was lost to such an extent that both here and abroad there are a lot of people, many of them sincere, who consider that great effort of ours a failure.

Volumes could be written about the reasons for this. Let me try to state it in an oversimplification: Except for the Governments and industrial leaders involved, the beneficiaries at the end of the line, millions of people all over the world, never did and still do not understand either *what* we did, or in fact *why* we did it.

Most recently, the President made another effort in the direction of world economic policy through the Randall Commission and his Message to the Congress on foreign economic policy. This was progress, but not sufficient to solve the problem, for two reasons.

In the first place, because of the composition of the Commission, its conclusions, though bolder than many previous attempts, nevertheless had to be politically "possible," and therefore what finally went to the Congress was already a fairly low common denominator.

In the second place, the terms of reference of the Commission were such that all they could address themselves to was a review of subjects which had already been reviewed and argued about many times before—subjects which did not have either the novelty or the drama to capture popular imagination both here and abroad in such a way as to start the kind of popular ground swell which so often brings about important and decisive political moves.

．．．

What the United States needs, in the development of its foreign policy, in its successful counter to Soviet expansion, in its determination to roll back Communism by peaceful means, is a bold, imaginative plan embracing not just one, but all, of the possible elements involved.

The essential element of such a World Economic Plan is that it will *work*. It must contain things to be done—things that can be done. We have had tons of theory, but hardly more than ounces of action. If a World Economic Plan is developed on this basis, it will then have sufficient dramatic appeal to be understood by *people* everywhere. And if *people* want it, *governments* will want it.

What is needed is not another report, but an imaginative synthesis of much that already exists, to which should be added a large number of action items which up to now Washington has either shied away from or which have become lost in the mass of papers after getting some kind of formalized policy approval.

It is my suggestion that a group of the best people we can find should sit down for a weekend to consider the broad shape such a synthesis should take. On the basis of that discussion, we might designate a small drafting committee to prepare a proposal for submission to the group, possibly at another session to be held early in the summer. Then, if the group considers that a worthwhile plan has been outlined, will be the time to submit it to the Government.

Recommendations should be made without regard to their political or legislative feasibility. Those checks and balances will have plenty of opportunity to exert themselves later, but they should be exerted on a *maximum* rather than a *minimum* proposition.

It is to be hoped that the President would see in the World Economic Plan the action fulfillment of his April and December speeches, and that sometime this fall, preferably in September, he could present the idea of a World Economic Plan to the United States and the world.

I am confident that if a World Economic Plan contains those ingredients which will unmistakably add to the welfare and prosperity of this country and of the free world, the fact that the grass is indeed greener on freedom's side of the fence will cease to be merely an American statement, and become a reality.

Invitation to the Princeton Meeting.

As a result of my year in the Administration with a special portfolio in international affairs, and after several private and unofficial discussions with some of my former associates in government, and with the knowledge of the President, I have become convinced that the time is overripe for some high caliber imaginative and bureaucratically unencumbered thinking and planning on what might best be described as a world economic plan.

This appears essential if the long term foreign policy of the United States, designed to lead the free world to victory and an enduringly prosperous peace without war, is to have weapons other than massive retaliation, military aid, and an endless vista of emergency grants.

Much thought has already been given to this in our government but for reasons too long to enumerate in this telegram such a project has not yet been organized or adequately presented or initiated.

Have therefore decided to ask a group of men from economics, agriculture, science, banking, industry, labor and government to spend the weekend of May 15–16 with me in Princeton, New Jersey, in a serious and concerted effort to make a start on the thinking and planning needed to generate a world economic plan.

All those attending would represent themselves and not their organizations and there is no personal or organizational commitment involved. There will be no publicity whatsoever.

Full details are following by mail but I wanted to alert you as one of those invited as soon as possible.
Sincerely,

C. D. Jackson
Time Incorporated
9 Rockefeller Plaza
New York, N.Y.

PRINCETON—MAY 15–16, 1954

Honorable Samuel W. Anderson
Assistant Secretary of Commerce

Mr. George B. Baldwin—MIT
Center for Intl. Studies

Dr. Lloyd V. Berkner, President
Associated Universities Inc.

General Robert Cutler
Special Assistant to the President

Mr. Allen W. Dulles, Director
Central Intelligence Agency

Mr. Arthur Flemming, Director
Office of Defense Mobilization

Mr. Robert Garner, Vice-President
The International Bank

Dr. Gabriel Hauge
Administrative Assistant to the President

Mr. C. D. Jackson
Time Incorporated

Mr. John K. Jessup
Time Incorporated

Professor Edward S. Mason
Harvard University

Mr. David J. McDonald, President
United Steel Workers of America

Mr. Thomas McKittrick
Chase National Bank

Professor Max Millikan, President
Center for Intl. Studies, MIT

Honorable H. Chapman Rose
Assistant Secretary of the Treasury

Professor Walt W. Rostow
Center for Intl. Studies

Honorable Harold E. Stassen, Director
Foreign Operations Administration

Mr. Charles L. Stillman, Vice-President
Time Incorporated

Mr. Abbott Washburn
U.S. Information Agency

SECRETARIAT:
  Miss Wanda Allender
  Miss Marie McCrum
  Miss Gertrude Neiderer (stenotype)

Appendix E

A *Reply to the Dodge-Humphrey Perspective*

[*Note*: The author replies, in effect, to Dodge's letter to Jackson late in 1954. The letter is from the author's files.]

December 27, 1954

Dear C. D.:

I just saw the copy of Joe Dodge's letter you kindly sent us. Also the rather pessimistic stories in today's *Times*. I can easily understand the roots of Dodge's and Humphrey's view; but it reflects a lack of imaginative understanding of the kind which leads to the fall of empires.

Let me begin by putting what may be their view in the most sympathetic form possible.

Economic development is a complicated matter. Other people's money is only one of the things involved, and perhaps the least important. You need orderly government, vigorous entrepreneurs, plant managers, foremen, engineers. You need tax systems that collect taxes, a forward-looking middle class, a hard-working working class. Any fool knows that, unless you are going to give the money away to finance imported Cadillacs and trips to Paris for some official's nephew, there are only limited openings for new capital investment in many areas, if you really mean investment. Any fool knows that the men in these underdeveloped countries are only too ready to talk and act as though U.S. dough will solve their problems when, in fact, they have to solve them at home. So let's keep cool and keep them cool. Let them work along at home. Let us help them with technical assistance. Let them learn that capital is other people's money which must be respected and put to use only under conditions which will yield a solid return.

What this view misses is:

1. The present position in *India*. They have gone a long way in a few years towards solving what looked like an insoluble problem: the food-population question. They are now turning, at this very moment, to how this success might be translated into industrial momentum. They need industrial advice and technical assistance; they can use some additional capital right now; in the course of five years they could absorb a helluva lot more. How much more depends in part on whether, at this crucial moment, we sense the dynamics of their situation, and get them to up their sights.

2. *Indonesia*. They are fussing about dangerously. They are not ready now for big industrial growth although the boys in Washington should look hard at the electricity-aluminum development possibilities with which the Japs have been playing on a small scale. The big point, though, is this. The odds are good that if the Indians follow through their agricultural break-through with a sound industrial phase it will get the Indonesians to stop fighting the Dutch all over again and begin to take economic development seriously. This at least is a decent hope, given the controversy between the two major parties.

3. *Japan*. How in hell are we going to give Japan anything like a hope for national dignity unless there is vastly more momentum in the Asian markets than there is now or there will be without a big American goose.

4. *Communist China*. A let-the-dust-settle economic policy in Asia is going to give Mao a chance to look awfully good, even if, in fact, his performance is mediocre and costly in human life. And on how good relatively Mao's performance looks to Asians may depend the fate of Asia, so far as we are concerned.

As you know these considerations do not lead to give-aways. They do lead to the following which Dodge and Humphrey should really understand before they reject:

1. Except for technical assistance and low level of grants, NO GIVE-AWAY.

2. Large investment sums available, IF SOLID CONDITIONS FOR IN-VESTMENT ARE FULFILLED.

3. A sufficient time perspective to give the boys in the Co-lombo Plan group a chance to create the preconditions we de-mand for investment.

4. Serious technical assistance on the scientific, engineering, and industrial side to help create the pre-conditions.

Basically, the Dodge-Humphrey view as I sense it fails to grasp two dynamic forces and their possibilities: first, the dynamics at work in Asia itself—we must ride with it and, in a sense, harness it, or it may well turn against us; second, the potential dynamics of a big U.S. investment offer, with hard-headed terms, combined with U.S. help in meeting our terms.

I don't think we should give up on this one partly because it's right, partly because the problem of economic development is so new that good men can misunderstand the possibilities. I write this urgently not only because I feel strongly, but because it would be vastly better if the Administration took the initiative after whatever internal hassles may be required, than if it became a public political controversy. Don't give up until you've talked personally with the Boss and had it out, even, with Dodge himself; although I feel a little like a towel boy urging his fighter from a seat on the bucket.

All the best,

W. W. Rostow

Appendix F

Jackson-Luce Memorandum of May 23, 1956

[*Note*: This reaction to a 1956 John Jessup (*Life* magazine) speech draft by members of the White House staff amounts to: wait until next year. The source is: C. D. Jackson Papers, box 56, "Log-1956" folder, Dwight D. Eisenhower Library.]

There assembled were Persons, Seaton, Hauge, Shepley, and Jessup, in order to discuss WEP and the Jessup speech draft.

The mood was gay and friendly, but the wisecracks had a slightly hollow ring, because the news had come through just a few minutes before that the House Committee had cut a billion dollars from the President's $4.9-billion foreign aid request (almost all of the billion out of NATO military), and another Committee had voted to dump five million bales of cotton on the world market and to hell with the price.

Everyone most appreciative of our effort, and particularly warm in their praise of the job Jessup had done.

Obviously Persons and Seaton obsessed with short-term tactical political considerations, to the exclusion of any real willingness or ability to grasp "the big picture," although Persons considerably more understanding than Seaton, probably due to Shepley's effective efforts over the past three weeks.

Hauge really understood what it was all about, and made a very incisive analysis of the Jessup draft against the twin practicalities of the political situation—that is, the temper of Congress—and the genuine necessity for the Administration getting on top of WEP. For instance, while he saw genuine value in a Presidential speech right now summarizing the Administration efforts to date, putting forward the American position, and urging renewed effort, including a strong intimation of something bigger and better as set down in four-fifths of the Jessup draft, he questioned the advisability, from a purely practical standpoint, of the President teeing off on either the escape clause or a convertibility fund at this time.

I gave them my "inspirational" five cents' worth, to the effect that

(1) We had been delighted to go through this exercise for them.

(2) If they could not put it to use, we would not feel that we had been put upon, but we intended to go ahead editorially, because

(3) This was the looming "great issue."

(4) It had been a great issue for a long time, which the Administration had not risen to, had been contented with an annual parade of shopworn economic cliches, compounded by Harold Stassen's international economic ambulance-chasing. Now, with the new Soviet economic offensive, a World Economic Policy, which was always important per se, became doubly important.

(5) While I recognized the practicalities of the political dilemma which faced them, at the same time I hoped they realized that this was something that they would either have the wisdom to stay on top of, or find themselves overtaken by it.

Upshot was that Jessup, who already had a second draft in mind, would go to work on a second draft with the added information and angles collected at the meeting, probably in the form of a informational and hortatory speech by the President in order to go to the people over the heads of the Congress to salvage his present program, but not to include any extra "nuts and bolts" beyond a general indication that there might be considerably more next year.

Three additional items emerged:

(1) Neither Persons nor Seaton have mentioned this to the President yet.

(2) There has been no coordination or contact between Persons and Bill Jackson, which Persons intends to remedy.

(3) The Rostow-Millikan memorandum which made such a press splash last Sunday and is supposed to be under consideration by the National Security Council, was something that these gentlemen just didn't know anything about.

Appendix G
A Vivid Portrait of Dulles' Frustrations, 1956

[*Note*: This Jackson-Luce letter, reporting Dulles' frame of mind in the spring of 1956, is not only a revealing document but reflects Dulles' willingness to confide in Jackson. Source: C. D. Jackson Papers, box 56, "Log-1956" folder, DDE Library.]

April 16, 1956
PERSONAL & CONFIDENTIAL

Dear Harry:

Following is a fuller report on my hour and a half with Foster Dulles Saturday afternoon, April 14th, at his home. On Sunday, I cabled you as follows:

"SOBERING AND SADDENING MEETING. HE HAS COMPLETE AWARENESS GRAVITY OF PROBLEM AND INTELLIGENT RATIONALE OF CAUSES BUT NO POSITIVE SOLUTIONS BEYOND PASSAGE OF TIME WHICH COULD INCLUDE FURTHER SETBACKS. FEELS VERY MUCH ALONE AND SOUNDS TIRED. I SHALL MAIL FULLER REPORT ROME REGARDS"

As I re-read the cable, it sums up the meeting, all right.

I found him elbow-deep in papers, working with his secretary on a speech, and commenting that he was trying to put together a speech which would explain the current Moscow goings on, although he was not too hopeful he would be able to pull it off because (a) it still was an enigma wrapped in a mystery, etc., and (b) the President was planning a foreign policy speech before the A.S.N.E. (American Association of Newspaper Editors) a few days before, which would probably interfere with his effort.

As an aside, he added that from what he had seen of the Presidential draft, he didn't think it was very good, and could not understand why Hagerty was promoting the speech so strongly: "I think it is a great mistake, because I don't think he is going to say very much."

By that time the secretary had left, and Foster was obviously waiting for me to open the meeting.

Jackson: In the past you have been generous enough from time to time to take me into your confidence and tell me when you thought things were going badly for you, and at those times you generally had ideas or plans which you would bat up to me for my reaction. Today, I am asking for that same generosity, although the twist is a little different this time. Sitting in New York observing things, I have the distinct impression that the foreign affairs of the United States, and therefore the foreign policy of the United States, are in a bad phase. In fact, it is sufficiently bad for me to say that I think you are in trouble, and the President is in trouble. Now you will know better than I whether this should be described as terrible trouble, or serious trouble, or just plain trouble—but I am sure you will agree that at least it is trouble.

I have several reasons for wanting to hear whatever you care to say. There is a great personal reason, arising out of my personal admiration and affection for you; there is also a Harry Luce reason, because in his own way he shares my personal feelings; and then there is a Time Inc. reason, because we have nailed two great big flags to our mast, and one of them has on it the letters J.F.D. and the other the letters D.D.E., and I would hate to have anything happen to those flags.

Dulles: (While I was talking about the "trouble" that he and the President were in, Foster had repeatedly nodded his head in agreement, so that his pick-up of the dialogue did not have explicitly to agree with my statement. He had already agreed and could take it from there.) We find ourselves in very difficult times. So long as the Soviets under Stalin continued to behave so badly in public, it was relatively easy for our side to maintain a certain social ostracism toward them—and I stress the word "social." The whole post–war relationship between ourselves and our allies and the Russians can be analyzed and described with great accuracy in terms of how a society, a community, a family, responds to the behavior of an obvious bad egg. The man who spits in your eye, puts poison in your soup, has impossible table manners, is the kind of person you don't want around. You don't want him in your house, you don't want him in your community, you don't want him in your club—you just don't want him. And what is more important, everybody else understands.

And behind that social ostracism, which everybody understood even though some did not necessarily applaud, it was possible fairly quickly and easily to reach mutual defensive agreements in order to see to it that this socially impossible person was kept out—and if he did threaten to break down the door or set fire to the house, that there would be sufficient friends and neighbors around to make him think twice.

Now all of a sudden the outward Soviet appearance, mood, behavior, has materially changed, and speaking in social terms, it is becoming extremely difficult to maintain the ostracism—and maybe we should not even want to maintain it. Frowns have given way to smiles. Guns have given way to offers of economic aid. Soviet industry has reached a point where they probably can start producing consumer goods if they want to.

Now I don't know if they are sincere or not, if this is a trick or not—but I do know two things. The first is that this "change" is not superficial, is not limited to a few speeches and Pravda editorials. It goes quite deep, and of course the deeper it goes the less chance the new collective leadership has to disregard it or reverse it. For instance, we know that some 6,000 workers' meetings have been scheduled in the Moscow area alone in order to hear the "new line." There is another little item I am trying to include in my speech about the Russian school system. Did you know that all history examinations have been suspended until they have time to rewrite the history books, or at least until the teachers have been told what the new right answers are? The other thing that I know is that with all of these outward improvements—with the repudiation of Stalin, with the rehabilitation of scores of officials, scientists, soldiers, dead and alive, with the apparent acceptance of Tito, and therefore of Titoism—with all these things going on, it is very difficult for the United States to say to its allies that all of this means nothing, that it is a trick, that the ostracism must be maintained.

Going back to the social angle, one of the deepest urges in men is the desire to be accepted, and it is perfectly possible that a large part of the new line could have as simple a motivation as that. Another strong human urge, particularly among Western peoples, is the desire to accept the bad man when he has repented and confessed and promised to be good.

I don't think anyone wants to try to turn the clock back and re-create Stalin's Russia, and furthermore I doubt if anyone could if he tried. We may be in very grave long-term danger because of the Soviets' new economic competition, but I would rather be trying to work out the answers to that one instead of trying to find answers to H-Bomb competition.

Back in 1950 or '51, I spent $1,000 to build a bomb-proof cellar in my New York house for Janet and myself and my documents. I would not have spent that much money if I had not been convinced at that time that it was necessary. Well, today I just would not spend that thousand dollars for that, because I don't think that is the way the struggle is shaping up any more.

This new economic competition is terribly serious, and frankly, I don't know the answer. One of the reasons that it is so serious is that ever since the dawn of industry—that is, for several hundred years—the West has had a real monopoly on industrial products, and it set what it called a world price on those products, and the underdeveloped areas just had to pay that price.

Today, for the first time in industrial history, there is a new and potentially tremendous industrial center—the Soviet Union—which has announced that it is prepared to compete. I know that the Western industrial nations compete among themselves, but this Russian competition is a different kind of competition. The Western industrial nations all have certain economic common denominators. There is such a thing as a profit. There are interest rates. There are all kinds of commonly accepted rules and techniques which establish not only a certain uniformity of trading procedures, but also a fairly narrow price range—which is why I said earlier that to the underdeveloped countries this looks like a monopoly, and as you know, nobody likes to buy from a monopoly if he can help it.

So these underdeveloped countries are very pleased to see this new competition spring up. It satisfies both their emotions and their pocketbooks. This new competitor, because of his economic setup, which includes slave labor, does not play according to any of the rules. If an interest rate is 5 percent, he can offer 2 percent. If he takes some Egyptian cotton in payment of some arms from Czechoslovakia, he doesn't have to worry about the Liverpool Cotton Exchange when he wants to unload his cotton. And so on.

We could be witnessing the beginning of economic piracy on a scale never before practised, and we frankly do not yet know what to do about it. But we do know that this economic piracy will be far too welcome in far too many parts of the world.

CDJ: Well, Foster, that is quite a gloomy picture, and it is understandable that on something as really tricky as this you and the President may not have worked out all the answers. On the other hand, the public—the American public—isn't going to be willing to sit still for the months or years needed to work this out. There is a national desire to see something being *done*, and from where I sit there is a growing impression that there is a virtual foreign policy moratorium in Washington.

You will recall that you yourself used the word "moratorium" the last time we had a major talk, which was shortly before the President announced that he would run again, and at that time you told me that since the President's illness you had been hamstrung because there was a foreign policy moratorium which would last at least until the President's political pronouncement. My impression is that it has lasted considerably longer. Knowing you and the President, I personally cannot believe what I hear—that this is a deliberate moratorium until after elections—but if that isn't it, then what is it?

JFD: The President is the last person in the United States to have that kind of political motivation. Just the other day, talking about the Arab-Israel business, the President said, "I don't want anybody bringing up the matter of votes in November in connection with the Middle Eastern problem. We will do what we think is right, and if because of that I don't get elected, I will probably be the happiest man around." And I know that he means it.

However, you know the President, and you know that he does not like to try to get his way by having rows. He prefers personal persuasion, even if it takes considerably longer, and he likes to be liked.

So although he himself would not move an inch either way for personal political considerations, he knows that the same does not apply to Congressmen and Senators in an election year. Therefore, he is not going to make any proposals, advance any ideas, which he thinks might run into strong opposition on Capitol Hill. So far as that type of "doing something" is concerned, there is in effect a moratorium.

It is a curious thing about Presidential personalities. When Congress laid its ears back, Woodrow Wilson took that as a sign to pour it on, and so did FDR. With Eisenhower, it is the other way around, and only history will tell which technique was right.

CDJ: Foster, I would now like to get into another aspect of the trouble, and since this involves specific people, I don't see how I can avoid naming names. I appreciate that this is highly indiscreet, but it just can't be helped, because if what I hear is correct, things are very bad. Again, I have to preface it by saying that I am on the outside looking and listening in, and I may therefore be completely wrong, although on some aspects of this I think my Intelligence sometimes works a little faster than your brother's.

The problem presents itself under two aspects, both of them under the heading of morale.

The first is the U.S. Missions abroad. Leaving out Rome, about which I have no information and have not tried to get any, my Intelligence tells me that the morale of the Mission Chiefs is very low. They are aware of the fact that U.S. stock in their particular country is on the skids, and being human beings they are not inclined to blame that phenomenon on themselves. The handiest scapegoat is U.S. foreign policy, and when they say "U.S. foreign policy" there are just two people in the background—yourself and the President. I am definitely not implying disloyalty or any conspiratorial gossiping—I am simply saying that there exists a general unhappiness which works against any team spirit or activity and must inevitably affect their personal diplomacy.

The second aspect has to do with Washington. When Nelson Rockefeller used to beef to me about his problems down here, and named the personal roadblocks he ran into in State and other Departments, I usually discounted his reports quite heavily, because I knew that many of Nelson's problems were self-induced. However, that is not the situation in the case of Bill Jackson, who knows the business, and Washington, much better than Nelson, and furthermore was prepared to find that most of what Nelson had told him about some of the local personalities was not true.

So when Bill tells me that the lack of Presidential follow-through, which you and I have discussed before, is worse than ever today because some highly placed individuals are deliberately exercising a pocket veto on the President's wishes and sometimes orders; that in the important areas of Defense and State there frequently is no functioning Government—I am inclined to take his words seriously.

More specifically, he says that Engine Charlie is worse than ever (nods from JFD), that his new Deputy, Reuben Robertson is just a junior replica of Engine Charlie (nods from JFD), that in State, with you away so much, Herbert Hoover, Jr. does not carry on as a representative of either yourself or the President, and conveniently forgets or reverses instructions. . . .

JFD: I am not away as much as all that, but that is really irrelevant because he does it even while I am here.

CDJ: . . . that this situation presents Bill with an almost impossible task, and that the Operations Coordinating Board and other mechanisms which were supposed to make things run better are now being used to prevent their running at all.

JFD: Herbert Hoover does present quite a lot of problems, partly because he approaches everything from the standpoint of a business engineering mind. But he is not as bad as all that. He has done some excellent things, and I frequently find him very useful.

The trouble is that outside of the President and myself—and I feel that I am running dry—nobody around here seems to have ideas. And if an idea of the President's or mine gets thrown into this huge Government machinery where everything has got to be coordinated sixteen times and in which these various Planning Groups reduce everything to the lowest common denominator, there is no one to pick it up and carry it through, the way you carried through Atoms-for-Peace—and God knows that took you long enough.

The various so-called idea mechanisms that we have, like my own Policy Planning Board, have become completely useless as producers of ideas, because they have to spend all their time arguing in NSC Board Meetings, for the ultimate purpose of producing a piece of paper which represents the lowest common denominator of agreement.

When a State Department representative finds himself in one of those inter-Departmental groups, he is just one person instead of being *the* person representing foreign policy, and I constantly find myself in a situation where I have to fight on foreign policy matters with people whose jobs and responsibilities are only one percent concerned with foreign policy—and yet whose vote is as good as mine or my representative's. This Government is being coordinated to death, and that is one of the reasons why there are no ideas.

Take this speech I am working on. I would naturally show it to the President and get his concurrence. But besides that, I will probably have to send it to half a dozen other Cabinet Members for their suggestions; it will go down to goodness knows what level in the State Department, where all the commas will be scrutinized; I may even have to send it for advance reaction and suggestions to three or four foreign Ambassadors. Well, by the time all those people have had their say, there isn't much left of either the original, or any enthusiasm I might have had.

Instead of coordinating machinery, we ought to have a few people around here who want to get things done. And that is what I hope Bill Jackson will consider his function, instead of coming around the way he did the other day to ask my advice on a letter he proposed to send Sherman Adams spelling out his coordinating functions. I told him what I thought about coordination. Do you realize that the only person around here on whom I can count to get something done reasonably quickly is Douglas MacArthur?

Take the current situation on NATO. Very bad. NATO could break up any minute unless somebody around here shows some imagination. [Nine lines excised from paragraphs 3 & 4 in accordance with the provisions of the Donor's letter of gift. DJH 4/25/75]

I have thought of getting Beedle back, but Beedle is so sick, living on his nerve, keeping himself going with coffee and whiskey, that I can't trust his judgment any more.

I wish there were some way of solving this problem of Government. Arthur Vandenburg told me that the real reason that he was praying that Eisenhower would become President was that the Government of the United States had become so tremendous, so unwieldy, practically so unworkable, that Vandenburg thought it would require someone with the prestige and personality and drive, and above all else the popular mandate, of Eisenhower, to come in and reorganize it and re-invigorate it—and of course that has not happened. The President let the early precious months go by, those months when he did have the leverage of a personal popular mandate. And anyhow, he never was, and is not today, a student of politics in the sense that Vandenburg meant. He doesn't understand, and he is not particularly interested.

CDJ: I agree with what you say on the size of Government and coordination, and all of those things, but wouldn't you agree from your own experience that an awful lot of that can be overcome if a very small handful of men—maybe not more than four or five—really want to get something done? And isn't it a sad fact that you have no allies?

JFD: Well, I have the President—and that is not an ally to be sneezed at. But other than that, I am pretty much alone. The really effective axis in Washington today is the Humphrey-Dodge axis, and Dodge's committee—another one of those coordinating things—is a disaster as far as getting any of the things I want done.

These are days when a great many of these problems cannot be approached from the viewpoint of a Middle Western banker-businessman, and that is the experience and the attitude of Humphrey and of Dodge, and in a sense of Herbert Hoover, and their many allies all over the place, including most of the Cabinet Members . . .

CDJ: . . . and including your own Mr. Hollister. (No comment from JFD.)

JFD: The other day I had what I thought was a pretty good idea, and still do, as a counter to Soviet economic warfare. They may be leading from strength inside their own country, but they certainly are not leading from strength in the European satellites, which is a place we could make an awful lot of trouble for them and keep them occupied. I thought that it might be a good idea while they are carpet-bagging around Afghanistan and places like that, for us to put together a really pretty package of food and goods and what have you, and offer it to Czechoslovakia—offer them a really beautiful deal. Goodness knows what we would take in payment, but that really doesn't make any difference. How could the Czech regime turn it down? And if Moscow ordered them to turn it down, they would have to put up something at least as good.

Well, right away, the lines began to form. The Attorney General's office thought that it was legally very difficult. The Treasury wanted to find out what it would cost the taxpayer. Somebody else was worried about something else. And so on. It is now being pawed over by one of these study groups—and goodness knows what if anything will ever reappear.

These things, if they are to be done, have got to be done quickly. Otherwise they have no impact.

Another idea I have had is in connection with the troubles in the Middle East. I frankly don't know if we would be able, if the American people would stand for real military intervention on our part in the war. We don't even know who we would be shooting at, and the circumstances under which the war might break out could be so confused that the question of who was the aggressor might not be at all clear. I proposed that we send a sizeable store of weapons—all kinds—to some nearby place, and let it be known that this military stockpile is there to be turned over immediately to the aggressed party. I think that that would be a real deterrent—much better than public argument as to whether or not 1500 Marines will be landed.

As far as I know, nothing whatsoever is being done about this.

CDJ: You have been very generous with both time and frankness, and I know you have a lot of other things to do, including that speech, so maybe I ought to close with one final question. Do you think I should be encouraged or discouraged by what you have told me?

JFD: Well, I think that there is some ground for encouragement. I told you at the start that I did not think anyone would want to turn the Communist clock back.

Ten years ago, in my article in *Life*, I said that if we could stay with this thing long enough and solidly enough, there would come a time when important internal changes would occur in the Soviet Union, and that any change from the rigid Stalin police state would probably be a step forward. Well, that has come to pass.

Six years ago, in my book, I wrote that it was conceivable that at some time the rulers of Russia might publicly repudiate Stalin and all his works. Well, that has come to pass also.

We are now entering a new phase, which may last decades, and it will present us with grave dangers. The world as we know it may be materially altered. Some of our existing arrangements may have to be discarded. We may even suffer what at the time will appear to be serious setbacks. But in the long run I do not see why we should not win. And after all, the fight that we are in now is, as I said, better than trading thermo-nuclear bombs.

. . .

While I was talking to Mrs. Dulles waiting for my taxi, Foster disappeared, then came back and beckoned me into the hall, where he said, "You appreciate, of course, that I have not tried to sell you anything, or to promote anything. That is because of our relationship. I think I could have given you a sales talk if I had wanted to."

. . .

Interpreting the above in terms of Time Inc.'s journalism, and the questions raised in your longhand letter of April 7th, this meeting with Foster has pretty well convinced me that we would be making a grave mistake, and committing a real unfairness, by unlimbering on JFD editorially. Although there is a lot for which he can be blamed; although the above dialogue indicates many times and places where he has sorrowfully acquiesced instead of himself doing something about it; although his personnel and administrative policies or lack thereof continue to be as bad as they were in the early days—nevertheless, to zero in on JFD would be shooting at the symptom rather than the disease.

If we are going to take this one on editorially, knowing what we know, feeling the way we feel, it would be cheap and superficial to indulge in the easy oversimplification of taking Foster over the jumps.

There is not any one villain, or even a pair of villains—but if I were ordered by you to choose between JFD and DDE as targets, I would pick DDE. But that, too, would be an oversimplification.

On the way back in the plane from Washington, I was trying to think of how best to package this situation for you, and at one moment I wished that I could draw like cartoonist Low. I would have shown a table, at the head of which sat the President. On his right sat Foster, looking lonely and forlorn. And then further down the table on Foster's side, separated by empty chairs, would be Herbert Hoover Jr., Hollister, Holland, and some other members of the Department's do-nothing club. This group would have its back turned to Foster, and would be shown busily conspiring and passing pieces of paper under the table to the other side, where, beaming, sat George Humphrey, closely surrounded by enthusiastic teammates

Dodge, Brownell, Weeks, etc., etc. And in a balloon over the President's head, would be the motto, "Decency will win in the long run."

I wonder if the handle to gain hold of this story isn't the Humphrey-Dodge axis.

All the best,

C. D. Jackson

Mr. Henry R. Luce
New York, New York

Appendix H

Kennedy and Cooper Defend Their Resolution in the Times, *July 29, 1958*

[*Note:* This joint letter responds to an article and editorial in the *New York Times* and keeps their project before its readers.]

New York Times
July 29, 1958
TO AID INDIA'S FINANCES
Senators Urge Support for 5-Year Plan's Objectives
TO THE EDITOR OF THE NEW YORK TIMES:

Edwin Dale's article of July 21 and your editorial of July 22 are urgent reminders—even at a time of the crisis in the Middle East—that India's economic position remains the pivotal test in our foreign assistance program.

It has been apparent for well over a year that the Indian Five-Year Plan requirements would leave a large foreign exchange gap to which foreign governments would have to contribute through loans. Today it is even clearer that the published figure of $1,200,000,000 is a minimum requirement over the next three years.

During this past year the United States Government has felt that it could not commit itself beyond the limited resources available through the Export-Import Bank, the inadequately capitalized Development Loan Fund and Public Law 480. Other governments—Germany, Canada and Great Britain in particular—have also extended commercial credits and loans.

Today India still stands precariously poised between danger and real progress. Today it is even more evident that China's economic success may overshadow India's with all of the implications that this will have for the whole Asian continent.

Danger of Stop-Gaps

Earlier this year, on the Senate floor, we stressed the compelling need for the United States and other free nations, including Great Britain, Germany, Canada and Japan, to mobilize their common resources in filling critical financial gaps in India. We stressed the peril of temporizing for yet another year with partial solutions and stop-gap remedies.

In the light of the fresh evidence it seems to us vital that the governments of the Atlantic Community, Japan and the Colombo Plan merge their thinking on this overshadowing problem in Asia. We should like to renew our suggestion for a free-nation mission to India, drawing on men such as John McCloy and Sir Oliver Franks to assess the areas of collaboration and to promote in India a panoramic yet precise appraisal of what is needed in the years ahead. Then Congress and other parliaments can early next year develop programs of effective assistance.

The Senate has already, after vigorous debate, stated its anticipatory concern regarding the Indian situation in the amendment to the Mutual Security authorization bill which it adopted.

In the meantime, the most urgent legislative requirement in this country is for the full restoration of the requested appropriations for the Development Loan Fund in the Mutual Security Appropriations Act. We feel that even this appropriation is too low for a fund which should be our dominant instrument in long-term aid. Unless the Development Loan Fund is given a real capital base, our foreign aid policy will only be driven to further expedients which will be peculiarly vulnerable to political blackmail and to the stresses of sudden crises.

Relieving Poverty

We would dissent with one thought expressed in your editorial. It is obvious that industrialization by itself is not an answer to poverty and to the economic facts of life in the underdeveloped world. However, we cannot agree that the present Indian effort is too ambitious and that its goals must be further curtailed.

Two facts in particular suggest that India should not attempt to do less:

First is the growing and ominous economic effort which Communist China has mounted. In India it can be established for Asia that democratic methods of planning and development can secure the central objectives of economic growth.

Second, each further cut in Indian goals imperils not only national morale but also further constricts private enterprise which has maintained a good economic performance in India.

There has been too little appreciation in this country that some of the most serious strains in the Indian economy today have arisen from the unexpected and wholesome momentum of the private sector of the economy. If private enterprise is to remain a decisive force, and if there is to be a vigorous private investment program, the fulfillment of the Five-Year Plan's objectives is essential.

Recent events in the Middle East have again raised the question as to whether we as Americans have yet learned to act in foreign affairs on our opportunities, before crisis has closed in. Even as the Middle East has exploded in crisis, there has been a less dramatic but equally deep-seated political erosion in the independent nations of Burma, Ceylon and Cambodia.

Nowhere do we have a better chance than in the Indian peninsula—including Pakistan—to act out of well-grounded hope rather than fear. Here, if we take advantage of our opportunities and capacities, the Western alliance need not become bedeviled in mere reflex action. Nowhere can we more effectively influence now the pattern of future events.

JOHN F. KENNEDY

JOHN SHERMAN COOPER

Washington, July 25, 1958

[Our disagreement with the opinions expressed in this letter has to do mainly with the question of the rate of industrialization. If this process is too rapid, it may create inflation and adversely affect the flow of trade.—Editor, *The Times*.]

Appendix I

Holborn Reminds His Boss of the Task for 1959

[*Note*: This undated memorandum, evidently written early in 1959, is a useful summary of where the Indian economy stood at the time. Evidently, the collapse of Mao's Great Leap Forward had not yet become clear in Washington.]

MEMORANDUM

To: Senator Kennedy

From: FLH

Future Legislative Moves on the India Situation

Recent Developments

During the past year India has received approximately $850,-000,000 in foreign loans, committed or promised. The Development Loan Fund has provided $100 million, P.L. 480 about $220 million, the World Bank a little over $100 million, Great Britain about $105,000,000 with smaller amounts from Russia, Canada, Japan, Czechoslovakia, and Germany. In the recent discussions between the United States, Canada, Germany, Great Britain and India there were statements that early next year there would be some supplementary loans.

Roughly, India has received in this one year the *minimum* amounts which she said were necessary in the fall of 1957. However, some unfavorable factors must be taken into further account in judging this performance: 1) India was forced to take several loans on poor terms—very high rates of interest and relatively short repayment periods. Only the Canadian loans were flexible and generous in their terms; 2) As matters now stand, far too many of these loans will have heavy repayment charges early in the 1960s—a critical point in the path to economic growth; 3) India was very much in the position this past year of "taking what it could get"— not always the type of aid with the best return or most necessary to good economic performance. Most of the aid and loans had to be applied against existing shortages and unpaid bills; relatively little towards new projects, private industry, or forward planning. Both the World Bank and the Development Loan Fund, as well as the EX-IM Bank are lending on a project-by-project basis—none help too much in furnishing growth momentum; 4) India has continued to suffer this past year from a *decline* in prices for Indian raw material exports (tea, textiles, jute, etc.), while there has been a continued *rise* in the cost of needed industrial imports—especially machines. This has not been true of India alone—the same is true in most of Latin America and Africa. This may improve somewhat this year and probably next year, when India's own steel production will be very much on the rise. What has been especially serious, however, has been India's inability to keep her food grain production in alignment with the rise in population—4,800,000 this year alone. India's agricultural performance in contrast to China's has been worsening—and must be more vigorously attacked, quite apart from what India is able to achieve in exports of steel, textiles, manganese, oil, etc. Therefore, the $850 million should not deceive: it must be set against the continued uncertainty of US's future plans, the high servicing costs of much of the assistance received, the poor agricultural situation, the relatively better showing by China, the population spiral, the fact that the tempo of growth has sagged.

The other inescapable fact is that the psychological climate has changed. Now—to a degree not true two or three years ago—Indian opinion and the Government of India are relying on the United States. Kennedy-Cooper has been taken seriously, and high hopes were raised by the "consortium" discussions of September between the U.S., Great Britain, Canada, Germany, Japan. All last year the Indians were told to wait until 1959—now it is here.

Appendix J

The Author Reports to Millikan from Cambridge (England), February 22, 1959

[*Note*: This letter is one of many which reflect the closeness of cooperation between B. K. Nehru and members of CENIS in 1958–1959. P. N. Rosenstein-Rodan, an old friend and contemporary of Nehru's at the London School of Economics in the 1930s, had many such contacts, as did Millikan.]

Dear Max:

B. K. Nehru came here to spend the day; and he has just left after five hours of intense and, for me, extremely interesting talk. Would you be good enough to have this copied for Fred Holborn, since there is not a piece of carbon paper in the house.

1. He has just returned from India having been protagonist in a fight concerning the general strategy of the Third Five Year Plan. The fight concerned shooting high versus shooting low. Shooting high demands a lot of foreign exchange. By the most prevalent calculation-deriving from a statistician on the planning staff of the order of $1 billion per annum. BK has fought for a policy of shooting high, and making whatever accommodations may be necessary to persuade US and others to lend the foreign exchange. He urged for two hours on the PM—he thinks successfully—the notion of making necessary accommodations in order to accomplish the take-off and achieve Indian economic independence. He thinks he has been successful, in the sense that certainly a high plan is now being drafted, at least as one of the two alternatives. Whatever its other effects, the Kennedy speech will re-inforce the examination of the high alternative.

2. He is convinced that the Communist line is to play for the failure of the Second and Third Plans; and simultaneously to posture as: a) a friend of a high plan; b) enemy of any foreign aid. Out of high expectations, domestic failure, and no external aid they plan the matrix for a take-over.

3. Domestically, the PM is feeling his way towards an understanding of the mutually re-inforcing role of social overhead capital in the public sector; agriculture; private industry; and private external capital; and he is doing fine except when foreign oil companies are involved or when he gets pin-pricked by equal belly-achers in the private sector. I outlined the great reconciliation speech I wanted the PM to deliver, freeing India from either 19th century Western slogans of the 30's; or Communist slogans, all centered around the conditions for a successful take-off.

4. Technically, BK is cheered by the momentum in both the public and private sectors; the will of the private sector to keep coming despite crippling foreign exchange restrictions; the likelihood of long period of gestation investment (dams and steel mills) coming soon into production; and (to my surprise) the view that the peasants are really latching on to water and chemical fertilizers. But he wasn't naively hopeful; merely confident that there are some underlying forces of momentum at work.

5. In London he presented in the past two days his high-low choice; Oliver Franks, Frank Lee, assembled financial journalists, assembled business-men working in SE Asia. . . . all, in fact, except Roger Makins, who was professionally (and responsibly) cautious, said the high choice was the only way to go. This accords with my soundings. Donald Tyerman* saw him the evening of my stages-of-growth lunch, which gave over more to India than my business (which was in any case in good shape) and it seems possible that he will hit the road on India and Kennedy, etc.; but we shall have to see.

6. Now an important point of timing. BK thinks that the optimum time for a serious Western team in India may be after the Indians have done quite a lot more homework, around the high plan. He

*Donald Tyerman was at this time editor of the *Economist* which was planning to publish a summary of my *Stages of Economic Growth*.

275

thinks a premature visitors' team may label the high plan foreign.

We agreed, in the light of this, that the West should maybe first spend some time getting its donors club in general in order; the DLF; a meeting to proportion other parallel contributions; criteria; etc.; and arrange an India go-to, maybe early 1960.

I still don't have the Kennedy text; so I don't know if he did the 7.5 billion in five years. I hope so. Until further guided I shall devote Operation Ernie to a generalized reaction, rather than an urgently Indian one.

So far as the Senator is concerned—and Doug Dillon: there is no problem, as I see it, if they wish to pass the resolution and leave the timing to the Executive Branch, so long as something serious is in motion by the next Congressional session, which it ought to be.

There was much more . . . but these are main points; and since you will soon be seeing him [B. K. Nehru] directly, will suffice.

Yours,

Walt

Appendix K

*The State Department Moves on May 4, 1959,
toward a Reconciliation with the Kennedy-
Cooper Resolution of February 1959*

[*Note*: This letter almost—but not quite—says the State Department
would support the Kennedy-Cooper resolution if Pakistan is included.
Source: Papers of John F. Kennedy, Pre-Presidential Papers, Senate Files,
Holborn Subject File, "India, 3/29/58—9/6/60" folder, box 562.]

Dear Senator Fulbright:

I have received your letter of February 26 requesting the Department's comments on Senate Concurrent Resolution 11 which was introduced by Senator Kennedy (for himself and Senator Cooper) on February 19, 1959, "To invite friendly and democratic nations to consult with India."

The Department is in sympathy with the interest shown by members of the Senate in the problems of countries such as the Republic of India. As you know, the Department has, for a number of years, supported the extension of economic assistance to India at levels which have contributed materially to the development of that country within the democratic form of government to which its present leaders are dedicated. In the Department's opinion, however, a resolution of this nature, which specifies a single country as the object of our interest, however important that country may be to us, could raise difficult problems with other countries that may believe they too merit priority consideration in their economic and social development, and we would oppose a resolution thus limited.

The economies of the five countries of South Asia—India, Pakistan, Afghanistan, Nepal and Ceylon—are closely entwined. The development, or the lack therefore, of one cannot fail to have a direct bearing upon the others. India and Pakistan particularly emphasize the regional nature of the many economic problems of the South Asian subcontinent. Any effort that the Free World can make to help both countries in broad development programs of mutual benefit will go far toward reducing the tensions which presently exist between them and which promote divisive tendencies in the area. The development of the water resources of the Indus basin on the basis of a mutually acceptable plan would be a possible illustration. In this connection, I am informed that the IBRD, which has been giving its good offices for a period of years in an effort to bring India and Pakistan together on a solution to the Indus Waters problem, is about ready to present to the Governments of the two countries a proposal which it has developed. It is hoped that the Bank's plan will be accepted by both countries.

If, therefore, it is decided to proceed with something along the lines of Senate Concurrent Resolution 11, the Department believes it essential that it cover the area of South Asia; so framed, it would serve a broader and more useful purpose.

Sincerely yours,
For the Acting Secretary of State:

William B. Macomber, Jr.
Assistant Secretary

Appendix L

Holborn-Kennedy Memorandum, July 13, 1959

[*Note*: Holborn summarizes the state of play before the final two sessions of the Foreign Relations Committee, which acted formally on the version of the Kennedy-Cooper resolution which embraced Pakistan and shifted the locus of action to the World Bank. Source: Papers of John F. Kennedy, Pre-Presidential Papers, Senate File, Holborn Subject File, "India" folder, box 572.]

MEMO TO SENATOR KENNEDY
FROM: Fred Holborn
SUBJECT: S. Con. Res. 11

1. S. Con. Res. 11 will be taken up by the Foreign Relations Committee in open session at about 10:15 on Tuesday. Later it will also be considered in executive session.

2. A revised draft of the resolution will be circulated to committee members at the meeting. It will be necessary for you to explain briefly this new version, which has been agreed to by the State Department.

3. This pilot mission, if established, would not supersede or run counter to any of the existing mechanisms through which we assist India and the other nations of South Asia. It makes explicit provision that representatives can be sent either by governments or by regional organizations. Therefore, the Common Market, the Colombo Plan, and the World Bank can all be represented. Its main purpose is to provide a vehicle by which there can be a more composite picture of these nations' needs over the next 5 or 7 years and

a better means of merging all of the disparate efforts already being made or proposed for this area. It is especially valuable in India because it provides an informal method for India to consult with its various creditor nations looking toward a longer span than one year and for these nations to have at the outset a clear image of India's Third Plan and its needs over the next 5 years.

4. The World Bank may be the best umbrella for such a mission, especially if the plans for IDA move forward, but this is left open in the resolution itself so that the views of other governments can be taken into account.

5. The Indian Government has been concerned that this resolution might be read in India as an effort to involve Western governments in the detailed planning and programming of the Third Plan. All we can do about this is to suggest in testimony that this is not the purpose, and we have added the phrase "in cooperation with the governments of South Asia" at the end of Section (a) of the resolution.

Appendix M

The New Republic *Comments Skeptically on the Bankers' Mission, January 4, 1960*

[*Note*: This bit of reporting and gossip is of interest mainly because the *New Republic*'s fears concerning the Bankers' Mission to the subcontinent proved to be unfounded.]

MISSION TO SOUTH ASIA

Shortly before adjournment the Senate, which had turned down one expensive aid-to-India proposal (long-term financing for the Development Loan Fund would have aided the Indian subcontinent more than any other single country), went along unanimously with Sen. John Kennedy's resolution calling on the Executive to

explore with other free and democratic nations and appropriate international organizations the advisability of establishing an international mission that would consult with governments in the area of South Asia on their needs . . . and . . . recommend methods by which the participating countries could jointly assist these South Asian governments in the fulfillment of their economic plans.

The idea had been cleared with the Administration in the person of Undersecretary of State C. Douglas Dillon, who had insisted only that the phraseology permit the inclusion of Pakistan and India's other immediate neighbors. What Mr. Dillon and Senator Kennedy (and co-sponsor John Sherman Cooper) had in mind was an autonomous commission of eminent men with standing in their countries who might, perhaps, avail themselves of World Bank technical advice but would not take the narrow banker's approach in which the have-not countries—and their ambitions—are treated much the same as Wall Street treats Osage City. Some of the broad-gauged men who have been sounded out over the past year about service on such a mission were, from the outset, Jean Monnet, the first chairman of the European Coal and Steel Community, a prime mover in the effort within the Common Market for a Western European aid program; the brilliant Sir Oliver Franks, chairman of Lloyds Bank and former Ambassador to the United States, and Escott Reid of Canada, former Ambassador to New Delhi. Sir Oliver is a banker, and so is the Chase Bank's John McCloy, who was the American desired for the mission. Both are also men of sophistication in world affairs whose interest in such an assignment would presumably derive from a positive commitment to the general objectives of Western assistance for South Asian development.

As the result of Senator Kennedy's persistent pressure this fall, Undersecretary Dillon finally in late November took up the matter seriously with World Bank President Eugene Black. To avoid direct US sponsorship, Dillon proposed (and Kennedy agreed) that Black should in his individual capacity take the leadership in constituting the commission. They did not bargain, however, for Mr. Black's personal animosity toward Mr. Monnet and his disposition to play ball with Treasury Secretary Anderson at this moment of the Anderson ascendancy within the Administration. The mission which was finally constituted last week and is scheduled to spend February and March in South Asia consists of Sir Oliver, Chancellor Adenauer's banker friend, Hermann Abs of the Deutschebank and, of all people, former Budget Director Joseph Dodge as the US member.

Mr. Black's veto of Jean Monnet and Secretary Anderson's pressure for Dodge (which was apparently governed, like the Diefenbaker Government's anxiety over the Reid appointment, by a desire to scale down the price tag on the mission's recommendations) have left Sir Oliver with two of the most conservative figures in the Western fiscal world as his collaborators. To be sure, the designation of a German as the Common Market's representative could conceivably have great value if Mr. Abs comes out for substantial government-to-government credits (as against the present German "aid" in the form of subsidies for private German business exports to the underdeveloped countries). And Joseph Dodge as a champion of large-scale aid to the South Asian governments might be influential with die-hard Congressional opponents of aid. This, at least, is the argument one hears in Mr. Black's defense, but it is difficult to swallow.

Appendix N

The Report of the Bankers' Mission to India and Pakistan

[*Note*: This historic document is, in a sense, the final result of the Kennedy-Cooper resolutions of 1958–1959. It is prefaced here by Black's covering letter to Kennedy. Source: Washington, D.C.: International Bank for Reconstruction and Development.]

INTERNATIONAL BANK FOR
RECONSTRUCTION AND DEVELOPMENT
Washington 25, D.C.

Office of the President

April 11, 1960

Dear Jack:

In view of the interest which you have always shown in the problems of economic development in India and Pakistan, and especially in view of your sponsorship of Senate Concurrent Resolution 11 last Fall, I have great pleasure in sending you herewith an advance copy of the report which has been submitted to me by the three Western bankers, Mr. Hermann Abs, Sir Oliver Franks, and Mr. Allan Sproul, who upon my suggestion visited India and Pakistan during February and March to acquaint themselves with the economic conditions and prospects there. This report has been read by the Finance Ministers of India and Pakistan and they have accepted our proposal that it be published as it stands. It would be issued by means of a press release from the Bank in the very near future.

I am sure that you will agree with me that this report will make a very important and illuminating contribution to public discussion in this country and elsewhere of the development problems of these two great countries.

With best regards,

Sincerely yours,

/s/ Gene
Eugene R. Black

Encl.
The Honorable
John F. Kennedy
United States Senate
Washington 25, D.C.

BANKERS' MISSION
TO INDIA AND PAKISTAN
February–March, 1960

A letter to
Mr. Eugene R. Black
President
International Bank for Reconstruction and Development
from
Mr. Hermann J. Abs
Chairman, Deutsche Bank of Frankfurt
Sir Oliver Franks
Chairman, Lloyds Bank Ltd., London
Mr. Allan Sproul
Formerly Chairman, New York Federal Reserve Bank

FOREWORD
by
Eugene R. Black

In response to my suggestion, three well known bankers visited Pakistan and India for six weeks in February and March of this year to study economic conditions there and acquaint themselves with the current and planned development programs in the two countries. The bankers were MR. HERMANN J. ABS, Chairman of the Deutsche Bank of Frankfurt, SIR OLIVER FRANKS, Chairman of Lloyds Bank Ltd., London, and MR. ALLAN SPROUL, formerly Chairman of New York Federal Reserve Bank.

In making this suggestion, which was prompted by the terms of a resolution introduced into the United States Senate by SENATORS JOHN F. KENNEDY and JOHN SHERMAN COOPER, and passed unanimously by that body, I was guided by the conviction that visits by prominent members of the business and financial communities of the industrially developed countries would help to achieve a wider understanding of the problems confronting the less developed areas of the world.

Mr. Abs, Sir Oliver Franks and Mr. Sproul were not asked to prepare a formal report, nor was a detailed assessment possible in the time available. But they had extensive opportunities during their visit to observe the economic conditions and problems of India and Pakistan, and to discuss with leaders of the two countries the issues involved in carrying out economic development programs. At the end of their visit the three bankers wrote a joint letter to me recording their general impressions; their letter is reproduced on the following pages.

In deciding to publish the letter, with the permission of its authors, I felt that it would make an important contribution to public discussion of the problems of economic development, both in India and Pakistan and in the industrialized countries which have been and expect to be providing assistance for economic development in the sub-continent.

New Delhi, India
19th March, 1960.

Dear Mr. Black:

The proposal that we should visit India and Pakistan was sponsored by you, as President of the International Bank for Reconstruction and Development, and was welcomed by the Governments of India and Pakistan. We accepted the invitation as independent private individuals. We received no terms of reference or instructions either from the International Bank, or from the Governments of our own countries. We have, therefore, had to consider what an independent Mission of this kind, with a limited amount of time at its disposal, could most usefully attempt. You told us that we were not expected to submit a formal report: and, indeed, it would have been impossible for us in the course of a month to undertake any detailed assessment of the economic situation and development programs of India and Pakistan. We have concluded that the most useful task which we can set ourselves is to try and form broad general impressions about the problems of development in these two countries. In doing so, we have approached the question of scale and balance of development plans in qualitative rather than quantitative terms, and we have tried to see how the kind of proposals for development which are at present under consideration in these two countries fit into the broad pattern of what has already been achieved. We hope that the bundle of impressions which we have formed will help towards the understanding of some of the problems of policy which seem to us to confront both the countries which we have visited and those countries and international institutions which are, or may be, concerned with providing finance for development.

Despite the many differences and contrasts between India and Pakistan, the basic economic problem confronting them is the shortage of capital resources in relation to the needs of development. In both countries there is the familiar vicious circle of low income, low savings, and continuing low income, which cannot be broken effectively without an inflow of capital funds from abroad. Both countries are suffering from a serious shortage of foreign exchange, and have been forced to impose strict import licensing. But perhaps the most striking feature of the sub-continent's development problem is its sheer scale: not only are real incomes low, but, with a population of about 500 million—about 90 million in Pakistan and over 400 million in India—the capital resources required to generate even modest increases in real income are very large.

The numbers already involved are large, but in both countries the problem is made much more intractable by the rate of growth of population. While precise information is lacking, it seems that the principal cause of the rapid growth of population is not an increase in the birth rate—the birth rate may be little higher than that in the United States—but a sharp decline in the death rate, which is the result of the provision in recent years of basic medical and sanitation facilities long familiar in more advanced countries. It is true that Governments have endorsed programs of education in family planning, though the results of this may not be realized for some time. Moreover, as the populations of both countries achieve a higher degree of literacy, and become aware of the possibilities of achieving an improved standard of life, the present trend towards smaller families in the urban areas may become more widespread. However, it is impossible to say when a significant fall in the birth rate will occur, and in the meantime both Governments are confronted with the task of providing the extra food and other necessities required by increases in population of the order of 18 to 20 per cent over the next ten years, while at the same time struggling to bring about an increase in *per capita* income.

In visiting India and Pakistan one of our first tasks has been to try and form a judgment about the qualities of character, vigor, and honest endeavor to be found in the two countries. On these questions we have gained a sense of considerable confidence from our discussions with the Ministers, officials and private individuals whom we have met. We have also been impressed by the capacity of the senior officials and prominent businessmen in both countries. Nevertheless, once one goes beyond this, managerial talent is scarce and it may prove difficult to carry through decisions effectively in their detailed application to the individual at the level of worker and farmer.

The shortages of foreign exchange, domestic saving and managerial capacity in both public and private sectors have caused both countries to adopt economic planning. Both countries are using the framework of Five Year Plans, with Pakistan embarking on its Second Five Year Plan in July 1960, and India beginning its Third Five Year Plan in April 1961. In both countries we have tried to review the broad outlines of these plans in the light of earlier experience and present economic policies.

The two sections which follow set out the impressions which we have formed in each of the two countries. The concluding section indicates briefly some more general ideas which we believe to be relevant when considering the problems of development and foreign assistance common to both countries.

Pakistan: The Second Five Year Plan

We began our tour of Pakistan on February 14th, and during the following ten days visited Rawalpindi, Peshawar, Lahore and Karachi, with brief stop-overs at several industrial and hydro-electric projects. We also flew over the Indus irrigation system in West Pakistan. We subsequently made a trip to East Pakistan from March 5th to 8th, visiting Dacca, Jessore and Khulna, where we were shown other industrial installations and given a flying tour over a number of flood-control and irrigation projects. During our visit, we met President Mohammad Ayub Khan and members of his Cabinet, most of the senior officials concerned with economic policy in the Central and Provincial Governments, and many private businessmen. In these meetings, we were impressed by the enlightened leadership which the present Government is bringing to bear on the problems of economic policy and development.

With the partition of the Indian sub-continent in 1947, Pakistan emerged as an independent country including both the semi-arid regions of Baluchistan, Sindh and the Western Punjab and, separated by more than a thousand miles of Indian territory, the subtropical area of East Bengal. The differences between East and West Pakistan are striking, but both provinces are predominantly agricultural, deficient in industrial materials, and since partition, hemmed in by frontiers which cut across the natural and traditional lines of communication and trade with India. After partition, Pakistan also faced the problem of receiving and integrating into its economy an influx of many million refugees; and the combined problems of physical separation, refugee assimilation, and economic development have created serious difficulties for a country in which there are shortages of skilled manpower stemming from educational deficiencies.

More deepseated has been the problem of the continuing loss of good agricultural land through waterlogging and salinity in West Pakistan. We were told that of about 30 million acres of cultivated land in West Pakistan about 70,000 acres are entirely lost each year and hundreds of thousands of acres are suffering losses in productivity as a result of the inroads of salinity and waterlogging.

Until the present Government came into power, a succession of governments had made only halting progress towards developing a more viable pattern in the economy. In 1955, the Government sought to introduce a more coordinated approach in the form of a First Five Year Plan, to cover the period 1955–60, but Ministers and officials have told us that the Plan failed in a number of important ways. The basic cause of the failure to make progress was the stagnation of agricultural output. This was due to an inadequate recognition of the priority of the agricultural problem, and to the lack of effective action to educate the farmer in improved production techniques, or to provide him with adequate supplies of seed, fertilizers, pesticides and credit. With food output stationary and population rising, food imports increased and the balance of payments deteriorated. At the same time, an upsurge of private import demand, which fiscal and monetary policy failed to control, led to the foreign exchange crisis of 1957/58.

In 1959, the new Government succeeded in regaining control over the economic situation. Firm action was taken to bring the budget into better balance and to restrain credit. Drastic restrictions on less essential imports effectively halted the decline in reserves, while the introduction of an export bonus scheme somewhat strengthened export incentives. The inflationary trend in prices was checked by price controls, which are being progressively relaxed now that the more fundamental financial measures are proving effective. Nevertheless, the economy remains heavily dependent on foreign aid, not only for supporting development but also for covering current import requirements. But, most important of all, the new Government has succeeded in restoring confidence.

Much has been learned from the failure of the First Five Year Plan, and this is reflected in the draft outline of the Second Five Year Plan which covers the period July 1960 to June 1965. In aggregate terms, the objective of the Plan is to achieve a 20 per cent increase in national output by 1965. With population expected to increase by 10 per cent during the period, the Plan thus envisages an increase in income per head of about 2 per cent per annum.

The Plan aims to spend about Rs. 19,000 million ($4.0 billion) over the five years. Of this Rs. 11,500 million is in the public sector and Rs. 7,500 million in the private sector. The general composition of the proposed expenditure is shown on the next page.

The Government has told us that it expects to be able to finance Rs. 11,000 million of this expenditure from domestic resources,

Total Development Expenditure

	Million Rupees	Percentage
Agriculture	5,530	28
Industry, fuels and minerals	4,170	22
Public utilities (transport, communications, power, water supply)	4,450	24
Commercial and residential buildings	2,710	14
Education, health, welfare, etc.	1,640	9
Inventories	500	3
	19,000	100

while direct private foreign investment is expected to provide about Rs. 1,500 million, leaving Rs. 6,500 million to be financed by foreign aid in one form or another. In addition to the aid needed to finance the development program itself, the Government estimates that a further Rs. 1,500 million will be required to cover the excess of ordinary imports not directly connected with development over export earnings, so that the total external assistance required (excluding P.L. 480 funds) is put at Rs. 8,000 million (or $1.7 billion).

The Second Plan gives first priority to achieving agricultural self-sufficiency by the end of the Plan period. Success in achieving this objective is a necessary precondition for the success of the whole Plan. This involves supplying the farmer with adequate amounts of fertilizer, improved seed, pesticides and credit, and ensuring their effective use. Warehousing and marketing arrangements will also have to be improved. If all this is to be done, the Government will have to overcome the extremely difficult problem of building up an effective organization that will reach down to the individual farmer. Next, the Plan proposes to take immediate steps to halt the progressive loss of agricultural output from waterlogging and salinity. Priority will be given to drainage in order to prevent further loss of good land. At the same time, a start will be made on longer term measures, some of which may still be experimental, to reclaim land which has gone out of use. There are also plans to bring new land under cultivation.

These proposals for conserving existing acreage and reclaiming lost land form part of a longer term overall water resources plan designed to make the fullest use of Pakistan's water supplies. This longer term plan includes proposals for the construction of dams, barrages, canals and tube wells, and will in the aggregate involve large amounts of capital expenditure over a decade or more. In certain instances these schemes form part of multi-purpose projects designed also to supply industrial power. A certain number of these large slow-maturing projects are essential to provide for the future growth of the demand for power and to extend irrigation over the wider area required by a growing agricultural population. But there is a risk that too much capital and technical resources can get locked up in these big schemes so that the investment program becomes inflexible. We feel that, in striking a balance between large projects and smaller schemes which yield more immediate returns, this problem of phasing should be kept under constant review.

The pattern of industrial development which the Plan proposes is largely directed to the need for supplying the agricultural sector with manufactured equipment and supplies, and providing for the processing of agricultural output such as jute, cotton and sugar cane. Of equal importance in determining the pattern of industrial development is the chronic shortage of foreign exchange which, as the Plan recognizes, must imply concentration on investment in industries which will either save imports or increase export earnings. In consequence, the Government will be forced to exercise a selective control over the establishment of new firms and industries for some time to come, and will hold the power to prevent expansion or enforce contraction in existing industries. The exercise of this power in a country in which administrative talent is spread so thinly obviously presents certain hazards.

A critically important aspect of the Second Five Year Plan is the problem which it poses for internal financial policy. We were told that, if the Plan is to be implemented without undue inflationary pressure, about 25 per cent of the projected increase in *per capita* income will have to be absorbed by saving, public or private. In a country such as Pakistan where real incomes are so low, and much of the increase in income will be widely spread over a population living near subsistence level, this is a formidable task. We were impressed by the determination with which the Minister of Finance is approaching the fiscal problem. We also feel that it is important that the fiscal and monetary authorities should be alert as to the part monetary policy can play in restraining inflationary pressure, and helping to bring about a more economic allocation of investment resources.

The Government is quite clear as to the role which it assigns to public and private enterprise within the Plan. Apart from certain social needs which are met in almost all countries by public expenditures, and apart from the qualification that whenever private funds and initiative are not forthcoming in other essential areas the State will have to undertake the investment itself, the Government believes that as much as possible should remain within the private sector. Again, officials have told us that outside the field of public utilities it is Government policy to return to the private sector any publicly-owned or operated enterprises as soon as feasible.

To summarize our main impressions. First, the rates of increase in output and *per capita* income envisaged by the Plan are modest. But if they are to be achieved the problem of mobilizing the necessary domestic resources will require strenuous efforts by the Government and continuing austerity for the people of Pakistan. On the assumptions of the Plan an increase in external foreign assistance of about 30 per cent will also be required for development purposes.

Secondly, we would like to endorse the priority which the Plan gives to increasing agricultural output. We have been impressed by the determination of the Government to achieve this objective. Our only uncertainty is whether the organizational problem of arranging adequate and timely supplies of fertilizer, seed and credit together with improved marketing arrangements will take longer than the Plan envisages.

Thirdly, the emphasis on industries which save imports or increase exports, and are based on local skills and resources, seems to be dictated by the realities of Pakistan's economic circumstances.

Finally, we have been told that, under the administrative procedure which the new Government has introduced all development expenditure will be reviewed annually, and that each year's Budget will only sanction development expenditure to the extent to which resources are available to meet it. We believe that this kind of year to year review of the progress of the Plan is essential if expenditure is to be adjusted to meet changing economic conditions, and we feel that we must stress the need for the Plan to be so phased that it can be kept flexible.

In making these observations we have not taken into account, indeed it would have been impossible for us to do so, the impact of the Indus Waters Scheme on Pakistan. We understand that while the Scheme is of great importance to both India and Pakistan, the finance planned under the Scheme is mainly for works in West Pakistan. It appears to us therefore that when the Scheme is being realized it must have a significant impact on the Pakistan economy. It will be of real importance to assess this impact correctly in relation to the Second Five Year Plan from the point of view of the incomes it will generate among a large labor force and the inevitable calls on technical and professional manpower which will arise even if the works are undertaken by foreign contractors.

India: The Third Five Year Plan

We arrived in Delhi on the 24th February and spent the next week in discussions with Ministers and officials. Between the 2nd and 5th of March we visited Jamshedpur, Rourkela, Maithon, Asansol, Sindri and Calcutta. After visiting East Pakistan, we returned to Calcutta on the 8th March, and then left for Southern India, visiting Madras, Bangalore and Mysore. During this time we were able to visit a range of industrial installations, community development projects and other development schemes, and to talk with many officials of State Governments and private businessmen. We returned to Delhi on the 12th March to complete our work. Pressure of time prevented us from visiting Bombay, as originally planned, and we very much regret that we did not have the opportunity of visiting this important centre.

The Indian Government just finished the preliminary draft outline of its Third Year Plan, to take effect from the 1st April, 1961. A great deal of work has already been done in bringing the draft Plan into a form in which decisions on it can be taken both by Union Ministers and by the State Governments, which is necessary under a Federal constitution. But, as these decisions are still in the course of being taken, the Indian Government has not been able to do more than explain to us the way in which they were approaching the Third Plan, and provide us with estimates of the general orders of magnitude in which they were thinking so that we could see broadly how the scale and balance of the Plan was taking shape. In these circumstances, we can do no more than discuss the problems of the Third Plan in rather general terms.

The problems facing those responsible for drawing up the Third Five Year Plan need to be looked at against the background of experience with the two preceding Plans. When India achieved independence in 1947, she was faced not merely with the problems left by the war and the consequences of partition, but with the need to speed up the process of development which would yield higher living standards for a population the bulk of whom were living near subsistence. The economy was largely agricultural, the main industries being the traditional manufacture of cotton and jute textiles, and, while some other industries had grown up in the decades before independence, their rate of expansion had not been strong enough to meet the needs of an increasing population, let alone provide an adequate base for further development.

In 1951 India embarked on its First Five Year Plan, although officials have told us that the word "Plan" is something of a misnomer since it did little more than pull together various schemes for economic development that had been started by the Central Government and the States in the postwar years. Although the planned increases in investment were relatively small and not entirely fulfilled, unusually good harvests during the last three years of the Plan contributed to an atmosphere of achievement. The expansion of agricultural output and income not only supported economic growth elsewhere in the economy, but also strengthened the balance of payments position and exerted a strongly stabilizing influence upon the price level.

Perhaps influenced in part by the good fortune attending the First Five Year Plan period, the Indian Government raised its sights considerably in developing the Second Five Year Plan. This called for major increases in investment in agriculture and there was a new emphasis on investment in basic industry and in various resource development projects in the public sector. Partly because the tempo of investment was stepped up so sharply, and partly because of the swing of fortune in the other direction, the Second Five Year Plan ran into difficulties. Unexpectedly heavy food import requirements appeared as lean years in agriculture succeeded the unusually good harvests during the First Five Year Plan; budgetary difficulties generated inflationary pressures; and a burst of private import demand so heavily drained India's foreign exchange resources as to force abrupt cutbacks in the program in 1957. Emergency assistance provided by a number of foreign countries prevented a breakdown of the Plan, and with this help the Indian Government has succeeded in carrying the Plan ahead on a somewhat reduced scale.

Despite the disruptive effects of the foreign exchange crisis, much of the heavy investment undertaken since 1956 is beginning to bear fruit. Three new steel plants are coming into operation and will shortly increase India's steel-making capacity from about 2 million tons to 6 million tons. There has also been a substantial growth in industries such as locomotives, vehicles, machine tools, chemicals and electrical engineering. Agricultural production has been rising, but the rate of increase has lagged considerably behind the growing food requirements of an expanding population. This is partly attributable to unfavorable weather, but also to delays in fertilizer production and various irrigation schemes, and to difficulties in securing effective action at village level.

In brief summary, India's experience with planning since 1951 has inevitably involved a number of miscalculations from which much seems to have been learned. Despite all the difficulties the basic result of the First and Second Five Year Plans has been to start the process of development moving at an accelerated pace. The Third Five Year Plan proposes to take this process one stage further.

The main objectives of the Five Year Plan as outlined to us by senior officials are:

(a) to secure during the Third Plan a rise in national income of at least 5 per cent per annum, the pattern of investment being designed also to sustain this rate of growth during subsequent plan periods;

(b) to achieve self-sufficiency in foodgrains, and increase other agricultural production to meet the requirements of industry and exports;

(c) to develop basic industries such as steel, fuel and power and, in particular, machine-building capacity, so that the requirements of further industrialization can be met within a period of 10 years or so mainly from the country's own resources;

(d) to ensure a substantial expansion in employment opportunities; and

(e) to bring about a reduction of inequalities in income and wealth and a more even distribution of economic power.

In framing the plan the Indian Government is faced with a number of exceedingly difficult decisions. On the one hand the Government feels that if it is to achieve the twin objectives of a gradually rising standard of life for the Indian people and reducing their dependence upon foreign aid, a very substantial investment effort is required now. In the mind of the Government the urgency of stepping up the investment effort during the Third Plan period is further reinforced by the expectation of a substantial growth in population over the next decade. On the other hand, both Ministers and officials recognize that the political pressures existing in a democratic society, which has only recently gained independence, impose a definite limit on the sacrifices of immediate consumption to the needs of the future which the Government can ask of its people. Further, even if the community is prepared to accept the maximum sacrifice called for by the Government, there would remain the complex administrative task of actually securing the requisite increases in taxation and saving from a population most of whom are living dangerously close to the subsistence level. This dilemma of choice between present and future needs is particularly acute in the balance of payments area where Indian officials are aware of the risk that an excessively high investment level might overtax India's foreign exchange resources, including whatever aid may be supplied by friendly foreign governments, and precipitate another balance of payments crisis.

In its present tentative form the Plan calls for a very substantial increase of investment from the $13.8 billion now scheduled for the Second Five Year Plan to $20.9 billion during the Third Five Year Plan, distributed as follows among the major sectors of the economy:

Investment in the Third Plan

Economic Sector	($billions)
Agriculture and Community Development	2.8
Irrigation	1.3
Power	2.0
Village and small industries	0.9
Industry and minerals	4.8
Transport and communications	3.5
Social services	3.4
Inventories	2.1
Total:	20.9

This volume of investment is expected to raise *per capita* income, after allowing for an expected population growth of nearly 50 million, from about 65 to about 74 dollars per annum. Mobilization of the internal financial resources required for an investment program of this magnitude would require an increase in the rate of saving, public and private, from 8 to 12 per cent, including substantial increases in taxation. On the balance of payments side, over the five year period this investment program is expected to open up a gap requiring $6.5 billion in foreign aid. In terms of annual rates, this would imply an increase of nearly 45 per cent over the amounts (including drafts upon exchange reserves) utilized by India during the Second Plan.

Without attempting an overall judgment on the dimensions of the Plan, we would like to put forward the following observations:

(a) the targets set by the Plan in terms of increasing per capita income and laying the foundations for self-sustaining growth are in themselves relatively modest;

(b) whether the volume of investment projected will reach, fall short of, or over-shoot the income and other targets specified depends on certain assumptions with respect to capital-output ratios, which inevitably involve a great deal of guesswork. Quite apart from the statistical difficulties inherent in estimating and applying such capital-output ratios, the unpredictable effect of changing monsoon conditions upon a predominantly agricultural economy introduces into the Plan an element of chance which should be realistically assessed both by the Government of India and by the Governments from which development assistance is sought;

(c) the Plan would unquestionably require sacrifices in the form of increased taxation and savings which present a challenge to the political possibilities and the administrative efficiency of the Indian Government;

(d) the Plan calls for a sufficiently large increase in external assistance to require detailed study of the Plan by aid-giving governments who have to consider domestic claims upon their resources, and the investment needs of a number of other underdeveloped countries.

On the question of the balance struck by the Plan in allocating investment expenditure among the various economic sectors in accordance with relative priorities, we can only put forward some tentative impressions. The principal ones are:

(a) agriculture is stated to have first priority. We have been told that if more could be done for agriculture by diverting additional investment resources to this sector, it would be done. We believe that this should be done if it proves to be appropriate, and we hope that regional and departmental demands upon India's limited resources will not override the order to priorities set by the national interest. In this context we have been impressed during our tour by the extent to which the demand for fertilizer by the farm community appears to have grown: we hope that every effort will be made to find within the Plan adequate resources for constructing the fertilizer plants upon which the objective of agricultural self-sufficiency so heavily depends;

(b) the industrial program is solidly founded upon the availability of domestic raw materials and power, and offers extensive scope for providing not only producer's goods, but also the kinds of consumer's goods which an expanding economy will need, while simultaneously saving foreign exchange. We are impressed with the comparative cost advantages India at present holds in producing steel and certain other metal manufactures, both heavy and light;

(c) the industrial program is likely to encounter difficult problems of phasing. For example, the plans for further expansion in steel making capacity do not seem to be ambitious when they are set against the present level of imports and the probable growth in the demand for steel. But it will probably be some time before the steel plants which are nearing completion are working at optimum rates, and the desirability of achieving the most efficient utilization of existing capacity needs to be looked at when deciding upon the desirability of expanding capacity further. Again, as an example, the expansion of coking coal output needs to keep pace with the growth in steel making capacity and the requirements of the fertilizer industry: efforts should be made to see that difficulties in expanding coal output do not prove a bottleneck;

(d) both the agricultural and industrial development programs will impose heavy demands upon scarce resources of managerial and technical skills. This is particularly true in the case of agriculture, where the problem of educating more than 50 million farmers in improved cultivation techniques must clearly be approached on a selective basis rather than thinly dispersed over the entire agricultural front.

In framing their development plans, the Indian Government has also faced a serious dilemma of choice between direct public action and reliance on private enterprise. While certain major projects of power and water development are beyond the capacity of private enterprise, it has proved extremely difficult to establish clear-cut dividing lines in other areas in which the relative efficiency of private as against public enterprise still remains to be tested. There has also been some tendency for cutbacks in development planning to fall primarily upon the private sector where relative priorities are less readily identifiable than in the public sector. On the other hand, the prevailing scarcity of all types of manufactured goods has created the risk that Government allocation of exchange, credit and other resources to individual private enterprises may confer a virtual monopoly position with the consequent danger of abuse. While recognizing the natural desire of the Government to prevent such abuse, it should be remembered that intervention in the form of extraordinary taxation or price controls designed to protect the general public may sometimes frustrate the normal market process through which high profits in one area attract capital and other resources from other less profitable uses. If the issue of public versus private enterprise has lost some of its sharpness, it is because it has become more widely recognized that both sectors of the economy have their contribution to make.

The pattern of industrial development in India has been primarily conditioned by the shortage of foreign exchange, and the consequent necessity of giving priority to industrial projects which either earn or save foreign exchange. In this stage of economic development, it is perhaps natural that import saving projects can be more easily defined and incorporated into policy than export projects for which markets still have to be found. On the import saving side, much progress is being made. In a number of important instances, moreover, import saving possibilities have coincided with major opportunities of exploiting rich natural resources in the way of iron and coal. India is now among the cheapest steel producers in the world.

The emphasis given in the program of industrial development to import saving by no means implies, however, that the import requirements of India will necessarily follow a declining trend over the next 5, 10 or 15 years. On the contrary, it is likely that, as the Indian economy moves towards progressively higher stages of development, new types of imports required to sustain this progress will outweigh the economies achieved in other areas. The greater the pressure for rapid industrialization and general economic development, the greater the likelihood that there may be a progressive racheting upward of import requirements. This further underlines the necessity of giving high priority to the investment of effort, money and talent in the export field where the development of markets often takes a considerable time. But in fact India's exports have tended to stagnate in recent years and we have found no firm basis for confidence that export performance will materially improve in the near future. It is beginning to be realized that India's export base must be extended well beyond the traditional export items if sustainable economic development is to be realized. But an adequate export effort will require not simply sufficient export incentives for specific items in which India holds a comparative advantage in the world markets, but the creation of a state of export-mindedness.

The achievement of a substantial increase in exports will depend, too, on securing an appropriate degree of control over domestic consumption. For years to come the Indian Government will be constantly confronted with the harsh decision of choosing between consumption and export earnings. Perhaps the most basic policy decisions involved in such a choice between exports and consumption are those of fiscal and monetary policy. It is clear that inadequate coverage of Government spending by taxation or savings can generate inflationary pressures which may be restrained by import controls from directly using up scarce exchange resources but may nevertheless indirectly impair reserve availabilities by diverting potential exports to domestic consumption. Quite aside from this basic consideration, it may well be that selective tax measures will be required to restrain domestic consumption of specific export items for which foreign markets are available.

Monetary policy is also relevant to the choice between consumption on the one hand and exports and investment on the other, and clearly has a useful role to play in restraining any buildup of inflationary pressure. In this connection, there would appear to be some scope for mopping up excess liquidity still remaining in the Indian economy, and for a consideration of the appropriateness of the present level of interest rates. It may be that the relatively low rates prevailing create an illusion that capital is not actually a scarce resource. In general, we feel that it would be worth examining ways in which monetary action might be made a more effective weapon of economic policy.

In seeking to summarize our impressions of key aspects and problems of the Plan, we should be inclined to stress the following:

(a) Our impression in talking to officials is that a good deal has been learned both about techniques of planning and techniques of economic control from the difficulties encountered during the Second Plan.

(b) The need for effort to ensure success in agricultural policy cannot be over-stressed, and we have found it difficult to be certain whether the implications of this have been fully realized in all quarters: success will involve not merely effective management and administration over a very wide area, but the coordination of the activities of a number of Government Departments working in conjunction with voluntary organizations, and perhaps most important of all ensuring that the overall policy of the Union Government is effectively implemented by the individual States with whom the executive responsibility for agricultural policy rests.

(c) If inflationary pressure develops as the program moves ahead, fiscal and monetary action will need to be prompt and decisive.

(d) A strenuous effort should be made to diversify the export base and enter foreign markets.

(e) Without passing judgment on the precise scale of the Plan we would suggest that during the process of finalizing the Plan it would be desirable to re-examine the importance of the marginal projects. To all appearances the Plan is a big plan, and if it can be made more manageable by the omission of some projects the need for which is less immediate this in our view would be worth doing.

Finally, we have tried to assess the extent to which the Third Five Year Plan will be flexible—*i.e.*, the extent to which it can be modified year by year to meet short run changes in the economic situation. Officials have told us that they are working out a detailed phasing of the Plan designed to allow the necessary room to maneuver; and that they are thinking in terms of different Plan variants which may be adopted to meet different circumstances; and that in terms of the allocation of foreign exchange they are trying to form a view about the relative priorities which will allow a hard core of essential industrial projects to go ahead, even if others have to be held back. We consider the maintenance of such flexibility critically important to the success of the Plan and to the effective utilization of such foreign assistance as may be made available to India.

Some Problems of Foreign Assistance

The development programs of India and Pakistan discussed above can only be made effective if a very substantial increase in foreign assistance above the amounts provided during the course of the Pakistan First Five Year Plan and the Indian Second Five Year Plan is forthcoming. The rough breakdown of figures of economic assistance both public and private required by India and Pakistan for their forthcoming Five Year Plan periods is as follows:

Development Imports		$ Billion
India		4.0
Pakistan		1.4
Balance of payment support		
(including foreign debt service)		
India		1.5
Pakistan		0.3
	Total:	7.3
Aid in food supply		
(in particular P.L. 480)		
India		1.1
Pakistan		0.2
	Total:	1.3
	Grand Total:	8.5

The decision as to how much aid should be provided is a matter for Governments and an independent Mission of private individuals cannot be expected to give a judgment on matters of this kind. There are, however, a number of general questions concerning the scale, character and organization of aid to which we feel we should draw attention.

The problems of the development of India and Pakistan cannot be approached in terms of a Marshall Plan concept embodying a fixed period of foreign aid assistance to highly developed industrial countries and designed to reach more or less visible targets of economic recovery. The fact that average per capita income in India and Pakistan is so low will inevitably mean that development will be a lengthy process possibly extending over a considerable period of time. It is possible that this process might be accelerated somewhat by political measures designed to operate the economy under forced draft with consequent grave loss of individual freedom. Both Governments have rejected this approach, but we recognize that this decision renders both countries more heavily dependent upon outside assistance than would otherwise be the case.

If the assistance required were made available entirely in the form of long or short loans on normal commercial terms, the resulting debt service liabilities would almost certainly impose an intolerable strain on the Indian and Pakistani balance of payments. This means that a substantial proportion of any aid provided would have to take the form of grants or loans not made on strictly commercial terms. The proposed International Development Association represents a recognition by Governments of the need for this kind of assistance to developing countries, but the IDA is still in process of being established and its resources will be too small for it to play more than a minor role in providing external resources for India and Pakistan during the next five years. This means that if aid is provided on a considerable scale, a substantial proportion of this aid would have to take the form of Government to Government assistance of one kind or another on liberal terms.

It is expected that a considerable number of Governments will participate in providing assistance for India and Pakistan, and this is likely to involve ultimately bilateral agreements between each of the aid-giving and aid-receiving countries. It will be of the first importance therefore to ensure that the policy of the aid-providing Governments with respect to the scale, form and terms of the assistance provided should be adequately coordinated. Otherwise there is liable to be a waste of resources and effort and unnecessary international friction. In the context of bilateral aid extended by a considerable number of governments, a reasonable measure of coordination should make possible the provision of aid which is not tied to the exports of a particular country. Multilateral aid of this kind provides the best way of getting the greatest benefit from a given volume of aid.

Foreign assistance on anything like this scale would create problems and responsibilities for both the countries providing and the countries receiving aid. It is the responsibility of the country providing aid to recognize the national sovereignty and aspirations of the countries that they are assisting. On the other hand, countries receiving aid must recognize that the Governments of the aid-providing countries must satisfy their legislatures, and that legislatures will require to be assured that the aid-receiving countries' methods of handling their economic policies are realistic and that aid provided is spent on the purposes contemplated by the aid-providing countries. It would be natural for the aid-providing countries to pay particular attention to the determination which the aid-receiving countries show in pursuing such tasks as growing enough food to meet their needs and expanding exports. The necessity for discussions between aid-giving and aid-receiving Governments which this implies must be accepted as a necessary consequence of the democratic process.

Now that postwar reconstruction has been completed and substantial progress has been made in restoring a measure of international equilibrium, a beginning has been made with the problem of providing assistance for the economic development of less advanced countries. This beginning has largely taken the form of the provision by the Government of the United States of funds to meet particular needs, together with relatively smaller measures of assistance by the United Kingdom and other Governments. The growing aspirations of developing countries and their desire to undertake larger scale development are becoming increasingly evident and seem to demand a broader basis of aid embracing a larger number of aid-giving countries. This is likely to pose major problems for international economic policy in the years ahead.

Governments such as those of India and Pakistan when formulating their development plans would naturally wish to have some assurance about the foreign aid that will be forthcoming over the periods of the plans. The Governments of aid-giving countries for constitutional reasons are not in a position to appropriate expenditure for more than one year. We draw attention to this problem because of the genuine difficulties it creates both for those who receive aid and those who give aid.

There is another point to which we should refer. Both India and Pakistan face the risk of crop failures from time to time. Over the period of the forthcoming Plans it cannot be expected that either country's foreign exchange resources will be large enough to finance imports of food on the scale which would be necessary. In recent years, the United States Government has made food supplies available under P.L. 480 to meet these needs. Should such crises recur, additional foreign assistance in some form over and above such support as may have been given to development plans, would be required if economic progress is not to be completely checked.

The role of private investment as a source of assistance for development must not be forgotten or underestimated although its immediate impact is not likely to be large. It is important that the Governments of countries seeking aid should recognize that the flow of private long term funds is one of the sources of investment finance which more developed countries wish to foster and that if they are to use the potential sources of aid to the full they will need to create conditions which will attract private capital from abroad. Private foreign investors on the other hand should be prepared to accept that the Indian and Pakistani balance of payments difficulties imply that these countries can in general only accept private foreign investment of a kind that will either be import saving or export earning. An increased flow of private foreign investment will also depend upon the willingness of the capital-supplying countries to foster such an outflow of private funds. We are the more concerned to stress the importance of private capital from abroad because, as the economic structures of these two countries is brought nearer to viability with the help of Government to Government assistance, it should be possible to substitute the ordinary flow of private investment for the more exceptional forms of aid.

The more highly industrial countries can further assist the course of development by removing the kind of barriers which restrict the export opportunities of developing countries. The process of development, and the growth of new areas of industry which it brings with it, must inevitably exert a profound influence on the whole pattern of international trade. If countries with longer established manufacturing industries resist this process of change by maintaining barriers to the free flow of trade, the pace of development will be retarded, and more aid will be required.

We should also emphasize the need for economic cooperation between the developing countries themselves. We have been impressed by the disruptive impact of partition upon the economies of India and Pakistan. While considerable progress has been made in cooperation between the two countries, we would like to emphasize the need for policies which would promote further cooperation and foster trade of a complementary character, and reduce the danger of economic separatism. The trend of the times not only in Western Europe but elsewhere in the world is strongly oriented towards international economic cooperation. Here on the subcontinent similar opportunities for cooperative efforts in the field of trade and exploitation of natural resources exist. It is obvious that such economic cooperation between India and Pakistan is not only to the advantage of both countries but also to the capital supplying nations of the Atlantic community.

Finally, whatever may be the final program developed by the two countries both Governments need to bear in mind that there can be no assurance that the Governments of the more highly industrialized countries will be in the position to provide aid over the period of the Plans to the full amount requested. This underlines the necessity to establish flexibility in both Plans so that cutbacks in expenditures of lower priority can be made without disrupting the whole Plan.

Before concluding, we should like to express our thanks to the Governments of India and Pakistan for the courtesy and hospitality with which they have received us. We are grateful for the opportunities which we have been given to see something of the progress of development in India and Pakistan, and we have been greatly helped towards better understanding of the problems confronting these two countries by the full and free discussions which we have had with Ministers, officials and private individuals. We were given every assistance in accomplishing the purpose of our Mission, and we would like to thank all those who have contributed to this end.

Yours sincerely
(signed)
Hermann J. Abs
Oliver Franks
Allan Sproul

Mr. Eugene Black,
President,
International Bank for Reconstruction and Development,
Washington, D.C.,
U.S.A.

Notes

1. *Khrushchev Remembers*, translated and edited by Strobe Talbott with an introduction, commentary, and notes by Edward Crankshaw (Boston: Little, Brown, 1970), pp. 481–483.

2. This strategy is described in more detail in Chapter 2 of Book 4 in this series, *Open Skies: Eisenhower's Proposal of July 21, 1955* (Austin: University of Texas Press, 1982). The best scholarly analysis of the economic dimensions of post-Stalin Soviet strategy is Joseph S. Berliner, *Soviet Economic Aid* (New York: Frederick A. Praeger for the Council on Foreign Relations, 1958).

3. It should, perhaps, be recorded that in a conversation with President Johnson, on the occasion of a refueling stop at the Karachi airport on December 23, 1967, President Ayub of Pakistan remarked that, if he lived long enough, he expected to see Soviet tanks move through Afghanistan to the Pakistani frontier along the highway built in Afghanistan with U.S. AID funds. The author was present when Ayub made this prediction.

4. Dillon's description and the illustrative quotation are included in a presentation to the Senate Committee on Foreign Relations of March 3, 1958, when he was Deputy Under Secretary of State for Economic Affairs. The text is to be found in the Department of State *Bulletin* vol. 38, no. 978, March 24, 1958, pp. 469–475. The quotation was from an unnamed Soviet speaker at an Afro-Asian conference in December 1957.

5. For a contemporary skeptical view of the long-run viability of the initial Chinese Communist development strategy, see, for example, W. W. Rostow, in collaboration with Richard W. Hatch,

Frank A. Kierman, Jr., and Alexander Eckstein, *The Prospects for Communist China* (Technology Press of MIT and John Wiley, 1954), especially pp. 271–274, 289–295, 299–314.

6. For such analyses, see, for example, ibid., especially Chapters 12–15; Kang Chao, *Agricultural Production in Communist China, 1949–1965* (Madison: University of Wisconsin Press, 1970); Alexander Eckstein, *China's Economic Development* (Ann Arbor: University of Michigan Press, 1975), especially Chapters 1 and 6–11; Dwight H. Perkins (ed.), *China's Modern Economy in Historical Perspective* (Stanford: Stanford University Press, 1975), especially pp. 1–18, 115–165, 203–233, 279–302.

7. See, for example, Benjamin Schwartz, "China's Developmental Experience, 1949–72," in Michel Oksenberg (ed.), *China's Developmental Experience* (New York: Academy of Political Science, vol. 31, no. 1, March 1973), pp. 18–21.

8. Op. cit., p. 49. An excellent technical account of the sequence of events and policies in agriculture is the chapter by Alva Lewis Erisman ("China: Agricultural Development, 1949–71") in *People's Republic of China: An Economic Assessment*, A Compendium of Papers submitted to the Joint Economic Committee, Congress of the United States (Washington, D.C.: Government Printing Office [G.P.O.], May 18, 1972), pp. 112–146.

9. Bauer's book on India is *United States Aid and Indian Economic Development* (Washington, D.C.: American Enterprise Association, November 1959). Some of Bauer's other writings during this period were: *West African Trade* (Cambridge: Cambridge University Press, 1954); (with B. S. Yamey) *The Economics of Under-developed Countries* (Chicago: University of Chicago Press, 1957); *Economic Analysis and Policy in Under-developed Countries* (Durham, North Carolina: Duke University Press, 1957). For a recent evaluation of Bauer's views, see my review of his *Equality, the Third World, and Economic Delusion* (Cambridge: Harvard University Press, 1981) in *Society* vol. 20, no. 1, November/December 1982, pp. 88–89.

10. P. T. Bauer, *United States Aid and Indian Economic Development*, p. 55. For a technical analysis and critique of the formal model used by P. C. Mahalanobis, see especially Jagdesh N.

Bhagwati and Sukhamay Chakravarty, "Contributions to Indian Economic Analysis: A Survey" in *The American Economic Review* vol. 59, no. 4, part 2, September 1969, Supplement *Surveys of National Economic Policy Issues and Policy Research*, pp. 5–12.

11. Ibid., pp. 75–76.
12. Ibid., pp. 103, 106, and 116.
13. Pre-presidential Papers, U.S. Senate files, Holborn research materials, Foreign Relations: India, box 573.
14. Russell Edgerton, *Sub-Cabinet Politics and Policy Commitment: The Birth of the Development Loan Fund* (Syracuse: Inter-University Case Program, 1970), pp. 77 and 80.
15. My return from Europe to MIT in 1950 and our joining to set in motion CENIS revived an old association between Millikan and me. We had been contemporaries and friends at Yale in the 1930s; learned our first economics together in a black market seminar taught to four of us by Richard Bissell, then a graduate student; worked together for a time on the student magazine, *The Harkness Hoot*; and wrote a joint column in the *Yale Daily News* when *The Hoot* was gently put to rest. Although we never lost touch, we worked over the intervening years, for the most part, in different places.

Millikan was, academically, an expert on national income analysis. His experience of government had included service in the War Shipping Administration, staff work with the Harriman and Herter committees in support of the Marshall Plan, and a stint as director of economic research with the C.I.A. where his interest in development economics and policy began. Rosenstein-Rodan was the senior in age among us and also the scholar with the oldest commitment in the field of development analysis. Out of his wartime work on postwar problems in London at Chatham House, he had published a distinguished germinal article in the *Economic Journal* in 1943, "Problems of Industrialization of Eastern and South-Eastern Europe." He served as Research Director in the early days of the World Bank before going to M.I.T. and had close ties with development economists and practioners throughout the world, notably in India, Latin America, and Italy. Everett Hagen, like Millikan, was a professional in national income analysis with government experience, who not only made the transition to development economics but also came to specialize in some of its psychological and sociological dimensions, especially as they bore on the quality of entrepreneurship. Wilfred Malenbaum was a statistician and expert in agricultural economics with both academic and governmental credentials. Benjamin Higgins, a Canadian economist, had a broad background in economic theory and policy which came to rest in the 1950s on development problems. He led the highly educational but abortive CENIS project in Indonesia. I came into development economics out of my work in economic history and in the theory of economic growth. The background and particular interests of our colleagues in political science and sociology were equally diverse.

16. An appendix to *A Proposal* included, as Table 1 (p. 155), the following data indicating how the additional $3.5 billion might permit per capita real growth rates of about 2 percent for most developing regions.

Possible Capital Formation and Income Growth in the Underdeveloped Countries by Regions

	South Central Asia	Rest of Asia	Middle East	Latin America	Africa	Total
National Income ($ billion) 1953	27.9	19.7	12.3	40.4	10.1	110.4
Gross Capital Formation ($ billion) 1953	2.8	1.7	1.5	7.1	1.2	14.3
Net Capital Formation ($ billion) 1953	1.7	1.2	0.9	4.3	0.7	8.2
Upper Limit of Proposed Annual Additional Capital Inflow	1.0	0.6	0.5	1.0	0.4	3.5
% Annual Income Increase	3.3	3.0	3.8	4.37	3.6	
Population (millions) 1953	459	231	90	173	173	1,126
% Annual Population Increase	1.3	1.6	1.8	2.25	1.5	
% Annual Per Capita Income Increase	2.0	1.4	2.0	2.12	2.1	

The regional grouping used in the table is as follows:

South Central Asia: India, Pakistan, and Ceylon

Rest of Asia: the balance of non-Communist Asia excluding the Middle East and Japan, i.e., Afghanistan, Burma, Cambodia, Formosa, Hong Kong, Indonesia, Laos, Nepal, South Korea, Malaya and Singapore, Philippines, Thailand, Vietnam, and the Pacific Islands.

Middle East: the Arabian Peninsula, Cyprus, Egypt, Iran, Iraq, Israel, Jordan, Lebanon, Syria, Turkey, and the Persian Gulf states

Latin America: all the countries of South and Central America

Africa: all the countries of the African continent except Egypt and the Union of South Africa

17. Ibid., pp. 128–129.

18. W. W. Rostow with Richard W. Hatch, *An American Policy in Asia* (New York: John Wiley with the Technology Press of MIT 1955), p. 50.

19. The complexity of the relationship between economic and political development was borne in on me since, starting in 1950, I taught regularly, as I still do, a course in the evolution of the world economy since the eighteenth century. Latin America figured substantially in that graduate seminar. My later reflections on the problem are incorporated in *Politics and the Stages of Growth* (Cambridge: Cambridge University Press, 1971). For a critical analysis of the views of CENIS and others on the allegedly automatic relation between economic development and democracy, see especially Robert A. Packenham, *Liberal America and the Third World, Political Development Ideas in Foreign Aid and Social Science* (Princeton: Princeton University Press, 1973). Packenham's judgments on CENIS' analysis of this complex relationship appear based more on paraphrase by others than on what members of CENIS actually wrote and said. We did, indeed, argue that societies which harnessed their strong nationalist aspirations to well-designed economic development programs, engaging the participation of all levels of the population concerned, would transit the inherently revolutionary process of modernization with less internal and external violence, less vulnerability to external intrusion, and a better chance of generating in time their own forms of democratic political life than those which turned

their nationalist political energies in other directions. We concluded (*A Proposal*, p. 131): "We do not seek societies abroad built in our own image. We do have a profound interest that societies abroad develop and strengthen those elements in their respective cultures that elevate and protect the dignity of the individual as against the claims of the state. Such elements of harmony with the Western democratic tradition exist in different forms everywhere. . . ." With the passage of almost three decades since those propositions were asserted, I see no reason to alter them.

20. The fact is that Mahalanobis' influence (and his model) proved a transient phase in the evolution of Indian planning concepts and policy. See, for example, Bhagwati and Chakravarty, op. cit., especially pp. 12–29.

21. See, especially, pp. 13–19.

22. In dealing with Kennedy's pre-presidential years neither Arthur Schlesinger, Jr. nor Theodore Sorensen has much to say about the formation of Kennedy's view of the world. James Mac-Gregor Burns (*John Kennedy: A Political Profile* [New York: Harcourt Brace and World, 1959]) provides brief, but useful, insights at each stage of his biography from Kennedy's undergraduate thesis (published as *Why Britain Slept*) forward, but he does not address the questions: Why the developing regions? Why India? Herbert S. Parmet (*Jack: The Struggles of John F. Kennedy* [New York: The Dial Press, 1980]) is useful and quite detailed down to Kennedy's speech on Algeria in 1957, but he does not deal with the Kennedy-Cooper resolution or, indeed, with any other aspect of Kennedy's foreign policy views in the period 1958–1960.

23. *Congressional Record*, 82nd Congress, 2nd Session, vol. 98, part 7, pp. 8492–8493.

24. Arthur Schlesinger, Jr., *Robert Kennedy and His Times* (Boston: Houghton Mifflin, 1978), p. 93. Herbert S. Parmet, op. cit., p. 228, quotes this observation of Robert Kennedy's. Parmet's account of the trip to the Middle East and Far East is quite full and sensitive to its meaning, notably the impact on Kennedy of the power of nationalism he observed; but Parmet does not pursue the lead he correctly identifies as it helped shape Ken-

nedy's subsequent foreign policy positions, except for those taken in his well known interventions on Indochina (1954) and Algeria (1957), to which Parmet does refer.

25. Quoted in the context of Kennedy's April 6, 1954, speech in the Senate on Indochina, *The Strategy of Peace* (New York: Harper, 1960), p. 60.

26. Ibid. A general but carefully elaborated statement on the need for the United States to detach itself from the colonial positions of its allies is included in Kennedy's speech at Rockhurst College, Kansas City, Missouri, June 2, 1956, to be found in the *Congressional Record*, 84th Congress, 2nd Session, vol. 102, pp. 9614–9615.

27. Ibid., pp. 63–64.

28. Ibid., pp. 74 and 79.

29. John F. Kennedy, "A Democrat Looks at Foreign Policy," *Foreign Affairs* vol. 36, no. 1, October 1957, pp. 44, 53–54.

30. Ibid., p. 45.

31. Dungan's other observations are also germane: "He was definitely trying to establish a record as a knowledgeable, dynamic and wise leader in foreign affairs; at that time support for India seemed sensible and in U.S. interest."

B.K. Nehru, in a letter to me of August 5, 1982, adds this *témoignage* from Kennedy himself in a conversation which probably took place in September 1959:

I asked him point blank the question why he, as a Presidential candidate, was sticking his neck out for foreign aid, particularly for India, when both such aid and the country for which he wanted it were unpopular issues and would certainly lose him votes. He gave me two reasons, the first of which was certainly the most impressive. It was, as I remember his words, "I support foreign aid because I think it is right." He then went on to say that it could be that he did lose some votes because this was an unpopular issue but the fact was that the people who were against foreign aid were generally against most things. The image they projected was a negative one; what the country was looking for in this view was a man with a positive outlook. By supporting foreign aid and by being positive in other matters he projected an image of a positive man which gained him votes.

32. Theodore Sorensen, *Kennedy* (New York: Harper and Row, 1965), p. 66.

33. The interview was conducted by Elspeth Rostow, my wife, and me. I have been unable to establish the precise date of the CENIS meeting to which Barbara Ward refers. It occurred when I was abroad on sabbatical leave and probably took place in 1958 when Kennedy was attending an Overseers meeting at Harvard. Historical conscience requires that I note that Malenbaum's memory of Kennedy's performance at this lunch (in a telephone conversation of July 15, 1981) is a good deal less impressive than Barbara Ward's.

34. For an extended reference to this occasion, see "The President's Toast at a Dinner Given in Honor of the King and Queen of Thailand, October 29, 1966," in *Public Papers of the Presidents, Lyndon B. Johnson, 1966*, vol. II, pp. 1279–1280. President Lincoln thanked King Mongkut for the offer and said it would have been gratefully accepted if the climate of the North was not too cold for the elephants to thrive.

35. World Bank, *World Development Report, 1980* (New York: Oxford University Press, 1980), pp. 140–141. The preliminary OECD figure for 1982 was about $28 billion in 1980 prices; for OPEC, about $8 billion in 1981 in current prices (*World Development Report*, 1983), pp. 182–183.

36. National Foreign Assessment Center, *Communist Aid Activities in Non-Communist Less Developed Countries, 1979 and 1954–79* (Washington, D.C.: Central Intelligence Agency, October 1980), p. 17.

37. A brief but authoritative account of the emergence of the Bank is to be found in Edward S. Mason and Robert E. Asher, *The World Bank since Bretton Woods* (Washington, D.C.: Brookings Institution, 1973), pp. 11–35. The authors supply full references to the primary sources.

38. Ibid., p. 28.

39. The Commonwealth embraced both advanced industrial coun-

tries (*e.g.*, Great Britain, Canada, and Australia) and developing nations. It was natural for the latter to press forward their development interests in the newly formed post-imperial club; and it was understandable that Britain, despite limitations on resources, would wish to make a positive response. The United States, South Korea, Japan, and some other Asian countries, not formerly part of the British Empire, joined the Colombo Plan which was an important pioneering venture in North-South collaboration although, in itself, it did not generate large resources for development.

40. The title of the report of the Gordon Gray Commission was: *Report to the President on Foreign Economic Policies* (Washington, D.C.: G.P.O., 1950); of the Rockefeller Report, U.S. International Development Advisory Board: *Partners in Progress: A Report to President Truman* (New York: Simon and Schuster, 1951). Acheson's speeches dealing with foreign aid in Asia are summarized accessibly in McGeorge Bundy (ed.), *The Pattern of Responsibility* (Boston: Houghton Mifflin, 1952), pp. 171–200.

41. Although it is clear that Communist policy had shifted prior to 1953 toward softer forms of aggression in Asia, the Middle East and Africa, and although it is clear that Moscow had every reason to maintain a soft policy until its missile delivery systems had matured, it is still possible, of course, that the ring of pacts helped to confirm in Moscow the correctness and to maintain the stability of that policy over the period 1953–1958.

42. *Europe after Stalin* (Austin: University of Texas Press, 1982).

43. Department of State *Bulletin* vol. 28, June 15, 1953, p. 831.

44. Clarence B. Randall, *A Foreign Economic Policy for the United States* (Chicago: University of Chicago Press, 1954), pp. 27–28.

45. *The United States in World Affairs, 1954*, p. 100. On Stassen's role in 1954 see also Burton I. Kaufman, *Trade and Aid: Eisenhower's Foreign Economic Policy, 1953–1961* (Baltimore: Johns Hopkins University Press, 1981), pp. 51–56.

46. Although Sherman Adams' account of the confrontation leaves a good deal to be desired, it is worth quoting as one of the few references in print to Jackson's world economic plan (*First-Hand Report* [New York: Harper, 1961], pp. 115–116):

When Jackson gave up the struggle in Washington after the agreed term of his enlistment had more than come to an end, he left with Eisenhower and Dulles a recommendation for a bold foreign program. While the central point of view of Jackson's proposal was becoming more widely shared by the best-informed foreign observers, it suffered from the competition of other more pressing programs and the realities of the federal budget. Jackson pointed out that the Soviets were making significant headway in the cold war because they were concentrating on economic and trade offensives. Recalling the tremendously successful effect of the Marshall Plan in winning friends overseas, he said that the United States, to stay abreast in the race, needed to launch a down-to-earth world economic plan that could be made to work. With the hard lessons learned during his experience as the administration's cold war idea promoter vivid in his mind, Jackson went on to warn that such a plan could win support only in the hands of people who understood the nature of the Communist competition and would keep it from the watering-down process which the compromisers would put it through to make it politically acceptable to Congress. This, said Jackson, would so dilute it that it would be quite useless.

Jackson's plan never reached even that stage. The problems of applying such thinking to the policies already in operation, together with the necessity of keeping some control over the ceilings of public expense, staggered the imagination of those who nevertheless believed in Jackson's approach. In that spring of 1954 those ideas became submerged in the more immediate urgencies of the Indo-China crisis and the supreme effort of Eisenhower and Dulles to persuade France to accept the proposed European Defense Community program.

Echoes of the Princeton meeting and its aftermath are to be found in a column by Sylvia Porter in the *New York Post*, "Asian 'Marshall Plan?'" June 8, 1954; and in an article in the *Wall Street Journal*, August 27, 1954, on C. D. Jackson's "new worldwide economic aid offer." Burton I. Kaufman deals with some aspects of Jackson's proposal and its vicissitudes, op. cit., pp. 49–51. Kaufman also discusses at some length the 1954 battle over the lending power of the Export-Import Bank, pp. 29–32. See also Robert E. Asher, "The World Bank, The Export-Import Bank of the United States, and the Developing Nations," in *International Review of the History of Banking*, no. 11, 1975, pp. 19–36.

47. Both Dulles and Jackson were Princeton graduates. That fact, plus Princeton's location between Washington and New York, made it a natural place to gather, in a time when the railroads were still a conventional means of travel. Jackson's reference to a "new" Princeton conference is to a Princeton gathering in May 1952 of government and non-government men concerned with psychological warfare policy.

48. C. D. Jackson [CDJ] Papers, box 56, "Log-1954" folder, Dwight D. Eisenhower [DDE] Library.

49. CDJ Papers, box 56, "Log-1954," August 7, 1954, DDE Library.

50. Ibid.

51. Ibid.

52. CDJ papers, box 41, "Eisenhower Correspondence through 1956" folder 1, DDE Library.

53. CDJ Papers, box 40, "Dulles, John Foster" folder, DDE Library.

54. Ibid.

55. Ibid.

56. CDJ Papers, box 64, "Millikan, Max" folder, DDE Library.

57. CDJ Papers, box 49, "Hoover, Herbert, Jr." folder, DDE Library.

58. CDJ Papers, box 38, "Dodge, Joseph" folder, DDE Library.

59. CDJ Papers, box 73, "Quantico Meetings" folder 5, DDE Library.

60. W. W. Rostow in collaboration with Richard W. Hatch, *An American Policy in Asia*.

61. *The Prospects for Communist China*, pp. 308–309.

62. *An American Policy in Asia*, p. 49.

63. *The United States in World Affairs, 1955*, published for the Council on Foreign Relations (New York: Harper Brothers 1957), p. 122.

64. J. F. Dulles [JFD] Papers, Correspondence Series, box 1, Dwight D. Eisenhower folder, Seeley G. Mudd Manuscript Library, Princeton University. Since this letter was written by Eisenhower the day after his talk with Rockefeller in Gettysburg, it

319

may reflect something of the latter's argument on behalf of the Quantico II report.

65. CDJ Papers, box 56, "Log-1956" folder, DDE Library.

66. Op. cit., p. 148.

67. U.S. Council on Foreign Economic Policy, Office of the Chairman, Dodge Series, Subject File, box 2, "Economic Aid—Multilateral" folder, DDE Library.

68. Ibid.

69. CDJ Papers, box 56, "Log-1956" folder, DDE Library.

70. Ibid., "Log-1957" folder. I should, perhaps add the following anecdote to supplement Jackson's account of the meeting on February 6, 1957. Eric Johnston, with whom I was closely in touch at this time, told me he had called Sherman Adams in the wake of Eisenhower's second Inaugural Address and asked what specifically the President had in mind in the key passage cited. Adams replied, according to Johnston: "Not a thing, Eric, not a goddamned thing. And don't you go about thinking he did."

71. Edgerton's monograph, already cited (Note 14), also contains a review of the evolution of foreign policy in the 1950s, with special attention to its congressional dimensions, that significantly supplements that presented here. His portrait of Dulles' views on development lending and of the Eisenhower-Dulles relationship on this matter differs from that presented here, mainly, I suspect, because documents are now available which were inaccessible to Edgerton when he assembled his data in the mid 1960s.

72. For a vivid account of these shenanigans, ibid., pp. 90−96.

73. The text of Dulles' statement of April 8, 1957, is to be found in the *Congressional Record* vol. 103, part 4, 85th Congress, 1st Session, pp. 5409−5411. A later forthright statement by Dulles in support of the DLF is in the *Congressional Record* vol. 103, part 7, 85th Congress, 1st Session, pp. 9123−9125.

74. At just about this time (in the spring of 1957) this theme was much on Eisenhower's mind. Quoting from one of Eisenhower's taped conversations, William Bragg Ewald, Jr. (*Eisenhower the President: Crucial Days, 1951−1960* [Englewood Cliffs, N.J.: Prentice Hall], pp. 97−99) presents the following account of a confrontation on foreign aid between Eisenhower and

Senator Styles Bridges which suggests, among other things, how effective Eisenhower could have been if he had chosen to crusade for a World Economic Plan including aid to India:

> If transcribed verbatim, tapes have a conspicuous merit, they relay the exact words spoken, in jest, in reflection, or (as on one May morning in 1957) in wrath.
>
> Through the spring of 1957 both Republicans and Democrats on the Hill had been making life hard for Ike, now a lame duck, by bellowing for cuts in his allegedly spendthrift budget and by denouncing foreign "giveaways." They would not see that the military defense of the free world depends upon the economic health of the free world. Senator Styles Bridges of New Hampshire, a crusty conservative, had made a speech calling foreign aid advocates "do-gooders." Jim Hagerty read the ticker and scribbled in ink on yellow pad a red-hot memo to Eisenhower recommending a woodshed hiding: a reminder to Bridges that "if anyone is getting sick of 'do-gooders' it's you—political do-gooders who can't or won't see the full picture and fulfill the obligations we have as a leader of the free world." The President, like Hagerty, also had had it up to here, and next morning, after the Legislative Leaders meeting, Ike called Bridges in on the carpet, switched on the gadget, and left historians with the only extended verbatim record extant of an Ike chewing-out.
>
> "I am convinced that the only way to avoid war," the President told the Senator, "the only way to save America in the long run from destruction, is through the development of a true collective system of defense.
>
> "It is pretty hard when I have to bear the burdens not only of the Presidency, but of the titular head of the party, to have said by one of the principal people in the party that this is nothing but a do-gooder act. . . . I think nothing could be further from the truth. I realize that as of this moment it is a very popular thing to talk about saving a dollar. Frankly, I would rather see the Congress cut a billion off . . . defense [than off foreign aid]—as much as I think it would be a mistake. . . . If we depend exclusively

on our own arms, we are headed for a war; there is going to be no other answer. . . .

"If I knew a cheap way out of this one, I certainly would take it. . . . If Mr. Truman (and, unfortunately, a Republican Congress in 1946 and 1948) had given us what the Chiefs of Staff authorized me to request—which was 15 billion dollars a year over and above stockpiling and pay increases—I believe there never would have been a Korean War.

"I begged them for 110 million dollars, but never could make them see the need for it. (I think you were among the group I went down to talk to.) I am not blaming anybody, but I want to say this is just another incident in a long lifetime of work on this.

"Finally, I think my party ought to trust me a little bit more when I put not only my life's work, but my reputation and everything else, on the line in favor of this. . . ."

Bridges, shaken, asked to see the ticker story. Then he started to explain: "What I meant by that statement was Yugoslavia, Indonesia, India and others—where I thought they in turn would contribute nothing to the mutual security, and therefore the money that you put into those countries was advocated particularly by do-gooders."

The President shot back: "Take some countries, like India for example. India has 350 million people. Suppose India said 'we take our stand with the West'—consider where we are, right up against an 1800 mile border against China.

"How much have we got to put into India to make it reasonably safe for them to even exist? Frankly, this is the one country I had in mind when I said that there are one or two countries in the world that I would want to be neutral. Now we have no obligation to defend them, and if the other fellow attacks them, they violate a world treaty because they are jumping on a neutral country. I had a long talk with Nehru about this, and he is up against the matter of 350 million people practically starving. You could put all the defenses in the world in there, and they will go Communistic. . . ."

Bridges backed and shuffled: "I don't blame you for being disturbed about that little statement given to you. That, in effect, is what I said, but it was only *part* of what I said."

Eisenhower's lecture did not, of course, keep Bridges from leading the fight in the Senate against the Kennedy-Cooper resolution on June 6, 1958 (see above, pp. 10–11 and Appendix B).

75. DDE Papers, Ann Whitman File, Dulles-Herter Series, Box 7, "Dulles, John Foster—Nov. '57" folder, DDE Library.

76. Stevenson was initially asked to go to Paris as the third-ranking man on the U.S. delegation. As one of his biographers correctly reports (Kenneth S. Davis, *The Politics of Honor: A Biography of Adlai E. Stevenson* [New York: G. P. Putnam and Sons, 1967], p. 371), Stevenson was wary:

> . . . Secretary of State Dulles, speaking, he said, for the President as well as himself, had approached Stevenson in early November to ask that the Democratic party's titular head participate to the fullest extent in the formulation of the U.S. position for the forthcoming meeting. Indeed, the words Dulles used could be interpreted to mean that Stevenson, if he accepted, would be responsible for drafting the new American position, which would then be passed upon by the President and Secretary of State. Further, Stevenson was asked to come to Paris as a member of the U.S. delegation, wherein he would be outranked only by Eisenhower and Dulles. The appeal (for it had that quality) was couched in terms of patriotic duty: at this juncture, a "bipartisan" approach was of the utmost importance.
>
> Stevenson, nevertheless was wary. He was not unmindful of the disadvantages he would suffer and of the advantages his political opposition would gain if he were tagged with public responsibility for final policies with which he might or might not agree. He therefore suggested for himself a much more modest role, that of mere adviser or "consultant." Thus his publicly assigned responsibility for the event would be no greater than his actual authority to determine it, and his freedom to criticize, if criticism seemed needed, would be unimpaired.

77. Adlai Stevenson Papers, box 733, NATO: Black Notebook (2 of 2) folder, Mudd Library, Princeton.

78. I had contributed some material to Stevenson's staff during the 1956 campaign, but our first meeting was at breakfast in the Commander Hotel in Cambridge on the morning of the Princeton-Harvard football game, November 9, 1957. I worked with him quite closely, helping as best I could with drafts and other suggestions over the next month until his responsibility was fulfilled and Eisenhower was off to Paris. Stevenson's papers at the Mudd Library in Princeton indicate that Thomas Finletter and Hubert Humphrey filed memoranda with Stevenson on the NATO Summit on November 29 and December 2, respectively. I remained in touch with Stevenson, helping with speech drafts, etc. through the winter until he left on a world tour in 1958. We were next in touch as the Kennedy administration assembled for business in the last week of January 1961.

79. Adlai Stevenson Papers, box 733, NATO: Black Notebook (2 of 2) folder, Mudd Library, Princeton.

80. The phrase is Robert Cutler's, in his *No Time for Rest* (Boston: Little, Brown, 1965), p. 375. Cutler was the first U.S. executive director of the IADB.

81. *Review of Foreign Policy*, Hearings before the Committee on Foreign Relations, Part I (Washington, D.C.: G.P.O., 1958), pp. 278–280.

82. The story of this enterprise is well, but briefly, told in James A. Robinson, *The Monroney Resolution: Congressional Initiative in Foreign Policy Making* (New York: Henry Holt, 1959). For a wider account of the origins of IDA and its evolution, see Edward S. Mason and Robert E. Asher, *The World Bank since Bretton Woods*, Chapter 12, pp. 380–419.

83. The differences between the resolution as Senator Monroney originally introduced it and as it was reported by the committee are shown in the following comparison, with deletions in italic type and insertions in capital letters:

> Resolved, That, recognizing the desirability of promoting a greater degree of international development by means of multilateral loans based on sound economic principles,

rather than a system of unilateral grants or loans, it is the sense of the Senate that *consideration* PROMPT STUDY should be given BY THE NATIONAL ADVISORY COUNCIL ON IN-TERNATIONAL MONETARY AND FINANCIAL PROBLEMS WITH RE-SPECT to the establishment of an International Development Association, *in cooperation with* AS AN AFFILI-ATE OF the International Bank for Reconstruction and Development.

In order to achieve greater international trade, develop-ment, and economic well-being, such *an agency* STUDY should *promote* INCLUDE CONSIDERATION OF the following objectives:

1. Provid*e*ING A SOURCE of long-term loans available at a *low* REASONABLE rate of interest and repayable in local cur-rencies, OR PARTLY IN LOCAL CURRENCIES, to supplement *World* INTERNATIONAL Bank *loans* LENDING ACTIVITIES and thereby permit the prompt completion of worthwhile de-velopment projects which could not otherwise go forward.

2. *Permit maximum use of foreign currencies* FACILITAT-ING, IN CONNECTION WITH SUCH LOANS, THE USE OF LOCAL AND OTHER FOREIGN CURRENCIES, INCLUDING THOSE available to the United States through the sale of agricultural surpluses and through other programs *by devoting a portion of these currencies to such loans.*

3. Insur*e*ing that funds *necessary* for international eco-nomic development can be made available by a process *which eliminates any possible implications of inter-ference with national sovereignty* WOULD ENCOURAGE MULTI-LATERAL CONTRIBUTIONS FOR THIS PURPOSE.

It is further the sense of the Senate that as a part of the United States economic aid program funds be subscribed to the capital stock of the International Development Association in cooperation with investments made by other participating countries.

84. I. G. Patel, *Foreign Aid* (Bombay: Allied Publishers, 1968), pp. 12–14.
85. Castro's deal with the orthodox Cuban Communist leadership and Moscow was probably struck in the summer of 1958. For a

brief account see the author's *Diffusion of Power* (New York: Macmillan, 1972), pp. 49–52, 99–103, and relevant notes for sources.

86. Dwight D. Eisenhower, *Waging Peace*, p. 520.
87. Ibid., pp. 269–270.
88. E. S. Mason and R. E. Asher, *The World Bank since Bretton Woods*, p. 514.
89. Escott Reid's name was ultimately dropped from the possible candidates because he was a Canadian ambassador. It was judged wise to include only private citizens in the mission to India. Reid later became a high official of the World Bank.
90. I. G. Patel, *Foreign Aid*, p. 17.
91. Letter to Millikan from author of December 10, 1958. From such records as I have, the period of most intense consultations in London was November–December 1958. The U.S. Embassy in London knew of and, to a degree, encouraged this enterprise in international crusading. Two officials at the British Treasury were particularly interested in the problem of mobilizing support for Indian development: Sir Denis Rickett and Chaim Raphael. The discussions were wide-ranging, including the British inflation-balance of payments problem which inhibited U.K.'s capacity to aid developing countries.
92. Box 718, Senate Files Legislation, Holborn, F. folder (1939), JFK Library. Writing to me in Europe on May 13, 1959, Millikan described his lobbying with the State Department on these residual issues:

> I have been politicking with the Department to try to get them to support the Kennedy resolution. This has been peculiarly frustrating because they have taken the line, first, that a resolution on India will get them into all kinds of trouble with all the other under-developed countries and, second, that the mission should be a U.S. Congressional one rather than an international wisemen's mission. This is partly based on the view that a Congressional mission will have more influence on Congress (which I doubt) and partly on some doubts as to whether the European countries would really come through with contribu-

tions to a cooperative effort. Your evidence from both your British discussions and those with Monnet has been extremely helpful, and I hope we have brought them around but it is not quite clear yet.

93. Joseph Dodge was to have been the American member of the three man team, backed by the Treasury which wanted a banker who would avoid excessive U.S. commitments. Dodge's illness led to the appointment of Sproul, who proved to be appropriately cautious but in no way obstructive. For press comment see Appendix M.

94. I. G. Patel, *Foreign Aid*, p. 14. In a letter to me of August 5, 1982, B. K. Nehru, now Governor of Gujarat, describes as follows how the Wisemen operated in India:

> The Wisemen operated at two levels. As far as I remember they used to have a meeting every day with one or the other section of the civil servants of the various Ministries concerned with economic development who explained their plans and programs to them and answered their questions. I do not recall who took these meeting on our side; it must, I should imagine, have been the Economic Secretary. They took place in the Finance Minister's room at his rather long conference table (I do not know what happened to the Minister!). The Wisemen did not have a formal leader but it was very clear that in fact Oliver Franks had been given the honour. He did most of the cross-questioning and was ably supplemented by Abs. As far as I can recall—and I was present at most, if not all, these meetings—Mr. Sproul was conspicuous by his total silence!
>
> The second level of operation was calls on the Ministers concerned. These were sometimes formal but sometimes, in the case of Ministers who knew their business, quite substantive. But I do remember Oliver Franks telling me at the very beginning that he would much rather spend time with civil servants who would know what they were talking about than spend it in discussing generalities with political leaders.

95. John F. Kennedy, *Public Papers of the Presidents, 1961* (Washington, D.C.: G.P.O., 1962), pp. 203 and 212.
96. Barbara Ward, J. D. Runnalls, and Lenore d'Anjou (eds.), *The Widening Gap: Development in the 1970s* (New York: Columbia University Press, 1971).
97. Ibid., pp. 11, 12, and 13.
98. See, notably, *U.S. Foreign Policy for the 1970s: Building for Peace*, A Report to the Congress by Richard Nixon, President of the United States, February 15, 1971, pp. 146–147.
99. I was probably the most explicit advocate of this approach in *The World Economy: History and Prospect* (Austin: University of Texas Press, 1978), part VI; *Getting from Here to There* (New York: McGraw–Hill, 1978), Chapter 13; *Why the Poor Get Richer and the Rich Slow Down* (Austin: University of Texas Press, 1980), Chapter 7; "World Agenda for a Disheveled World Economy," CHALLENGE, March/April 1981, pp. 5–16; and in a speech in Maracaibo, Venezuela, on July 21, 1982, entitled "The World Economy and the Tasks of Economic Statesmanship in the Hemisphere."
100. The chairman of the group was Filipe Herrera, former president of the Inter-American Bank. It consisted of six from Latin America, one from the Caribbean, one from North America (myself). The report is dated August 1980 (OEA/Ser. T/II).
101. *Statement by the President at the Opening of the International Meeting on Cooperation and Development*, Office of the White House Press Secretary, Cancún, Mexico, October 22, 1981, p. 4.
102. *Economic Report of the President Transmitted to the Congress February 1982* (Washington, D.C.: G.P.O., 1982), p. 184. This report (pp. 181–189) articulates clearly the Reagan administration's doctrines on trade, the central role of private enterprise and private capital movements, aid, and international finance.
103. I. G. Patel, *Current Crisis in International Co-operation* (New Delhi: Reserve Bank of India, March 15, 1982), p. 16.
104. Jean Monnet, *Memoirs* (Garden City, New York: Doubleday, 1978), p. 109. Burton I. Kaufman, *Trade and Aid*, p. 198, notes an experience which might, at last, have converted Eisenhower to unambiguous support for enlarged development aid

and which might account for the substantially enlarged final aid budget he submitted to the Congress which was of considerable assistance to Kennedy (see above, p. 172); that is, the strong impact on Eisenhower of his visit to India and other parts of Asia in 1960.

105. For an account of Kennedy's view of this problem and the actions he undertook, see my *Diffusion of Power* (New York: Macmillan, 1972), pp. 203–206. The fact is that Nehru's visit to Washington in November 1961 was a grave disappointment to both U.S. and Indian officials. Nehru was passive and unresponsive, quite possibly because his health was already failing.

106. For elaboration of this theme, see my *Stages of Economic Growth*, pp. 26–30.

107. *Economist*, "India, Treadmill or Take-off: A Survey," p. 8. The special supplement was written by Rupert Pennant-Rea.

108. W. W. Rostow, *Why the Poor Get Richer and the Rich Slow Down*, pp. 266–267.

109. For a systematic effort to measure the improvement in "basic needs" see David Morawetz, *Twenty-five Years of Economic Development: 1950 to 1975* (World Bank, Baltimore: Johns Hopkins University Press, 1977), especially pp. 31–58.

110. I. G. Patel, *Current Crisis in International Cooperation*, p. 11.

111. I would not attribute to the existence of food imports under P.L. 480 the primary reason for the systematic neglect of agricultural and rural life which was—and remains—one of the most troubling features of policy in developing countries. That neglect flowed mainly from a convergence of political realities and understandable, but misguided, intellectual biases within developing countries. In the short run, the cities were more volatile and, in a sense, politically dangerous. There was a powerful temptation, therefore, to provide the cities cheap food even at the cost of wise, longer-run agricultural policies. P.L. 480 loans were evidently attractive to many political leaders in developing countries and to their finance ministers as well because they provided a prompt increase in current governmental revenues. Meanwhile, intellectuals argued that agriculture was a quasi-colonial activity, value added was higher in industry than in agriculture, industry was needed urgently to underpin military strength, etc.

112. The historians of the World Bank, E. S. Mason and R. E. Asher, share my view of the importance of this point but more wistfully: "The Bank can ally itself with the development-minded elements in the country and reinforce their efforts. But the Bank's biggest handicap is its inability to guarantee that development-minded officials will come into power or remain in power" (*The World Bank since Bretton Woods*, p. 648). My point is, of course, that many more development-minded officials rose to power and stayed in power than would have been the case if development aid had not been institutionalized.

113. In terms of development theory and policy as my colleagues and I conceived of it in the 1950s—and I conceive of it now—the criterion of the proportion of GNP allocated by the advanced industrial countries to developing countries is irrelevant and misleading. Measuring ODA in this way implies that the objective is the transfer of resources from rich to poor. The "correct" criterion is to assure that absorptive capacity is matched by the availability of capital for development programs which are in appropriate sectoral balance. This would not, of course, exclude emergency aid, on a human welfare basis, to countries experiencing one kind or another of economic emergency.

114. I. G. Patel, *Current Crisis in International Co-operation*, p. 3.

115. Donella H. Meadows, Dennis L. Meadows, Jørgen Randers, and William W. Behrens III (New York: Universe Books, 1972).

Index

Humphrey, Hubert H., 4, 68, 324

Senate Foreign Relations Committee: JFK assigned to, 64; and Kennedy-Cooper Resolution, 162; 1958 hearings of, on development aid, 140–141
Senate Resolution 264. *See* Monroney Resolution
SHAPE, 60, 82
Sino-Soviet split, 32
Sixth Fleet: in Lebanon intervention, 146–147
socialism: and aid under Reagan, 193–194; CENIS' views on, 52–54; criticized by Bauer, 40
Sorensen, Theodore: and aid increase, 172; on JFK's search for ideas, 67–70
Southeast Asia Treaty Organization. *See* SEATO
South Korea, 180
Special United Nations Fund for Economic Development (SUNFED), 115
Sproul, Allan, 327; and international mission to India, 163
Sputnik, 13; Dulles fears impact of, 135; impact of, 33–35; influence of, on aid, 203
Stages of Economic Growth, The, 221
stagflation: affects development aid, 188
Stalin, Joseph: and JFK, 59; and Mao, 13–14; and Yugoslavia, 19
Stassen, Harold: and "Arc of Free Asia" program, 109; heads FOA, 91; and neutralism, 135; and regional development in Asia, 93–94
State Department: critical of Eisenhower's policy, 92; and Kennedy-Cooper initiative, 10–11; and Kennedy-Cooper Resolution, 161–162; and Monroney Resolution, 143
Stebbins, Richard: on Stassen's

Asian initiative, 93–94
Stevenson, Adlai, 92; and CIEG, 159; and NATO proposals, 136–137; and post-Sputnik foreign economic policy, 135–138, 323; and WWR, 324
Strategy of Peace, The, 57
Strauss, Lewis: and 1958 Middle East crisis, 148
Suez crisis: Soviet role in, 19
Sukarno, 206; and modernization, 51
SUNFED. *See* Special United Nations Fund for Economic Development
supply and demand: effects on aid programs under LBJ, 174–179; under Nixon, 180–183; under Reagan, 191–195
Symington, Stuart, 69
Syria: Communist assistance to, 15, 17–18; U.S. assistance to, 18

Taiwan (Republic of China), 180; and U.S. security, 90
take-off: in Millikan-Rostow report, 46; unsettling effects of, 50
technical assistance: early programs of, 79; in Soviet aid program, 16
technology, new: and China and India, 212
Thailand, 180; foreign assistance to, 18
Time: favors WEP, 107
Tinbergen, Professor Jan, 5
Trade Agreements Extension Act: and JFK, 58
Treasury Department: and Kennedy-Cooper Resolution, 162; opposes WEP, 105
Trezise, Philip: importance of, 134; and Owen-Trezise proposal, 127
Truman, Harry S: and CIEG, 159; enunciates Point Four, 78–79; foreign policy of, and JFK, 58
Truman Doctrine, 90

Turkey, 180; Communist assistance to, 16–18; and Eisenhower initiative, 150–151; signs pact with Pakistan, 90; U.S. assistance to, 18

Union of Soviet Socialist Republics. *See* U.S.S.R.

United Nations: General Assembly debate of 1974, 185; of 1975, 186; and 1958 Middle East crisis, 148; and technical assistance, 79

Uruguay: Communist assistance to, 15

U.S.: in Aid-India Consortium, 154; pledges aid to India, 168; and take-off, 52

U.S.S.R.: aid policy of, alarms Monroney, 142; aid policy of, evaluated, 212–215; arms deal with Egypt of, 111, 112; and Chinese Five Year Plan, 28–29; First Five Year Plan of, and Mahanalobis, 51–52; and Indochina settlement, 14; and 1958 Middle East crisis, 148–149; and take-off, 52; and tension with P.R.C., 32

Vandenberg Resolution: and JFK, 58

Venezuela, 193

Vietnam: and JFK, 62–63; war in, 176

Waldenström, Erland, 6

Ward, Barbara, 316; and CIEG, 159–160; on India as a test case, 50; on JFK and CENIS, 71–72

Weeks, Sinclair: hears WEP presentation, 122–124

WEP (World Economic Plan): advocated by Jackson, 118–120; difficulties of, 98–108; opposition to, characterized by Jackson, 124; proposed, 97–98; and Randall group, 121–125; and the Treasury, 105

West Germany, 173; and Aid-India Consortium, 154; WWR lobbies in, 160–161

wheat, 177

While England Slept, 59

Whitman, Ann, 98

Williams, Maurice, 186

Woods, George, 220

World Bank, 79–80, 158; and "basic human needs" doctrine, 182; and consortium for India, 152–154; and India, 204; and institutionalization of aid, 220; and international mission to India, 163–168; and JFK, 155; and Kennedy-Cooper Resolution, 162; and Millikan-Rostow report, 48; and Monroney Resolution, 142–143; and *North-South*, 187; origins and early character of, 77–78; and Reagan, 191–192; regional role of, suggested, 190

Yalta: criticized by JFK, 58

Yemen: Communist assistance to, 15–18; U.S. assistance to, 18

Yugoslavia: Communist assistance to, 15–17, 19

Zhdanov, Andrei A.: and Communist objectives in developing regions, 13